Samuel Beckett and trauma

Manchester University Press

Samuel Beckett and trauma

EDITED BY MARIKO HORI TANAKA,
YOSHIKI TAJIRI AND MICHIKO TSUSHIMA

Manchester University Press

Published by Manchester University Press
Altrincham Street, Manchester M1 7JA
www.manchesteruniversitypress.co.uk

British Library Cataloguing-in-Publication Data is available

ISBN 978 1 5261 2134 9 hardback
ISBN 978 1 5261 4809 4 paperback

First published by Manchester University Press in hardback 2018

This edition first published 2020

Typeset by Servis Filmsetting Ltd, Stockport, Cheshire

Contents

Part III: Historical and cultural contexts

List of contributors

Julie Campbell was Senior Lecturer in English at the University of Southampton and co-convenor (2011–12) and then convenor (2013) of the Samuel Beckett Working Group under the auspices of the International Federation of Theatre Research until her death on 21 May 2014. She had published widely, in books and scholarly journals. Her articles on Beckett appeared in *Samuel Beckett Today/Aujourd'hui* and *Beckett and Animals*, edited by Mary Bryden (Cambridge University Press, 2013). Her chapter in this book derives from a lecture delivered at Aoyama Gakuin University, Tokyo, in December 2012.

Conor Carville is Associate Professor of English at Reading University. His book on Irish cultural theory, *The Ends of Ireland: Criticism, History, Subjectivity*, was published by Manchester University Press in 2012. He has published many essays on Beckett, most recently 'Murphy's Thanatopolitics' in *The Irish Review*. His book on Beckett and the visual is forthcoming from Cambridge University Press. He is currently working on a book about Beckett and the concept of life.

Robert Eaglestone is Professor of Contemporary Literature and Thought at Royal Holloway, University of London. He works on contemporary literature and literary theory, contemporary philosophy and on Holocaust and genocide studies. He is the author of six books, including *Ethical Criticism: Reading after*

Levinas (1997), *The Holocaust and the Postmodern* (2004) and *The Broken Voice* (2017). He is the editor or co-editor of seven volumes, including *Derrida's Legacies* (2008) and *The Future of Trauma Theory* (2013). His work has been translated into five languages, including Japanese. In 2014 he won a National Teaching Fellowship Award.

Mariko Hori Tanaka is Professor of English at Aoyama Gakuin University, Japan, and co-convenor (2011–12, 2014–18) of the Samuel Beckett Working Group under the auspices of the International Federation of Theatre Research. She has published widely, in books and scholarly journals. Her essays on Beckett have appeared in *Samuel Beckett Today/Aujourd'hui* and several collections of essays such as *Samuel Beckett and Pain*, co-edited by Yoshiki Tajiri and Michiko Tsushima (Rodopi, 2012) and *The Edinburgh Companion to Samuel Beckett and the Arts*, edited by S. E. Gontarski (Edinburgh University Press, 2014). She co-translated James Knowlson's *Damned to Fame: The Life of Samuel Beckett* and published *Beckett Junrei [Pilgrimage]* in Japanese.

Nicholas E. Johnson is Assistant Professor of Drama at Trinity College Dublin, as well as a performer, director and writer. Recent Beckett projects include dramaturgy for *Cascando* (Pan Pan, 2016) and direction for *No's Knife* (Lincoln Center, 2015). He co-edited the *Journal of Beckett Studies* special issue on performance (23.1, 2014) and co-founded the Samuel Beckett Laboratory in 2013 (both with Jonathan Heron). His research has been published in several edited collections including *The Plays of Samuel Beckett* (Methuen, 2013) and *Staging Beckett in Ireland and Northern Ireland* (Bloomsbury, 2016). He is a co-director of the Beckett Summer School and head of the Creative Arts Practice research theme at Trinity College Dublin.

David Houston Jones is Professor of French Literature and Visual Culture, University of Exeter. His publications include *Installation Art and the Practices of Archivalism* (Routledge, 2016); *Assessing the Legacy of the* Gueules cassées: *from Surgery to*

Art, a special issue of *Journal of War and Culture Studies* (2017) (with Marjorie Gehrhardt); *Paddy Hartley: of Faces and Facades* (Black Dog Publishing, 2015) (with Marjorie Gehrhardt); *Samuel Beckett and Testimony* (Palgrave Macmillan, 2011); *Jean Genet, Journal du voleur* (University of Glasgow, French & German Publications, 2004); and *The Body Abject* (Peter Lang, 2000).

Anna Sigg is a professor of English at John Abbott College in Quebec. She completed her PhD in the Department of English at McGill University, Montreal. Her article on Beckett's *Krapp's Last Tape* was published in *L'Annuaire théâtral*. Her FQRSC-funded dissertation, 'Therapeutic Theatre: Trauma and Bodily Articulation in Post-War European Drama', explores the connection between trauma, body and sound in post-war European theatre (Beckett, Artaud, Brecht, Bond and Kane). She teaches modernist and Romantic drama. She is also passionate about performance and directing and has worked as an acting coach and music director.

Yoshiki Tajiri is Professor of English at the University of Tokyo. He has written extensively on Samuel Beckett, modernism and contemporary English literature. His Japanese translation of Beckett's *Dream of Fair to middling Women* appeared in 1995. He is the author of *Samuel Beckett and the Prosthetic Body: The Organs and Senses in Modernism* (Palgrave Macmillan, 2007) and co-editor of *Samuel Beckett and Pain* (Rodopi, 2012). He has also translated a selection of J. M. Coetzee's critical essays into Japanese (2015) and published articles on his work in *Journal of Modern Literature* and *Textual Practice*. More recently he co-edited a Japanese book on Yukio Mishima (2016).

Michiko Tsushima is Associate Professor in the Faculty of Humanities and Social Sciences at the University of Tsukuba, Japan. She is the author of *The Space of Vacillation: The Experience of Language in Beckett, Blanchot, and Heidegger* (Peter Lang, 2003) and *Hannah Arendt: Reconciling Ourselves to the World* (in Japanese, Hosei University Press, 2016). She has also published a number of articles on modern literature and contemporary thought, including articles on Beckett and Arendt. Her articles on Beckett have appeared in *Samuel Beckett Today/Aujourd'hui* and *Samuel Beckett and Pain*, co-edited by Mariko Hori Tanaka and Yoshiki Tajiri.

Acknowledgements

On 11 March 2011, north-eastern Japan was hit by a huge earth-quake followed by a *tsunami* that caused the deaths of 20,000 people. What shocked us most, however, was not the disaster itself but the news of a nuclear catastrophe that happened at the Fukushima Daiichi nuclear power station. People living within twenty kilometres of the station were forced to leave their homes and literally lost their hometowns. Those who sustained their lives through fishing lost their jobs because the sea was contaminated with radioactive waste which leaked out of the plant. The high level of radioactivity was scattered as far as the Tokyo metropolitan area. This calamity, which reminds us of the aftermath of Hiroshima, annihilated by an atomic bomb, threatened many people in Japan. It was the most traumatic event to have occurred in post-war Japan.

A year after this irremediable catastrophe, in April 2012, we received a three-year grant (Grant-in Aid for Challenging Exploratory Research) from the Japan Society for the Promotion of Science, which made it possible to start this project on 'Samuel Beckett and Trauma'. Having experienced the earthquake and Fukushima's nuclear catastrophe, studying trauma in relation to Beckett became an issue that impinged on us. What Beckett writes made us think of the way we could overcome our own trauma. Struggling with trauma of our own, we could philosophise about the trauma within Beckett and his works.

During the course of the three years' grant period, we planned to publish a book of essays on 'Samuel Beckett and Trauma'. We first disclosed our idea to the late Mary Bryden, ex-President of the Association of University Professors and Heads of French, and ex-Head of the Department of Modern Languages and European Studies, University of Reading, who had always been very kind in giving us sincere comments and advice during the decades when she was an important staff member at the Beckett Archive, University of Reading. Despite being ill, she encouraged us through emails to develop our idea until she passed away in November 2015. It is very sad that she could not live to see this book's publication, and we would like to dedicate the book to her.

The grant enabled us to invite to Tokyo three contributors to this book: Julie Campbell, ex-Senior Lecturer at the University of Southampton, Robert Eaglestone, Professor at the University of London, and Nicholas Johnson, Assistant Professor at Trinity College Dublin. Julie Campbell sadly passed away in May 2014. Her essay in this book, therefore, is our edited version of her lecture given at Aoyama Gakuin University in December 2012. We thank Samantha Campbell, Julie's daughter, for finding her essay files and permitting us to include the essay here. We also thank Robert Eaglestone for letting us use in the earlier part of our introduction his unpublished essay on the history of trauma theory. This book could not have been realised without their kind help and advice.

In April 2015, our grant was renewed for another three years. Fortunately, three other people with brilliant achievements in Beckett scholarship agreed to contribute to our book: David Houston Jones, Professor at the University of Exeter, Conor Carville, Associate Professor at the University of Reading, and Anna Sigg, Professor at John Abbott College. In the meantime, Manchester University Press agreed to publish this book during our second collaborative research process. We thank Matthew Frost, the commissioning editor at the press, for his kind efforts to realise our project. We also thank Daniela Caselli, Professor at Manchester University and President of the Samuel Beckett Society (2017–20), whose friendly support and encouragement were indispensable for our communication with the press.

We would like to thank the members of the Samuel Beckett

Research Circle of Japan and colleagues from the Samuel Beckett Society for their help and advice. We are also grateful to the scholars in other fields, from philosophy to literature, theatre to art, psychology to history, who offered their kind suggestions and assistance. We are particularly grateful to Miryam Sas, Professor at the University of California, Berkeley, for her encouragement and helpful advice regarding the Introduction. Our gratitude extends also to Marianne Kimura, Associate Professor at Kyoto Women's University, for her kind editorial assistance. We are also indebted to the editors of enago and editage for their editorial work to create a complete manuscript. Lastly, we wish to note with gratitude that this work was supported by JSPS KAKENHI Grant Number 15K12855. This book could not have materialised without the efforts, cooperation and patience of the contributors, to whom we would like to express our gratitude.

Mariko Hori Tanaka
Yoshiki Tajiri
Michiko Tsushima
Tokyo, March 2017

Introduction

*Mariko Hori Tanaka, Yoshiki Tajiri and Michiko Tsushima,
with Robert Eaglestone*

Roger Luckhurst argues that the modern concept of trauma developed in the West through the interlocking areas of 'law, psychiatry and industrialized warfare' (2008: 19). However, over the twentieth century, trauma as a concept became increasingly medicalised and simultaneously significantly linked with wider political frameworks: with survivor and testimony narratives, with responses to persecution and prejudice, to the Holocaust, and other acts of mass atrocity and genocide. In such discourses, the concept of trauma is not fully material or bodily, nor simply psychic, nor fully cultural, nor simply historical or structural, but a meeting of all of these. As Luckhurst usefully suggests, it is precisely because it is a knot, or a point of intersection, of turbulence, that 'trauma' is such a powerful force and is impossible to define easily.

In terms of its growth in literary studies, the study of trauma and trauma theory also has a range of antecedents. As Kerwin Lee Klein from the discipline of history demonstrates, there was a turn to 'memory' in the 1980s, in part stimulated by the work of Pierre Nora and David P. Jordan (2009) and Yosef Yerushalmi's influential book *Zakhor: Jewish History and Jewish Memory* (1982). Michel Foucault, too, invoked a politics of memory and, tracing this out, Ian Hacking explored what he named 'memoro-politics'. This turn to memory involved a rediscovery and translation of Maurice Halbwachs's work from the 1920s on collective memory (Halbwachs was murdered at Buchenwald in 1945). This shift in historical discourse seems not only to align much in that field with similar questions about representation, politics and ethics and historical understanding in literary and cultural studies, but also to raise questions about trauma. Hacking, for example, wrote that 'there are interconnections between group memory and personal memory. One obvious link is trauma' (1995: 211).

Literary and cultural theory in the 1980s and 1990s seemed to turn towards trauma for other reasons as well, beyond the widely acknowledged 'turn to history' in the 1990s and 2000s. Research in the nascent fields of the medical humanities, sometimes inspired by Judith Lewis Herman's *Trauma and Recovery* (1994) or Arthur Frank's *The Wounded Storyteller* (1995), focused on traumatic events and the ways in which individuals may come to terms with them. The work of theorists inspired by Lacan, or by Slavoj Žižek's Hegelian-Lacanian politicised psychoanalysis (or, perhaps psychoanalytic politics), often uses trauma as a core concept. Judith Butler, too, turned to issues of trauma, grief and mourning in books such as *Precarious Life* (2004) and *Frames of War* (2009).

However, perhaps the most powerful source of trauma theory has been the work of Cathy Caruth and Shoshana Felman, developing on works of deconstruction by Jacques Derrida and Paul de Man. Many have argued that there is something profoundly traumatic in the impulse that underlies deconstruction and Derrida's work, and that this work both enacts and responds to trauma (see Critchley, 1999; Eaglestone, 2004; Ofrat, 2001). A recent Derrida biography suggests political trauma in the events of his life (see Peeters, 2013). However, it is also the case that in the late 1980s and early 1990s, Derrida and those inspired by his work were widely criticised by both the right and the left because many found his work overly textual and distant from the 'real world', unable to address political or ethical issues. This was aggravated by the Paul de Man scandal, when the influential Belgian-born critic was discovered to have published a handful of literary articles in a collaborationist newspaper in occupied Belgium during the Second World War. Much of Derrida's work in the 1990s and afterwards, and much scholarship on his work, aimed to correct this impression. It is in this context that Caruth's and Felman's work developed.

Shoshana Felman and Dori Laub's *Testimony* (1992) also had a huge impact. *Testimony* shows an explicit debt to psychoanalysis and deconstruction, having at its core a sense of oddness and peculiarity connected to trauma: texts 'that testify do not simply *report facts* but, in different ways, encounter – and make us encounter – *strangeness*' (Felman and Laub, 1992: 7). Laub and Felman argue that the strangeness of trauma cannot be easily domesticated. While some of the claims of the book have been questioned, its impact remains powerful (see Trezise, 2008; Laub, 2009), not least in the academy itself, where so many have followed Felman's lead in organising their teaching modules around questions of trauma, testimony and witnessing.

The collection *Trauma: Explorations in Memory* (1995), edited by Caruth, draws on a wide interdisciplinary range of critics and theorists, film-makers and medical experts and practitioners. Her introduction to the volume serves almost as a 'mission statement' for this form of 'trauma theory' and is, perhaps, the most widely cited piece in this field. It claims that trauma consists 'in the *structure of its experience* or reception: the event is not assimilated or experienced fully at the time, but only belatedly, in its repeated *possession* of the one who experiences it' (Caruth, 1995: 4). Caruth's understanding of trauma as a belated experience of the event that defies representation has had a great influence in the development of trauma studies.

The essays in the present volume consider the psychoanalytically based post-deconstructive theories of trauma not as ahistorical contributions to a universalised idea of 'the psyche', but as historically and culturally contingent articulations of issues crucial to the twentieth and twenty-first centuries. Yet we perceive that theories of trauma and the arguments about them have reached an impasse that involves oppositional poles – trauma as the 'unrepresentable' vs. trauma as historical representation, or a broader sense of the 'wounded' subject that exists outside of history vs. the specificity of historical catastrophes in particular places and times. For example, in the introductory essay in the collection *Contemporary Approaches in Literary Trauma Theory*, Michelle Balaev criticises the model of trauma introduced by Caruth in which she thinks '[t]he unspeakable void became the dominant concept in criticism for imagining trauma's function in literature' (2014: 1). According to Balaev, one of the limitations of this model is that it 'moves away from the fact of the lived experience of trauma', 'forgetting that trauma occurs to actual people, in specific bodies, located within particular time periods and places' (7). She argues for a shift from 'the classic model of trauma' to 'the pluralistic model', from 'the focus on trauma as unrepresentable' to 'a focus on the specificity of trauma that locates meaning through a greater consideration of the social and cultural contexts of traumatic experience' (3). Like this argument, many arguments about trauma are based on seemingly oppositional poles.

Samuel Beckett's work manages to walk the line between these two poles in unique ways: though often seen as abstract and anti-representational in many ways, it has connections to the historical and cultural contexts from which it emerged. The experience of trauma found in Beckett's work is characterised by its resistance to representation. Yet this cannot be understood superficially. *Samuel Beckett and trauma* attempts to regard the anti-representational aspect of Beckett's work as something that testifies to a profound question that involves a traumatic experience. Beckett explores the 'force and truth' (Caruth, 1995: vii) of trauma that cannot be resolved or assimilated. In this sense, Beckett's attempt can be read in relation to what is questioned in the post-deconstructive approaches of Caruth and Felman. As mentioned above, Caruth thinks that the pathology of trauma 'consists … solely, in the *structure of its experience* or reception: the event is not assimilated or experienced fully at the time, but only belatedly, in its repeated *possession* of the one who experiences it' (1995: 4). This 'belatedness', or in other words, the structure of trauma as 'afterwardsness', is an important element in Beckett. We need to 'look closely and more carefully not simply at the trauma, but at the structure of experience within which trauma is made manifest' (Eaglestone, 2014: 18). Each essay in this book attempts to 'look closely and more carefully' at the structure of traumatic experience in Beckett's work and to show how it is expressed as an unresolvable force of trauma.

This anti-representational aspect of Beckett's work cannot be grasped in terms of 'the use of experimental, modernist textual strategies' (Craps, 2014: 50). One of the critiques of current trauma theory lies in 'its investment in fragmented modernist aesthetics' (Rothberg, 2014: xiii). Stef Craps, Luckhurst and others have suggested that trauma theory – influenced by Theodor Adorno – has valorised and even often prescribed 'a modernist aesthetic of fragmentation and aporia as uniquely suited to the task of bearing witness to trauma' (Craps, 2014: 46). Craps criticises 'the notion that traumatic experiences can only be adequately represented through the use of experimental, modernist textual strategies' (50). He holds that this assumption of current trauma theory may 'lead to the establishment of a narrow trauma canon' (50) and a 'rush to dismiss whatever deviates from the prescribed aesthetic as regressive or irrelevant' (51). He argues that trauma theory needs to be open to a wide range of cultural forms that bear witness to traumatic events.

Beckett's work sits at the intersection of these contemporary debates in trauma studies. It cannot be denied that his work is characterised by 'a modernist aesthetic of fragmentation and aporia'. However, the modernist aesthetic found in Beckett cannot be understood as mere 'textual strategies' (as suggested by Craps's characterisation). Beckett does not attempt to represent the psychic experience of trauma through the use of anti-narrative, fragmented, modernist textual strategies. For him, artistic expression is never an employment of certain means or strategies. Rather, as he articulated in his oft-quoted dictum from 'Three Dialogues', the artist should prefer 'the expression that there is nothing to express, nothing with which to express, nothing from which to express, no power to express, no desire to express, together with the obligation to express' (1984: 139). Beckett's theatre even enacts this challenge through embodiment and ethics, going far beyond 'mere' text.

While Beckett's work testifies to the profound dimension of traumatic experience, it is closely linked to the historical specificity of trauma. As Andrew Gibson points out, Beckett had 'an unusually profound grasp of the *zeitgeist*, and a power of conveying it unrivalled by any other contemporary artist': 'for all the ostensibly ahistorical character of much of Beckett's writing, it is above all *via* his works that the historical connection makes itself felt' (2010: 21–2). A range of Beckett's works are responses to the historical and cultural situations of his times.

The essays in this volume try to move beyond the impasse that has come to characterise the more orthodox uses of trauma theory in literary studies, taking inspiration from Beckett's own paradigm-shifting formulations of physical and psychic trauma to find new ways of understanding the viewpoints that trauma theory can reveal. Drawing on insights from psychoanalysis, performance studies, philosophy, history and literary studies, *Samuel Beckett and trauma* attempts to open Beckett's work as an avenue for new insights and methodologies for the understanding of cultural trauma. Our selection of contributors and essays, emerging out of the Samuel Beckett Research Circle of Japan and also drawing in prominent and promising Beckett scholars from England, Ireland and Canada, creates a unique frame for viewing Beckett and trauma in historically specific ways as well as in transhistorical ways.

Reflecting the recent scholarly interest in trauma theories, some academics have related trauma to Beckett's work. Erik Tonning's essay 'Not I and the Trauma of Birth' (2006) discusses Beckett's idea of birth-trauma as a state of being unable to leave the womb, in relation to the Freudian 'death drive' depicted in the thematic content and structural build-up of *Not I*. Graley Herren's 'Mourning Becomes Electric: Mediating Loss in *Eh Joe*' in *Samuel Beckett and Pain* (2012) brings into play the writings of Freud, M. Klein and Abraham and Torok to read *Eh Joe* as a mediation on personal loss, comparing it with Shakespeare's *Hamlet* in terms of a meditation upon the vicissitudes of melancholy. Lois Oppenheim's essay 'Life as Trauma, Art as Mastery: Samuel Beckett and the Urgency of Writing' (2008) explores Beckett's urge to write in order to heal his psychic pain. These essays focus on Beckett's work, taking into account the author's personal psychological disorder and incorporating psychoanalytic theories into literary analyses of his work. They examine Beckett's work according to psychoanalytic texts, not the texts of trauma theory.

A scholarly work that concentrates more on Beckett's work in relation to trauma theories is Alysia E. Garrison's '"Faintly

Struggling Things": Trauma, Testimony, and Inscrutable Life in Beckett's *The Unnamable*', in *Samuel Beckett: History, Memory, Archive*. This essay explores Beckett's text's 'undecidability between the "transhistorical" and the "historical" dimensions of trauma' (2009: 105), using Dominick LaCapra's definition of '"testimonial art" or "post-traumatic writing"' that 'bears witness to trauma … "transmitted from intimates, or sensed in one's larger social and cultural setting"' (LaCapra, 2001: 105, quoted in Garrison, 2009: 91). It is an undeniable fact that Beckett's experience working within a Resistance cell and then hiding from the Gestapo during the Second World War affected his postwar writings. Many scholars have referred to these experiences, from Adorno to Ihab Hassan, and in Beckett studies from S. E. Gontarski to Jackie Blackman. However, David Houston Jones's *Samuel Beckett and Testimony* (2011) is the sole book on Beckett that focuses on this central theme of Holocaust studies. Garrison and Jones are successful in analysing the effects of trauma on Beckett's post-Holocaust work, but they may be limited in the sense that their discussions are based on the past trauma theories that addressed events in the West, not least the Holocaust, as opposed to more broad and transcultural discussions of recent years, of which this volume aims to be a part.

Perhaps the most provocative essay concerning trauma in Beckett is Jonathan Boulter's 'Does Mourning Require a Subject? Samuel Beckett's *Texts for Nothing*'. Boulter examines how the concepts of trauma and mourning play out in relation to the narrating subject in Beckett's *Texts for Nothing*, 'a subject without history or memory' (2004: 333). He observes that the Freudian paradigms of trauma and mourning require a stable, unified subject, a subject 'unified enough to perceive the originary shock, if only retroactively' (336) and that 'history – the process by which experience enters and becomes memory – is crucial to the workings of trauma and mourning' (337). Boulter argues that since the subject in the Beckett text has no coherent sense of personal history or memory, its 'ontology denies the viability of mourning and trauma' in that sense (337). Further, he suggests that Beckett's work fundamentally calls into question the value of trauma as a theoretical concept at work in contemporary literary and cultural studies. He writes: 'Beckett's work, in its continual interrogation of the workability of the concepts of trauma and mourning, may in fact be read as a generalized critique of the use of trauma and mourning as interpretive tropes' (345).

However, Russell Smith responds critically to Boulter's reading of subjectivity and mourning in '*Endgame*'s Remainders', in *Dialogues: Samuel Beckett's Endgame*. Smith argues that Boulter's view that the Freudian paradigms of mourning and trauma require a unified subject is 'the attribution to Freud of an unsophisticated notion of the unified subject' which is 'one of the more unfortunate solecisms of orthodox post-structuralist thinking' (2007: 105). He also argues that Boulter's 'insistence on the impossibility of mourning is, precisely, the expression of melancholia' (107). Summarising LaCapra's account of the distinction between absence and loss, Smith writes, 'For LaCapra, absence tends to be non-specific and ahistorical, a kind of logical or even ontological category, whereas losses are always specific, historical events' (111). Boulter reads *Texts for Nothing* with an emphasis on the absence of the subject, therefore denying the existence of a specified subject and its historical meaning, whereas Smith warns that such an interpretation is dangerous because it ignores 'the ethical capacity to confront historical loss' (113). Michael Rothberg, the author of *Multidirectional Memory: Remembering the Holocaust in the Age of Decolonization*, also quoting LaCapra, comments that 'LaCapra's distinction between absence and loss and historical and structural trauma allow us to ask what it means to write ruins' (2009: 152). This suggests that absence and loss, or structural and historical trauma, are inseparable but must be considered separately. Smith holds that 'in *Endgame* Beckett is always careful to maintain the distinction between absence and loss'. While LaCapra's reading of Beckett as 'a novelist and dramatist of absence and not simply loss' (LaCapra, 2001: 67) 'may be true of much of Beckett's fiction (and here LaCapra's reading of Beckett's dismantling of ontological categories seems broadly to accord with Boulter's)', *Endgame* is a play of historical losses, not absences (Smith, 2007: 113–14). Smith reads *Endgame*'s end, wherein Hamm severs melancholic attachments to the remainders of lost objects, as a process of mourning. Smith interprets

Hamm's abandonment of these remainders as 'an ethical act of betrayal that constitutes the accomplishment of the tragic work of mourning' (115). By refusing melancholia, Beckett finally found 'a thoroughly humanistic acceptance of the work of mourning' (117).

While admitting that these different interpretations of trauma in Beckett's work between Boulter and Smith may correspond to the difference between the texts they approach, we could also think that it points to the ambiguity peculiar to Beckett's work. Beckett's work can be read as what involves the lack of history, memory or a subject (or LaCapra's idea of absence) on one hand, *and* as what addresses itself to historical situations (or LaCapra's idea of loss) on the other. It allows the two seemingly opposing approaches to exist, and we might say that thence comes its special appeal.

Building on and extending these preceding works, *Samuel Beckett and trauma* offers new ways of reading and understanding Beckett's work in relation to trauma. Beginning with biographical and intertextual readings of instances of trauma in his work, the essays take up a range of innovative approaches to Beckett, inspired by theories of trauma. The volume consists of three parts that are interrelated and together cover important aspects of the representation of trauma in Beckett's work.

Part I, 'Trauma symptoms', analyses the trauma symptoms that are shown in Beckett's characters, or that are experienced by performers enacting them, the audience watching them or the radio listeners hearing them. According to James Knowlson, Beckett when young was afflicted with symptoms such as insomnia, panic attacks, racing heartbeat and night sweats (1996: 64). Another comment by Knowlson reveals that Beckett had 'obsessional' images of the County Dublin coastline he visited with his family that 'permeated his imagination and pervaded his work' (29). 'The Bailey Lighthouse near Howth flashing across Dublin Bay … Dún Laoghaire and the Forty-Foot were to stay deeply etched in Beckett's memory' (29), but these locations are often described in his work as suggesting something negative: darkness, death, fear, vexation, shame, remorse, etc. Julie Campbell, in 'Beckett

and trauma: the father's death and the sea', focuses specifically on
the fear of diving that Beckett experienced at six years old, which
recurs from the early poem 'For Future Reference' (1930) to the
later fiction *Company* (1980), and analyses how and why it was
traumatic for him. It was one of the most fearful and shameful
experiences Beckett had, exposed not only to his father's eyes but
also to the many other eyes upon him. Hesitating to dive, he felt
ashamed of letting his father down. The incident, together with
the shame and the sense of guilt he felt in mourning his father's
death, traumatised Beckett. The author's trauma, caused by his
remorseful feeling that he had betrayed his father's expectations,
is perhaps most strongly reflected by the character of Henry
in *Embers*. Henry is obsessed with the death of his father, who
drowned at sea but whose body was not found. The main focus
of Campbell's essay is this radio play. According to Campbell,
Henry denies his father's death as if trying to expunge it from
his memory. His distress, anger, bitterness and confusion are
expressed in his commands of his own actions and of the story of
Bolton and Holloway. The radio listeners witness Henry's inner
feelings and share in his suffering.

Nicholas E. Johnson, in '"Void cannot go": trauma and actor
process in the theatre of Samuel Beckett', seeks to develop a new
mode of attention in discussions of Beckett and trauma by fore-
grounding the lived experiences of actors performing Beckett.
It is well known that Billie Whitelaw experienced panic and
vertigo when she performed Mouth in *Not I*, partly because the
play demands a great speed in speaking the lines, which caused
Whitelaw to have difficulty breathing. Others of Beckett's plays
demand physical stillness or constraint, often including stances
that operate as 'stress positions' when sustained over time, such as
in *Endgame*, *Happy Days*, *Play*, *That Time*, *A Piece of Monologue*
and *Catastrophe*. In the rehearsal process, many actors report
traumatic symptoms such as panic, fear, anxiety and nightmares,
but it can be difficult to disentangle the overdetermined origins
of these feelings: are they ingrained in the source material, individual to the actor's process, specific to the performance context,
or simply authentic physiological responses to the physical
demands? Working through these questions first in terms of

contemporary acting theory, Johnson introduces qualitative data from both experienced and early-career practitioners of Beckett. Alongside historical and theoretical explorations of acting, the chapter emphasises the concept of the 'void' as one possible key to navigating the potentially traumatic terrain within Beckett, as well as naming it as one of the tools at the actor's disposal. By connecting to urgent contemporary debates in the medical humanities and positing Beckett as core to a unified theory of acting that takes account of the 'cognitive turn', Johnson's focus on the materiality of these experiences extends a discussion beyond the fictive space of the texts and the biographical, currently the two most common approaches to Beckett and trauma.

Part II of the volume, entitled 'Body and subjectivity', moves on to the deeper questions of traumatic body and subjectivity. According to Ananya Kabir's arguments in 'Affect, Body, Place: Trauma Theory in the World', trauma studies should attend to the presence of 'affect-worlds within which the space of trauma is located'. These affect-worlds are 'epidermal and haptic' and 'invoked through the processes of embodiment'. She argues: 'the body, therefore, must be returned to the centre-stage of analysis; the original meaning of "trauma" – a bodily wound – must be revived in our considerations of how people cope with traumatic histories' (Kabir, 2014: 71–2). Three essays in this part return to the original meaning of 'trauma' by discussing the language of trauma related to bodily wounds.

For David Houston Jones, the privileged site of the body is the face. In his '*Insignificant residues*: trauma, face and *figure* in Samuel Beckett', Jones considers the face as a vector of the expressive capabilities of testimony. He examines a range of dramatic and narrative situations in which the expressive capabilities of the face are pitted against the epistemological problem of testimony, from the deterritorialised face of *Not I* to the inexpressive face in *Watt* and the later prose. This chapter helps to problematise trauma theory by critiquing and extending Agamben's theory of testimony in his *Remnants of Auschwitz*. Indeed, Jones says that 'Agamben casts a long shadow over this essay as a thinker of trauma'. Building on his detailed discussion of the impossibility of speech in Beckett's work in relation to Agamben's account of testimony in his book *Samuel Beckett and Testimony*, Jones turns in this chapter to the question of the face, which Agamben himself left undeveloped after his article 'The Face'. Jones analyses the relation between the impossibility of speech and the expressive uncertainty of the face in Beckett's work. The face is of particular importance because it 'is seen here as the visual figure that best illuminates the interface between Beckett's work and trauma theory and, equally, in Beckett, as a visually coded response to unspeakability'. This analysis constitutes a unique critique of Agamben's idea of testimony and contributes to a rethinking of trauma theory with reference to the realm of the visual.

Michiko Tsushima's chapter, '"The skin of words": trauma and skin in *Watt*', discloses the relationship between trauma and skin in considering *Watt* as a 'skin of words' woven by Beckett – a psychic skin that he tried to recover – and, at the same time, as something that reveals the 'force and truth' (Caruth, 1995: vii) of trauma. In medical and psychiatric literature, especially in Freud's work, the term 'trauma' is used to mean 'a wound inflicted not upon the body but upon the mind'. However, trauma originally meant 'wound' in Greek, 'an injury inflicted on the body' (Caruth, 1996: 3), implying something from the outside that tears, cuts or wounds the skin. Tsushima's chapter tries to return to the original relationship between trauma and skin and understand that relationship as it is presented in Beckett's novel, *Watt*. First, with the help of Didier Anzieu's concept of 'the Skin Ego', Tsushima explores the possibility that Beckett's act of writing *Watt* can be considered an attempt to recover the psychic skin by weaving a 'skin of words'. This act of writing has a therapeutic aspect: by writing *Watt*, Beckett tried to overcome his traumatic experiences and mental crisis during wartime. She also argues that *Watt* explores the 'force and truth' of trauma which cannot be resolved or assimilated. Reading *Watt*, with the help of Caruth's explanation of 'the structure of the experience' of trauma, this chapter discusses how the 'force and truth' of trauma is revealed by the subject 'possessed' by the traumatic experience. Watt, possessed by the traumatic event and alienated by the existing linguistic system, becomes a subject whose existence embodies the force to disrupt existing institutions or traditions. Tsushima shows how the 'force and truth' of trauma manifests itself as a violence to the surface of language, a force that disrupts the apparatus of linguistic representation, in light of Steven Connor's idea of 'an assault upon the skin'.

In 'Bodily object voices in *Embers*', Anna Sigg argues that in this radio play Beckett represents trauma most of all through internal bodily sea sounds. The play effectively 'blinds' its listener and places him or her in a mental cave – a ghostly place of darkness from which the sound of *Embers* emerges. *Embers* focuses on Henry, who is tortured by a roaring 'tinnitus', an internal sea-like sound, which reminds him of the death of his father and his own mortality. Henry re-enacts the stories of his past, but is unable to finish them through the use of words. However, they can be completed by listening to the internal sea sound, which in the 1959 BBC production can be heard during the pauses. This chapter illuminates the connection between Henry's loss and the listener's perception of the 'tinnitus' by drawing on Mladen Dolar's idea of the acousmatic object voice and Jacques Lacan's concept of the *objet petit a*. Dolar states that the object voice is 'a voice whose source one cannot see … [i]t is a voice in search of an origin, in search of a body' (2006: 60). Thus, Henry's 'tinnitus', Sigg argues, is a bodily object voice manifesting an uncanny intimation of the unconscious. It expresses Henry's mourning and his confrontation with mortality, while also generating countermelodies to the traumatic losses inside the listener's head. Sigg suggests that Henry's bodily countermelodies and object voices originate from what Dolar calls 'a blind spot' (2006: 4), a traumatic place of otherness. The BBC's first production of *Embers*, by inserting Donald McWhinnie's roaring sea-like tinnitus sound in the pauses and removing pure silence in the performance, proves that Henry's 'tinnitus', a disturbing head noise, is a powerful bodily internal sound which demands to be heard and reveals its potential for resistance. Inside the listener's head, Henry's 'tinnitus' re-enacts, speaks back to and destabilises the original malleable sonic sound memories.

Part III widens the scope and considers relevant historical and cultural contexts. Yoshiki Tajiri's chapter, 'Trauma and ordinary objects in Virginia Woolf and Samuel Beckett', explores the connection between a traumatised psyche and the ordinary objects surrounding it. While a traumatised subject is compelled to return to the original shocking event, it also needs to cope with the flow of everyday life. In the process, ordinary objects may assume unexpected significance. In Virginia Woolf's *Mrs Dalloway*, Clarissa is haunted by a sense of the precariousness of life. This mental instability derives from the trauma of the First World War. On the other hand, she pays constant attention to the ordinary objects she encounters by chance, as if to reassure herself that she is still alive. In the case of her 'double', Septimus, who is suffering directly from shell shock, the perception of ordinary objects becomes more unstable and problematic. Beckett's work shows the human psyche more radically destroyed than Woolf's. However, as humanity seems to be reduced to its barest minimum in the aftermath of the Second World War and the Holocaust, ordinary objects again become oddly meaningful. In *Happy Days*, for example, Winnie continues to use and even examine her toothbrush in an improbable ruin-like setting, thus stressing the absurdity of ordinary life against the trauma of the calamity. By discussing these two authors, who represent high and late modernism, this chapter illuminates the ways in which trauma and ordinary life are correlated rather than opposed. It also aims to demonstrate that trauma theory and everyday life studies can stimulate each other. Trauma is far from an everyday phenomenon, but it can shed light on the nature of everyday life after calamities of modernity as in the cases of Woolf and Beckett. Conversely, there may be ways of enriching trauma studies by incorporating reflections on everyday life. This chapter thus offers a close and careful look 'not simply at the trauma, but at the structure of experience within which trauma is made manifest' (Eaglestone, 2014: 18). To consider trauma in relation to the way a traumatised subjectivity comes to terms with everyday life may be conducive to such a project to open up trauma studies, particularly when it is applied to literature.

Conor Carville's 'Smiling tigers: trauma, sexuality and creaturely life in *Echo's Bones*' approaches the trauma in Beckett from a unique perspective. It is well known that Beckett was deeply interested in Otto Rank's 1924 book *The Trauma of Birth*. Its influence is particularly conspicuous in Beckett's early works, including the early poems collected in *Echo's Bones and Other Precipitates* (1935). By analysing 'Sanies I' and 'Serena II' meticulously, with special attention to the animal imagery, Carville links Rank's theory of the trauma of birth with Eric Santner's recent idea of 'creaturely life' – the life that is exposed to biopolitical power at moments of trauma. Trauma is here considered as constitutive of the subject, not as an exceptional phenomenon, and also as providing the raw material for biopolitical power. In the process of Carville's analyses emerge hitherto uncharted networks concerning Beckett's fixation on the trauma of birth and contemporary biopolitical concerns with birth, reproduction and population in Ireland and Britain. Carville's chapter not only provides original close readings of those difficult poems in light of Rank, but also illustrates how a highly personal unease about sexual identity caused by birth trauma can be connected to biopolitical discourses by the use of Santner's idea of 'creaturely life', which itself draws on the ideas of Benjamin, Foucault, Lacan, Agamben and other theorists.

Mariko Hori Tanaka, in 'The global trauma of the nuclear age in Beckett's post-war plays', focuses on how Beckett responds to the imagined nuclear winter inherent in the global competition in the production of nuclear bombs and energy during the Cold War years. In his biography of Beckett, Andrew Gibson writes, 'From the mid-1950s onwards, there is a strain in Beckett's art which seems less abstract than global. [… His works] clearly respond to a historical condition, that of the Cold War' (2010: 133). Many of his post-war plays, including *Endgame* and *Happy Days*, are clearly set in a post-apocalyptic world, where the only human survivors are the onstage characters. The earth uninhabited and the landscape of ruins with the last remaining human beings barely alive are suggested in many of Beckett's works. During the Cold War, science fiction that dealt with global calamity became popular. Porter Abbott categorises Beckett's works after *Endgame* as 'utopian fictions' (1996: 133), while Veronica Hollinger finds in the play the sense of forever unending, an end endlessly deferred. Such a sense is found in the post-9/11 novel by William Gibson, *Pattern Recognition*, set in the endless endtimes of the future-present (Hollinger, quoted in Mousoutzanis, 2014: 125). Our post-Holocaust world is filled with repeated calamities such as wars, conflicts and natural disasters, so that we endlessly feel a sense of apocalypse. Beckett's sense of men and women living in worsening conditions towards the unseen ending is the global anxiety shared in the late twentieth and twenty-first century. Beckett's imagination of dead victims ruined and suffering in some traumatic event (which he never clarifies) reminds us, the audience and the readers, of those who have suffered and died in apocalyptic disasters. This chapter thus deals with the recent globally shared cultural traumas in our age. It will open up the discussion of the future of trauma studies and Beckett.

In his essay 'Future Shock: Science Fiction and the Trauma Paradigm', Luckhurst considers science fiction as the best place to examine the future of trauma, arguing that the technological transformation of subjectivity itself in science fiction may necessitate a reconsideration of the notion of trauma (2014: 161). In a similar manner, the transformation of subjectivity itself is inseparable from the unique representation of trauma in Beckett's work. In this collection, we thus present subjectivity in Beckett's work, such as the subject exposed to biopolitical power that Carville reads in his analysis of Beckett's poems, the subject as a ruin in the 'apocalyptic' time that Hori Tanaka examines, or 'the void' navigated by actors when performing Beckett's work in Johnson's chapter. The post-traumatic state of Beckett's new subject is explored in Campbell's biographical discussions of Beckettian characters, in Sigg's examination of 'tinnitus' and in Jones's study of testimonial potentials of the face, whereas Tajiri and Tsushima focus on how such a post-traumatic state influences behaviour in everyday life and its linguistic representation.

As we argued earlier in this Introduction, the anti-representational subject in Beckett transforms the concept of trauma itself. In his work, the concept of trauma is tested at the intersection of material, bodily, psychic, cultural, historical and structural concerns. The representation of trauma in his work traverses these and goes beyond simple binary oppositions. It also hints at, to borrow James Berger's words about sites of apocalypse, 'sites of unrepresentability out of which representation emerges, sites of absolute rupture that impel transmission, sites of the destruction and generation of structures' (1999: 119). It marks a no-man's land suspended in void where silence and screams coexist, and yet it is not separable from historical particulars.

References

Abbott, H. Porter (1996). *Beckett Writing Beckett: The Author in the Autograph*. Ithaca, NY: Cornell University Press.

Agamben, Giorgio (2002). *Remnants of Auschwitz: The Witness and the Archive*. New York: Zone Books.

Balaev, Michelle (ed.) (2014). *Contemporary Approaches in Literary Trauma Theory*. Basingstoke: Palgrave Macmillan.

Beckett, Samuel (1984). *Disjecta: Miscellaneous Writings and a Dramatic Fragment*. Ed. Ruby Cohn. New York: Grove Press.

Berger, James (1999). *After the End: Representations of Post-Apocalypse*. Minneapolis, MN: University of Minnesota Press.

Boulter, Jonathan (2004). 'Does Mourning Require a Subject? Samuel Beckett's *Texts for Nothing*', *Modern Fiction Studies* 50.2, 332–50.

Butler, Judith (2004). *Precarious Life: The Power of Mourning and Violence*. London: Verso.

Butler, Judith (2009). *Frames of War: When Is Life Grievable?* London: Verso.

Caruth, Cathy (ed.) (1995). *Trauma: Explorations in Memory*. Baltimore, MD: Johns Hopkins University Press.

Caruth, Cathy (1996). *Unclaimed Experience: Trauma, Narrative, and History*. Baltimore, MD: Johns Hopkins University Press.

Craps, Stef (2014). 'Beyond Eurocentrism: Trauma Theory in the Global Age'. In Gert Buelens, Sam Durrant and Robert Eaglestone (eds), *The Future of Trauma Theory: Contemporary Literary and Cultural Criticism*. London: Routledge, pp. 45–61.

Critchley, Simon (1999). *Ethics–Politics–Subjectivity*. London: Verso.

Dolar, Mladen (2006). *A Voice and Nothing More*. Cambridge, MA: MIT Press.

Eaglestone, Robert (2004). *The Holocaust and the Postmodern*. Oxford: Oxford University Press.

Eaglestone, Robert (2014). 'Knowledge, "Afterwardsness" and the Future of Trauma Theory'. In Gert Buelens, Sam Durrant and Robert Eaglestone (eds), *The Future of Trauma Theory: Contemporary Literary and Cultural Criticism*. London: Routledge, pp. 11–21.

Felman, Shoshana, and Dori Laub (1992). *Testimony: Crises of Witnessing in Literature, Psychoanalysis, and History*. London: Routledge.

Frank, Arthur (1995). *The Wounded Storyteller: Body, Illness and Ethics*. Chicago: University of Chicago Press.

Garrison, Alysia E. (2009). '"Faintly Struggling Things": Trauma, Testimony, and Inscrutable Life in Beckett's *The Unnamable*'. In Seán Kennedy and Katherine Weiss (eds), *Samuel Beckett: History, Memory, Archive*. Basingstoke: Palgrave, pp. 89–109.

Gibson, Andrew (2010). *Samuel Beckett*. London: Reaktion Books.

Hacking, Ian (1995). *Rewriting the Soul: Multiple Personality and the Sciences of Memory*. Princeton, NJ: Princeton University Press.

Halbwachs, Maurice (1992). *On Collective Memory*. Ed. and trans. Lewis A. Coser. Chicago: University of Chicago Press.

Herman, Judith Lewis (1994). *Trauma and Recovery: From Domestic Abuse to Political Terror*. London: Harper Collins.

Herren, Graley (2012). 'Mourning Becomes Electric: Mediating Loss in *Eh Joe*'. In Mariko Hori Tanaka, Yoshiki Tajiri and Michiko Tsushima (eds), *Samuel Beckett and Pain*. Amsterdam: Rodopi, pp. 43–65.

Hollinger, Veronica (1992). 'Playing at the End of the World: Postmodern Theater'. In Patrick D. Murphy (ed.), *Staging the Impossible: The Fantastic Mode in Modern Drama*. Westport, CT: Praeger Publishers, pp. 182–96.

Jones, David Houston (2011). *Samuel Beckett and Testimony*. Basingstoke: Palgrave.

Kabir, Ananya (2014). 'Affect, Body, Place: Trauma Theory in the World'. In Gert Buelens, Sam Durrant and Robert Eaglestone (eds), *The Future of Trauma Theory: Contemporary Literary and Cultural Criticism*. London: Routledge, pp. 63–75.

Klein, Kerwin Lee (2000). 'On the Emergence of Memory in Historical Discourse', *Representations* 69, 127–50.

Knowlson, James (1996). *Damned to Fame: The Life of Samuel Beckett*. London: Bloomsbury.

LaCapra, Dominick (2001). *Writing History, Writing Trauma*. Baltimore, MD: Johns Hopkins University Press.

Laub, Dori (2009). 'On Holocaust Testimony and Its "Reception" within its Own Frame, as a Process in its Own Right: A Response to "Between History and Psychoanalysis" by Thomas Trezise', *History & Memory* 21.1, 127–50.

Luckhurst, Roger (2008). *The Trauma Question*. London: Routledge.

Luckhurst, Roger (2014). 'Future Shock: Science Fiction and the Trauma Paradigm'. In Gert Buelens, Sam Durrant and Robert Eaglestone (eds),

The Future of Trauma Theory: Contemporary Literary and Cultural Criticism. London: Routledge, pp. 157–67.

Mousoutzanis, Aris (2014). '"Soul Delay": Trauma and Globalization in William Gibson's *Pattern Recognition* (2003)'. In Monica Germanà and Aristeidis Mousoutzanis (eds), *Apocalyptic Discourse in Contemporary Culture: Post-Millennial Perspectives of the End of the World*. London: Routledge, pp. 117–29.

Nora, Pierre, and David P. Jordan (eds) (2009). *Rethinking France: Les Lieux De Memoire*. Trans. David P. Jordan. Chicago: University of Chicago Press.

Ofrat, Gideon (2001). *The Jewish Derrida*. Trans. Peretz Kidron. Syracuse, NY: Syracuse University Press.

Oppenheim, Lois (2008). 'Life as Trauma, Art as Mastery: Samuel Beckett and the Urgency of Writing', *Contemporary Psychoanalysis* 44.3, 419–42.

Peeters, Benoît (2013). *Derrida: A Biography*. Trans. Andrew Brown. Cambridge: Polity.

Rothberg, Michael (2009). *Multidirectional Memory: Remembering the Holocaust in the Age of Decolonization*. Stanford, CA: Stanford University Press.

Rothberg, Michael (2014). 'Preface: Beyond Tancred and Clorinda – Trauma Studies for Implicated Subjects'. In Gert Buelens, Sam Durrant and Robert Eaglestone (eds), *The Future of Trauma Theory: Contemporary Literary and Cultural Criticism*. London: Routledge, pp. xi–xiii.

Smith, Russell (2007). '*Endgame*'s Remainders'. In Mark S. Byron (ed.), *Samuel Beckett's* Endgame. Amsterdam: Rodopi, pp. 99–120.

Tonning, Erik (2006). '*Not I* and the Trauma of Birth', *Journal of Beckett Studies* 15.1&2, 21–34.

Trezise, Thomas (2008). 'Between History and Psychoanalysis: A Case Study in the Reception of Holocaust Survivor Testimony', *History & Memory* 20.1, 7–47.

Yerushalmi, Yosef Hayim (1982). *Zakhor: Jewish History and Jewish Memory*. Seattle, WA: University of Washington Press.

Part I

Trauma symptoms

1

Beckett and trauma: the father's death and the sea

Julie Campbell

Recent discussions of trauma

This chapter begins by focusing on trauma in relation to recent discussions concerning the causes and symptoms of a traumatic reaction to an event. The website 'Emotional and Psychological Trauma: Causes, Symptoms, Help' contends that '[i]t's not the objective facts that determine whether an event is traumatic but [the] *subjective emotional experience* of the event' (Robinson, Smith and Segal, 1). This is very useful, as it cautions against thinking about trauma in terms of a limited set of definitions in relation to the causal episode, and this corresponds with many recent discussions of trauma. Trauma does not only result from the death of a loved one or a near-death experience, but from an experience that is felt as terrifying, and also transforms the subject's perception of the external world. Robert Scaer, for example, says the following:

> I attempt to redefine trauma as a continuum of variably negative life events occurring over the lifespan, including events that may be accepted as 'normal' in the context of our daily experience … [T]he traumatic nature of those experiences is also determined by the *meaning* the victim attributes to them. That meaning is based on the cumulative burden of a myriad of prior negative life events, especially those experienced in the vulnerable period of early childhood. (2005: 2)

He also contends that symptoms of trauma involve a far broader spectrum than past definitions allow for:

The varied symptoms of trauma ... fall under the definition of conditioned responses. These symptoms are incredibly varied. They include abnormal memories (flashback images, intrusive conscious memories, recurring physical sensations, nightmares), abnormal arousal (panic, anxiety, startle), and numbing (confusion, isolation, avoidance, dissociation) [...]. The core of this problem is the fact that procedural and declarative memories for the traumatic event, and the conditioned sensory perceptions and reflex motor responses associated with those memories, continue to replicate the failed efforts at successful fight or flight responses. (2005: 42)

Beckett was himself subject to many of the symptoms noted by Scaer: nightmares, panic attacks, isolation and numbness. He described to James Knowlson how his racing heartbeat kept him awake at night and how he experienced 'dreadful night sweats and feelings of panic' (Knowlson, 1996: 64). In a letter to Thomas McGreevy on 10 March 1935, he wrote about his 'misery & solitude & apathy' and the 'terrifying physical symptoms' (Beckett, 2009: 258, 259) he had suffered from for many years. These personal experiences gave him not only a comprehensive understanding of the fearfulness and panic that trauma elicits, but also a strong sympathy and compassion for sufferers, which is clearly evident in his work.

Scaer explains that intense life experiences change 'the brain permanently in the way that it specifically reacts to subsequent similar experiences'; brain-imaging studies have shown that 'unconscious patterns of learned behaviour' are created (2005: 17). The result is that experiences perceived as threatening 'prompt unconscious conditioned responses related to cues from that experience' (31). Mardi Horowitz (1986) and Ronnie Janoff-Bulman (1992) have examined the ways in which traumatic events shatter pre-existing ideas about the world. The perception of a safe and reliable world is transformed and replaced; the world appears fragile, unpredictable and full of danger: 'the sense of having control' over life and events is lost (Harvey, 2002: 17).

This recalls Sigmund Freud, in 'Beyond the Pleasure Principle', where he describes 'as "traumatic" any excitations from outside which are powerful enough to break through the protective shield' (Freud, 1991: 301). This shield allows us to perceive an illusory external world which is benevolent, safe, predictable and within our control; the shattering of this shield creates access to the unpleasant truth that there *is* danger out there and much that is beyond our control: the sudden shock of such knowledge through a traumatic event can be completely debilitating. In 'Mourning and Melancholia' (1917), Freud suggests that the process of mourning is the working through of the loss of the loved object, while his nephew in 'Beyond the Pleasure Principle' is described as playing a game in order to retain a sense of mastery over the lost object, his mother: in fact, to gain a sense of mastery over the unmasterable. In a sense the fort/da game enables a return to the illusion, the comfort of illusion: a comforting sense of control.

Slavoj Žižek, in 'Melancholy and the Act', makes an interesting critique of Freud's position in 'Mourning and Melancholia':

> Freud opposed normal mourning (the successful acceptance of a loss) to pathological melancholy (the subject persists in his or her narcissistic identification with the lost object). Against Freud, one should assert the conceptual *and* ethical primacy of melancholy. In the process of the loss, there is always a remainder that cannot be integrated through the work of mourning, and the ultimate fidelity is the fidelity to this remainder. Mourning is a kind of betrayal, the second killing of the (lost) object, while the melancholic subject remains faithful to the lost object, refusing to renounce his or her attachment to it. (2000: 658)

Žižek is describing how the subject keeps the lost object 'alive' through memory, through choice, through a refusal to forget, but there is more than conscious choice involved, for, as Scaer explains, the '[m]emory that is associated with intense emotional states is relatively permanent and the brain pathways that mediate it are partly unconscious' and 'readily retrievable into conscious memory' (2005: 40). This relative permanence is an important factor, as it suggests that a conscious desire to forget and 'move on' is not within a traumatised person's control. The melancholic subject may well have no choice but to remain 'faithful to the lost object', with an inability 'to renounce his or her attachment', as the memories return unbidden, in nightmares, or in unsolicited responses to external stimuli. John H. Harvey doubts 'if closure is possible' and disagrees with the idea that closure should be sought

(2002: 5). It may be that working through trauma is not just a difficult and problematic process but, ultimately, an impossible one. Jonathan Boulter references Žižek's questioning of Freud's views on mourning and melancholia in *Melancholy and the Archive*, and points to Freud's admission in 'Mourning and Melancholia' that the melancholic 'has a keener eye for the truth than other people who are not melancholic' (Freud, 1991: 255). The process of mourning, in effect, results in a denial of the truth, a forgetting of the past. As Boulter maintains, there is an ambivalence in Freud's thought here in relation to his emphasis on facing the truth of the past elsewhere in his theoretical discourse. Mourning is a working through towards 'an eventual erasure of the past – or at least its resonance – [and this] is at explicit odds with Freud's own sense, repeatedly demonstrated, that the past truly is inescapable' (Boulter, 2011: 22).

In an earlier work, 'Does Mourning Require a Subject? Samuel Beckett's *Texts for Nothing*', Boulter suggests that trauma 'in relation to Beckett, manages to avoid [the] ghostly metaphysical haunting, [the] nostalgia for an originary subject and scene of loss' (2004: 333) which are a central focus of discussions of trauma. He considers that Beckett's work 'avoids this haunting precisely because the Beckettian narrator is unable to present itself as a stable, unified (or potentially unified) subject. My interest here is to explore how trauma and mourning play out in relation to a subject without history or memory, without, that is, those preconditions for trauma and mourning' (333).

Boulter is discussing *Texts for Nothing* specifically, and presents an interesting and convincing argument, but does mistakenly generalise the way trauma can be read in relation to other works by Beckett. The intention of this chapter is to not to present Beckett's poetic voices, narrators or characters as 'stable, unified (or potentially unified)' subjects, as they definitely are not. Disunity and lack of stability are symptomatic of traumatic reactions. But the texts I will discuss *do* portray subjects haunted by personal history and memory, where characters *are* preoccupied by 'ghostly metaphysical haunting [and the] nostalgia for an originary subject and scene of loss'.

Forty-Foot

Knowlson, in *Damned to Fame*, describes a persistent memory of Beckett's which featured

> his father in the sea below inviting him to dive in from the rocks of the Forty-Foot at Sandycove. Diving through the air was an experience that entered into his dreams as a child and returned to him often as an adult. Dreams frequently turned into nightmare as he saw himself diving into too narrow a pool between jagged walls of a rock face. (1996: 20)

The recurring nightmares suggest that this experience was of a traumatic nature, as they have the characteristic Freud described 'of repeatedly bringing the patient back into the situation ... a situation from which he wakes up in another fright' (1991: 282). Lawrence E. Harvey describes how 'Beckett was plagued by a recurring nightmare in which he was required to dive into a small and distant pool closely ringed by jagged rocks [...]. He attributes such dreams to diving lessons he received at the age of six from his father at the "Forty-Foot Hole," a rocky swimming pool on the coast south of Dublin' (1970: 298).

Beckett described the nightmares as exaggerating the danger, as they 'shrank the pool, sharpened the rocks, and elevated the diving board' (Harvey, 1970: 298). What this process demonstrates is not the perception of the 'Forty-Foot' by the adult Beckett in the 1960s, who had returned and made the dive on many occasions, but the perceptions of the six-year-old boy, and the terror that this little boy must have felt. In a recent email exchange Knowlson explained that, as far as he knew, there was a successful dive at the Forty-Foot on that day.[1]

However, as Scaer observes, '[u]nder certain circumstances ... the intense arousal that was associated with a traumatic event is conditioned to the cues derived from sensory messages from the body at that moment' (2005: 18), and he stresses the fact that 'childhood is the life period of greatest helplessness' (262). And, as the event involved the father he loved and trusted, and thus the source of his sense of safety, it involved a terrifying transformation: this benign figure suddenly, and shockingly, became the source of threat. Patrick Bracken describes how subjects faced with a perceived threat 'in situations where they felt safe were more likely to suffer severe reactions' (2002: 54).

Eoin O'Brien contends, matter-of-factly, that Beckett's father 'who swam in the all-male preserve known as the Forty Foot at Sandycove deemed it a fitting place to introduce his children to the water' (1986: 85). It must be remembered that Beckett was only six years old when he stood so high up on the diving board with his father urging him to jump, and it is intriguing to explore the ways in which this experience entered into his writing.

Company (completed in 1979, published in 1980) includes a description of a young boy, standing perilously on a diving board. The use of the second-person 'you' encourages the reader to share imaginatively in the experience, and to judge how this 'fitting place' would have been perceived by the young boy:

> You stand at the tip of the high board. High above the sea. In it your father's upturned face. Upturned to you. You look down to the loved trusted face. He calls to you to jump. He calls, Be a brave boy. The red round face. The thick moustache. The greying hair. The swell sways it under and sways it up again. The far call again, Be a brave boy. Many eyes upon you. From the water and from the bathing place. (Beckett, 1980: 23–4)

The precariousness of the position is emphasised: 'you' are at the 'tip' of the 'high board' with the 'high' repeated: 'High above the sea'. The father is looking up, there is his 'upturned face' and all importantly it is 'Upturned to *you*' (my emphasis). 'You look down', a long, long way, from the height of the high board, and see the 'loved trusted face' – a face 'you' love, a face 'you' trust. 'You' are being called 'to jump'; 'He calls'; 'He calls, Be a brave boy.' So this is a test, a test of 'your' bravery, 'your' masculinity. 'You' can't let him down, but 'you' are terrified. It's that familiar face, the face 'you' associate with love and protection: 'The red round face. The thick moustache. The greying hair.' 'Your' father is asking 'you' to jump into the 'swell [that] sways [his face] under and sways it up again'. The 'far call' comes again: 'Be a brave boy.' Your father is watching 'you', and 'many eyes [are] upon you' – 'you' are being judged; 'you' must be brave; 'you' must jump. 'You' feel the shame of 'your' fear, 'you' need to be brave: brave for 'your' father, brave for all those people watching 'you'.

Bracken contends that '[a] traumatic event presents information which conflicts with pre-existing schemas. There is thus an incongruity which gives rise to distress … [and a] revision of the schemas', a process which can be very prolonged (2002: 55). The young boy's 'pre-existing schemas' included a father who he loved and trusted, who would protect him from danger, and who was proud of him, and a self who was brave and fearless and who would never let his father down. Although readers will not share this actual childhood event, they will also have memories of significant childhood episodes when they have felt the shame of letting a parent down, and even of occasions when their idealised perception of a parent has been challenged. It communicates to a reader through their own memories of the shattering of pre-existing schemas, memories of those moments that alter fondly held perceptions, memories that in fact make us who we are, that construct our sense of the self and others and our perception of the world we live in.

It is of interest to turn to other occasions when the Forty-Foot incident finds its way into Beckett's work. It is first alluded to in the poem 'For Future Reference' (completed in 1929; first published 1930). As Seán Lawlor and John Pilling elucidate, the poem has the 'first occurrence of the diving board imagery, re-used in "Spring Song" (line 15)', *Dream of Fair to middling Women*, *Watt*, *Eleutheria* and *Company* (Beckett, 2012: 303). The repeated references to the Forty-Foot episode fit with the repetitive return of the past, symptomatic of trauma (Scaer, 2005: 59). The poem can be related to Scaer's description of trauma as 'an aberration of memory': '[t]he past event is ever-present, awaiting its chance to intrude on our daily life based on the subtlest of cues' when the 'old memories' are 'fragmented, distorted, at times terrifying, at times confusing' (2005: 252).

In 'For Future Reference' (Beckett, 2012: 28–30), the poem presents a memory of a fight when the adversary was successfully overcome, as were the fears: 'I stilled my cringing/ I did' (lines 12–13); 'I smote him/ ah my strength/ smashed/ mashed/ peace my incisors/ brayed him and flayed him' (lines 14–19), but this is followed by the question, accentuated by standing alone as a three-word stanza: 'But did I?' (line 22). The memory is challenged, destabilised, and this leads to the memory of a dive:

And then the bright waters
beneath the broad board
the trembling blade of the streamlined divers
and down to our waiting
to our enhanced buoyancy
come floating the words of
the Mutilator. (lines 23–9).

Ruby Cohn describes these lines as revolving 'around a terrifying plunge into deep water' and how, '[a]s in nightmare, one image floats into another [...]' (2001: 8). Beckett told L. E. Harvey of how he 'was plagued by a recurring nightmare' concerning the Forty-Foot dive. Traumatic memories invade the dreams of the subject, but, as Scaer reports, they also intrude into the subject's consciousness unbidden. The poem describes the subject's bravery, and then questions it – 'But did I?' This could be seen as the subtle cue that brings to mind the trauma of the Forty-Foot experience, when fear was experienced (would the young boy be brave?), and the shame at this fear (a shame exposed to the father's and the many other eyes that are upon him). Was the 'cringing' described in 'For Future Reference' really 'stilled'? This question seems to prompt and intermingle with the memory of the earlier event: the dive. In this poem the distortion and intermingling of past and present that is symptomatic of trauma are presented (Scaer, 2005: 253). L. E. Harvey suggests that the 'Mutilator' would 'seem to be a professor giving a lecture on anatomy' (1970: 300, n. 87). The 'displacement' (line 3) can be related to the transformation of the father into the professor, which fits with Cohn's idea of one image floating into another. Harvey sees the '[f]ear of the teacher ... associated with fear of high places' (1970: 298). Scaer contends that '[a]ll threatening experiences ... will prompt unconscious conditioned responses related to cues from that experience' (2005: 31); conditioned responses have developed which shape future reactions, which are stored, it could be said, 'for future reference'. Fear prompts

the memory of the fear felt on that diving board at Forty-Foot, yet
the poem describes the successful entry into the 'bright waters'
that follows the dive. Maybe, unconsciously, the question 'But did
I?' hangs over this event, too. It seems to present a successful dive
which should have alleviated the fear felt on the tip of the diving
board, but this question ('But did I?) undercuts any triumph, and
the fear is still fixed, as if indelibly, in the memory. 'Into the water
or on to the stones?' (line 60) presents a question that would have
been a fearful concern when looking down from high up on that
diving board.

In Victor Krap's dream, at the beginning of Act III of *Eleutheria*
(completed 1947; first British publication, 1996), there is a return
to the diving scene:

> *Victor* [is] *alone, lying down. He is asleep.* [He is being watched by]
> *The glazier in the doorway.*
> Victor (*in his sleep*) No … no … too high … rocks … my body
> … Papa … be brave … brave boy … I am brave … a brave boy …
> brave boy … (Beckett, 1996: 118)

Victor seems to be reliving Beckett's own recurring nightmare
of standing on the diving board at Forty-Foot; he is experiencing
the fears that must have assaulted Beckett as a six year old as he
stood precariously on the tip of that diving board: there is fear
for his body, fear of failing his father, fear of not being brave,
fear of death. It is significant to note that with the words 'be
brave' the father's voice enters the dream, although these words
can also be interpreted as the dream self's identification with the
father, which is in line with Freud's contention in 'The Ego and
the Id' that 'an individual's first and most important identification [is] his identification with the father' (1991: 370). The play
continues:

> *Silence.* [Victor] *tosses and turns. Louder:*
> Fathom … full fathom five … at low tide … low tide … fathomless
> … fathomless … wild waves. (Beckett, 1996: 118)

Now the memory has become intermingled with *The Tempest*.
Ariel is singing a song, and this is listened to by Ferdinand, who
describes himself 'Sitting on a bank,/ Weeping again the King my

father's wrack' (I.ii.392–3). Ariel sings: '*Full fadom five thy father lies*' (I.ii.399).

The connection being made in the dream no doubt concerns the fear of death by drowning in the sea inspired by the diving event, and it is an interesting recognition of the way that drama can summon up deep memories in audience members, often existing beneath fully conscious awareness, which form a part of the identification that arises and aids the shared experience with dramatic characters that spectators experience. However, it is interesting that it is the father's presumed death and the son's grieving that this allusion points to, though the father, Alonzo, also grieves for his son, who he presumes was drowned in the sea (II.i.102–9). The reference to 'low tide' may well be referring to the memory of the fear that the water at the Forty-Foot will not be deep enough to safely dive into. The dreaming continues: '*Silence. Enter the glazier. He goes to the bed.* Those ... eyes ... a thousand ships ... towers ... circumcised ... fire ... fire ...' (Beckett, 1996: 118). And now the play alluded to is *Doctor Faustus*, and the eyes that launched a thousand ships, and perhaps the connection being made is with the Father's eyes and the '[m]any eyes upon you' referred to in *Company*, and again the image of the sea is present with the 'thousand ships'. The 'towers' and the 'circumcision' may perhaps allude to the threat he felt to his perception of his own masculinity if he failed to act bravely. This is followed by '*Silence*' (118). And then the Glazier shouts, shakes him and wakes him up. This is a short but significant reference, which gives a strong sense of how the images associated with the event haunted Beckett.

In *Dream of Fair to middling Women*, again the reference to the diving scene is connected to dreaming (as it is later in *Watt*). Here, it is swathed in romantic dream images. Belacqua is sharing the diving scenario with the Syra-Cusa, whose body is described in images of water: her body is 'more perfect than dream creek, amarynth lagoon'; she flows as she moves. It is a lush, romantic description undercut by the admission that '[h]er neck was scraggy and her head was null' (Beckett, 1993: 33). Belacqua imagines walking with her in terms of musicality. He pictures her 'dream-dive', whereas Belacqua, it would seem, remains alone, '[h]igh over [the] dream-water':

> To take her arm, to flow together, out of step, down the asphalt bed, was a foundering in music, the slow ineffable flight of a dream-dive, a launching and terrible foundering in a rich rape of water. Her grace was supplejack, it was cuttystool and cavaletto, he trembled as on a springboard, jutting out, doomed, high over dream-water. (33–4)

That the dream-dive is 'ineffable', beyond description, fits with other references to the diving incident, as, although the fear is conveyed to the reader, it is never verbalised. In *Company* the facts and the actions are recounted: 'You stand [...] You look [...] He calls [...]'; in 'For Future Reference' it is the blade that trembles rather than the young boy. In *Eleutheria* the situation is displaced on to references to Shakespeare and Marlowe. The dive itself is not recounted (except in 'For Future Reference', when it is challenged), and here it is the Syra-Cusa's dive that is described, watched by Belacqua, who remains high up on the diving board, trembling. Here there is a 'terrible foundering' when the water is entered, while the words 'rich rape' to describe the water perhaps allude to Belacqua's desire for a violent sexual encounter, 'foundering' in the flowing water and music of the Syra-Cusa's body. The reference to the fear instilled by the diving board, described as 'jutting out' (which could be a phallic allusion), 'doomed' and 'high', is expressive of the fearfulness also felt towards attempting such a sexual encounter. The connection with the Forty-Foot event may well be that the sexual act is anticipated as a leap into the unknown, a long, long fall, in fact a doomed fall: envisaged as doomed before the leap takes place.

In *Watt* (competed in 1945; published in 1953) the image of diving follows a period of great fatigue, with a 'desire for rest so strong' that Watt seems to want to rest and to put 'his arms on the table' and bury 'his head in his arms ... perhaps even of falling, after a moment or two, into an uneasy sleep' (Beckett, 1963: 221). He does not do this, and perhaps the fear is that his sleep will be 'lacerated by dreams, by dives from dreadful heights into rocky waters, before a numerous public' (221). But the reader can't be sure. This is *Watt*, after all, and the tortuous method by which the narrator, Sam, receives the story from Watt means that he 'missed ... much ... of great interest' when noting down Watt's report (166). But it seems that sleep, for Watt, is accompanied by nightmares of diving, as it was for his creator.

Why did Beckett bring his own nightmares into his work? It could be suggested that it was part of a therapeutic process – to deal with his troubled dreams by recollecting them consciously and externalising them in his writing – but I find this unconvincing. In a letter to Thomas McGreevy, dated 16 January 1936, Beckett quotes from a letter he received from his analyst Wilfred Bion, following the end of his analysis. Bion wrote that he '"trusted I had now taken up my work with pleasure and satisfaction", as he was sure I must "even though not entirely free from neurosis"' (Beckett, 2009: 299). The first quotation implies that Bion had suggested that creativity would be a therapeutic activity, whereas the second recognises that Beckett had not reached closure. I think it may well have been the case that Beckett realised that closure was not possible. He told McGreevy that '[i]ndeed I do not see what difference the analysis has made'; he still has difficult relations with his mother, the difficult nights and the heart palpitations (300). But he has learned something about himself: the '2 years have taught me who I am' (300). I would contend that a very significant reason why Beckett is a great writer is because he was writing from his own experience. Not, of course, in any realist way, but writing from his *inner* experiences. He realised that there is much beyond understanding, apprehended the ineffable nature of inner experience, and intimated that life, inner and outer, is not a tidy, simple affair with everything in the right place, safe, ordered, reliable and cosy. Bracken considers that when, as a result of trauma, the perception of a safe and reliable world is transformed and replaced, this 'can lead to the opening up of new imaginative and artistic paths', and he contends that '[s]ome of the great artistic achievements of the twentieth century … have emerged directly from a confrontation with the naked contingency of our situation as human beings' (2002: 2).

During the 'Beckett and Brain Science' symposium at Warwick University (18 September 2012), delegates discussed the ways in which Beckett's drama impelled his actors to embody suffering and communicate intense feelings. The visual and sound images, the restricted movements and entrapment were viewed as taking the experience beyond words, which so often fail to convey hidden inner states, and this was seen as encouraging audience members to share in and recognise, in their own inner selves, similar feelings and affects to those portrayed by the drama. His work manages to convey truths that are hidden and often repressed and unacknowledged in conscious life.

His father's death

Beckett's father died on 26 June 1933. He wrote to Thomas McGreevy on 2 July:

> Father died last Monday afternoon after an illness lasting just under a week, and was buried on the following Wednesday morning in a little cemetery on the Greystones side of the Bray Head, between the mountains and the sea. Mother and I nursed him while he was ill. The doctor saw him the morning he died and told us that he was much better. I was so delighted that I got into the brightest clothes I could find. The doctor was scarcely out of the house before he collapsed. I fear he suffered a great deal before he died about 4 o'clock in the afternoon. We were all with him. He was very beautiful when it was all over. I thought Mother would go to pieces, but she was and is wonderful. It is a very blank silent house now.
> [...]
> I can't write about him, I can only walk the fields and climb the ditches after him. (Beckett, 2009: 164–5)

Knowlson describes Beckett as '[d]evastated by the loss of his father [...] feeling a crushing sense of guilt at having, as he saw it, let his father down' (1996: 171). His letter to McGreevy makes it clear that the death was sudden and unexpected, following the reassuring words of the doctor. The suddenness, the unpreparedness and the lack of ability to prevent the death are all prominent elements in discussions of traumatic grief and its preconditions. Beckett told Knowlson that '[a]fter my father's death I had trouble psychologically' (Knowlson, 1996: 172); and Knowlson describes how 'nothing seemed to calm his nerves. He was disturbed, sad, depressed' and he made the decision to undertake a course in psychotherapy, starting 'shortly after Christmas in 1933' (174). Beckett's feelings of guilt along with his anxiety, racing heartbeat, palpitations, chest pains, nightmares and withdrawal from others (Knowlson, 1996: 172–4; Bair, 1980: 184–5) are consistently cited as symptomatic of traumatic grief.

There are three poems, 'Malacoda', 'Da Tagte Es' and 'Echo's Bones', which Lawlor and Pilling consider 'may be regarded as successive attempts to come to terms with the death of the father Beckett loved deeply' (Beckett, 2012: 294). He began 'Malacoda' very soon after his father's death (Beckett, 2012: 293). L. E. Harvey points to the way that, in both 'Malacoda' and 'Da Tagte Es', death is depicted as a sea journey; in the former the poem ends with a departure: 'all aboard all souls/ half-mast aye aye' (Beckett, 2012: 21, lines 27–8), with a final, one-word stanza, redolent of denial: 'nay' (line 29), as if the voice is refusing to accept that this is the end, that the lost one has really gone for ever, never to return. In 'Da Tagte Es' the bed sheet becomes the sail of a ship, 'the sheet astream' (Beckett, 2012: 22, line 2); the sea-voyager has 'no more for the land' (line 3), a line which Harvey sees as reversing the on-board call before departure: 'Any more for the land' (1970: 84). The bereaved are left alone on the shore, watching the departure of the loved one, with nothing to be done.

The association of his father's death and the sea may well stem from a variety of factors. There was, of course, that scene on the diving board at the Forty-Foot, when the six-year-old Beckett feared for his own death, and perhaps also his father's, seen waiting far down below, with his upward-turned face repeatedly swamped by the waves of the sea. This would help to explain the reference to *The Tempest* in Victor's nightmare in *Eleutheria*. There is also the cemetery where his father was buried, between the sea and the mountains, which would mean that the sight and sound of the sea would always be associated with the death of his father, through his memories of the burial and his visits to the graveside. At the beginning of October 1933, Beckett joined his mother in a rented house by the sea, and found it a difficult experience. He wondered 'how people had the nerve to live so near, *on* the sea. It moans in one's dreams in the night' (letter to McGreevy, 1 November 1933, quoted in Knowlson, 1996: 173).

By 1959, when Beckett completed *Embers*, he had lost both his mother and his brother. His mother died on 25 August 1950; she was buried in the same grave as Beckett's father, with 'the view looking down and across Greystones harbour' (Knowlson, 1996: 384). His brother died four years later, on 13 September 1954. A month before his death the doctor informed his brother 'that there was nothing more that could be done for him' (Knowlson, 1996: 401). Beckett listened to 'the sound of the sea on the shore', remembering his father's death and his mother's death (letter to Pamela Mitchell, 5 June 1954, quoted in Knowlson, 1996: 402). Every bereavement, with its intense grief and feelings of hopelessness and despair, is accompanied by all the pain and suffering of former losses, making it all the more intense and overwhelming. For Beckett, the sound of the sea was entangled indelibly with his losses: Knowlson describes how 'he would lie awake listening to "the old sea still telling the old story at the end of the garden"' (1996: 402; Knowlson is quoting from a letter to Pamela Mitchell, 19 August 1954). The sound of the sea, so often perceived as a relaxing and soothing sound, was clearly something very different for Beckett, as it was associated so forcefully with the loss of those closest to him. His description of the sea 'moan[ing] in one's dreams at night' gives it a ghostly haunting sound (letter to McGreevy, 1 November 1933, quoted in Knowlson, 1996: 173).

He gave a similar perception of the sea to Henry in *Embers*, his second radio play. Henry is tortured by the sound of the sea and the memories of his father, thought to have been drowned at sea. *Embers* dramatises a whole range of traumatic sequelae. The listener hears the intrusive voices, the haunting memories of the past, and shares the experience of the temporal distortions. The play demonstrates the way in which '[e]xperiences of trauma become freeze-framed into an eternal present in which one remains forever trapped, or to which one is condemned to be perpetually returned [...] all duration collapses, past becomes present, and future loses all meaning other than endless repetition' (Stolorow, 2008: 118). Robert Stolorow describes how 'trauma so profoundly alters the universal or shared structure of temporality [that] the traumatized person quite literally lives in another kind of reality' (118). The radio listeners share this alienated, altered state for the duration of the play.

Henry sits on the pebble beach, gazing out to sea, all alone, dissociated from the external world, solely fixated on his inner thoughts, apart from the sound of the sea, which he tries to block out, though it continuously intrudes. He is subject to traumatic symptoms such as the denial or disbelief of his father's death: as his father's body was never found he may be alive (although this seems highly unlikely). Henry's father's disappearance/death was sudden and unexpected, and the listener listens to him talking to his lost father, which enacts Freud's observation in 'Mourning and Melancholia' that 'the existence of the lost object is psychically prolonged' (1991: 253). Colin Murray Parkes describes the way in which the bereaved often speak of talking to their lost loved one, which achieves a 'feeling or impression' that the lost object 'is nearby although he may not be seen or heard' (1972: 57).

When Henry speaks to his father, the shame and the sense of guilt he feels is apparent: Henry feels he has let his father down. He recalls the last words he ever heard from his father, calling him a 'washout' (Beckett, 1990: 256). 'Washout' is repeated five times, and this would seem to be a pivotal memory: Henry feels that he has disappointed his father, and his memory returns to this again and again; but he cannot change it, resolve it, or make his father proud of him now. This is the way of traumatic memories, which cause the subject to re-experience the pain of a moment that cannot be relived in reality and thus cannot be overcome; the memory is relived again and again in the traumatic subject's present. This harsh rejection, it can be imagined, is of the kind that the six-year-old Beckett feared when up on the diving board, if he did not make the Forty-Foot dive: the fear of rejection as a 'washout' rather than the praise for having been a 'Brave boy'. The harsh words of Henry's father are linked directly to the sea; he imitates his father asking: 'Are you coming for a dip?' – his reply is 'No', and 'No' again to his father's encouragement: 'Come on, come on' (256). This, alongside the father's presumed death at sea, means that the sound of the sea is a trigger, 'a memory-based sensory cue' which brings the past traumatic event into the present (Scaer, 2005: 18). Henry is unable to block the constant intrusion of the sound of the sea, except by talking to himself, or playing a gramophone – the sound of the sea intruded even when he went to Switzerland to escape it (Beckett, 1990: 254). The intrusive sound of the sea is accompanied by intrusive thoughts, voices and flashbacks to the past, which form part of the 'broad spectrum of somatic and cognitive reexperiencing' that plague the subjects of trauma (Scaer, 2005: 65).

Freud, in 'The Ego and the Id', describes the incorporation of the lost object that 'occurs in melancholia': 'a setting up of the object inside the ego' (1991: 368) through a process of interjection. In *Embers* there are instances that suggest that Henry is identifying with his father, but it is as if in a mirror – a reversed image. Henry lives on the other 'side of the bay' (Beckett, 1990: 253) from his father, and when he speaks to his absent father he tells him: 'when I got the money I moved across' (253); thus he takes up his position on the opposite side of the bay after his father is lost, believed drowned. Like his father, he 'can't stay away from' the sea, but unlike his father 'he never go[es] in' (254). Henry can be imagined sitting in the same pose that Ada describes his father adopting: 'sitting on a rock looking out to sea'; Ada comments on the 'stillness': it was 'as if he had been turned to stone' (262). This may well be the posture of Henry at the end of the play, following his final words that predict the nothingness he perceives as awaiting him.

Scaer describes a traumatised subject as suspended in time with only a 'dim sense of a future': 'Because past experience remains of prime importance ... [the subject is] frozen in that past event [...]. It is almost as if victims cannot perceive a future when they will not be continuously preoccupied by a battle with their past demons' (2005: 70). The presentness of the past in which the subject is frozen and lacks any perception of a future is eloquently evoked at the end of *Embers*, when Henry checks his 'little book':

This evening ... [*Pause.*] Nothing this evening. [*Pause.*] Tomorrow ... tomorrow ... plumber at nine, then nothing. [*Pause. Puzzled.*] Plumber at nine? [*Pause.*] Ah yes, the waste. [*Pause.*] Words. [*Pause.*] Saturday ... nothing. Sunday ... Sunday ... nothing all day. [*Pause.*] Nothing, all day nothing. [*Pause.*] All day all night nothing. [*Pause.*] Not a sound. (Beckett, 1990: 264)

'Nothing' is repeated seven times, accentuating the idea of a future that holds nothing, except the waste – the waste of words that resolve nothing.

Pilling has pointed to the 'structural slackness' and the way
the play fails 'to blend' its materials (1976: 98). However, Beckett
told Lawrence Shainberg that he realised that 'what I had to do
was investigate the not-knowing, not-perceiving, the whole world
of incompleteness' (Shainberg, 1987: 106). Trauma shatters the
unity, the structures and patterns that provide comfort and a
sense of safety and containment; a traumatised subject is faced
with a world that is alarmingly lacking in narrative structure
and shape, and it is this fragmentation and lack of meaning that
Embers dramatises.

Henry, it could be suggested, is attempting to bring sense and
shape to his life, but he is failing. Not only are the elements 'failing
to blend' for the radio listener, they are for him, his own listener.
He is talking to himself, even though he is attempting to summon
up listeners from his past. Henry talks to himself, and it seems
that he has been doing this for a long time. He claims that he
has been 'Roaring prayers at God' (Beckett, 1990: 260); he is at
first apparently speaking to his father, who 'must hear me', but
'doesn't answer me' (253). Ada, his wife, does answer, and is able
to tell him things he has forgotten. She also warns him that 'The
time will come when no one will speak to you at all, not even
complete strangers. [*Pause.*] You will be quite alone with your
voice, there will be no other voice in the world but yours' (262).
It could be suggested that this has already happened. Henry is
recalling voices in his mind: Addie's, the Music Master's and
the Riding Master's. He no longer hears his father's voice, who
'doesn't answer any more' (262). Ada's voice supposes that he
has 'worn him out' (262). He imitates his father's voice (256), and
later his daughter Addie's (256), though she is also heard (258–9),
but intriguingly not by Ada ('You are silent today'; 'What are
you thinking of?' are Ada's questions following the memory of
Addie's music and riding lessons [259]).

Repetition is an important feature of the play, and also a
persistent affliction suffered by victims of trauma. Pilling notes
that the play 'relies very considerably on repeating a cluster of
phrases' (1976: 98). The repetition of phrases is evidence of past
moments which, like a scratched record, play over and over in his
mind, and cannot be erased. Pilling writes of the confrontation

'of the configuring mind of the artist' (98), and the repetition
of phrases is also striking in respect of the fictional story that
Henry composes, as he tests out certain phrases to judge if they
'work'. The fictionalising can be envisaged as a welcome relief
from Henry's actual past, a fort/da game that gives him a sense of
control, blocking out the sound of the sea which is so entangled in
his memory with both his father's death and his harsh rejection,
a rejection that produces an ambivalence that Freud considered
'among the preconditions of melancholia' (1991: 260).

Henry can be envisaged as attempting to take control, in an
attempt to mitigate the hopelessness and helplessness he feels
about the past he cannot change, and cannot escape. This recalls
the '*active* part' Freud's nephew adopted in the fort/da game,
to gain a sense of mastery over the unmasterable (Freud, 1991:
285). This idea also brings to mind the radio studio, and the processes that lie behind the radio play the listener hears. Katharine
Worth contends that 'Henry functions as controller of the radio
medium' (1981: 203). It is certainly very evident that he is striving
for mastery, and it is as if the inside of his head becomes a radio
studio, with all the requisite sound techniques at his disposal.
Like a director, he commands, at the beginning of the play, his
own actions: 'On […] On!'; 'Stop […] Stop!'; 'Down' […] Down!'
(Beckett, 1990: 253); it is as if he were both director and actor
devising and producing his own radio play in his head (which
recalls *Company*: 'Devised deviser devising it all for company. In
the same figment dark as his figments' [Beckett, 1980: 64]). He
introduces his silent listener, his father, and explains the sound
of the sea, in case it is not understood. He then summons up
the sound of hooves, and the sound person can be imagined
obeying this command by tapping two halves of a coconut shell
together. It seems that each command needs to be repeated before
there is a response. The sound effect of the drip follows a similar
sequence 'A drip! A drip! […] Again!' yet this is suddenly cut off
with Henry's 'No!' (Beckett, 1990: 255). It is as if Henry is also
commanding the listener with his repeated: 'Listen to it!' He is
able to summon up the violent slamming of the door (twice),
and Addie's '*loud wail*', and his wife's presence with 'Ada […]
Ada!' (256). However, the flashbacks of Addie with her Music and

Riding Master come into being without Henry's explicit direction, including the sound of the hooves '*trotting*', '*cantering*' and '*galloping*' (259). When Henry 'wants thuds' it is as if he takes over the role of the sound person, dashing two big stones together. The sound of the second clash is '*amplified*', then suddenly '*cut off*', as were the drips (260). Ada is more difficult to control, a figment with a seeming autonomy, but this can all be Henry's devising. Most significant are the times when Henry insists that she 'Drive on, drive on!'; 'Keep on, keep on!' (262) as, although she speaks for a little while longer, he fails to keep Ada with him, and fails to summon the hooves again (263). His control is failing.

The story of Bolton and Holloway features control, a control Henry would have as the inventor of the fiction, although this is a qualified control, as it clearly does not come easily. When he begins to tell his story for the first time, there is the same repetition as there is for the sound effects and the voices, in what could be designated as the narrative situation, on the pebble beach. He calls twice for his fictional character to appear: 'Bolton [...] Bolton!' (Beckett, 1990: 254). The second time he begins to tell the story there are no such commands, and there is a sense of Henry's command fading now, and of the compulsion that drives the constant talking becoming stronger; Henry is attempting to drown out the sound of the sea, and the rhythm of the words takes on the rhythm of the waves breaking on the pebble beach. The first segment ends with a rhythmic repetition: 'white world, great trouble, not a sound, only the embers, sound of dying, dying glow, Holloway, Bolton, Bolton, Holloway, old men, great trouble, white world, not a sound' (255). In attempting to escape the sound of the sea he emulates its rhythm, but fails to escape the image of death that the sea, an 'old grave' (258), evokes; it is still heard in the 'sound of dying' of the embers. The 'dying glow' (255) of the embers strongly evokes fading towards the end of life. In the second segment the fire is out (264), the 'embers [are] cold' and Bolton's 'eyes [are] drowned', and this fictional world is diminished to a rhythmic, staccato list: 'not a sound, white world, bitter cold, ghastly scene, old men, great trouble, no good' (264). The listener has been commanded again and again to listen, 'Listen to it! [*Pause.*] Close your eyes and listen to it' (255), and to listen to the silence ('not a sound'), which is a strange request, as is the even more baffling command: 'Listen to the light' (253). But the listener is witness to the distress, the need, the compulsion, which drives Henry. He begins in command, and ends with the recognition of nothing, of 'the waste' and, again, nothing: 'All day all night nothing. [*Pause.*] Not a sound' (264). Henry's world at the edge of the sea, his dialogues with memory and his story all fade to nothing and silence. The radio play is over.

Listeners to a radio play have no visual images, but only the sounds and silence out of which to imagine the situation presented. The radio presents the listener with disembodied voices, and this fits this play particularly well. Henry is talking to himself and also summoning up disembodied voices inside his head; these voices, alongside the sound of the sea, enter the heads of the listeners, and thus, although the listener can imagine Henry sitting on the pebble beach from an external perspective, the play also encourages a strong identification with him. His distress, his anger, his bitterness and his confusion enter into the mind of the listener, who experiences the voices, the sounds and the silences in a way that can be shocking in its invasiveness, its intrusiveness, its intimacy – in its insistence on involving the listener so directly. The listener, in a sense, is sharing in the trauma.

Embers is concerned with the inner world, an ineffable world; the listener enters Henry's world and in the process enters her or his own. This is a disturbing, confusing and unsettling place to be, and it is understandable that many readers and listeners would prefer to be in a place redolent of safety and control. However, as Beckett makes clear in *Proust*, art is very much about jolting us out of the safe, habitual world of 'preconception' (Beckett, 1987: 23) and recognising its illusory nature. Henry is suffering, and the listener shares in this suffering, and in the process faces the distressing truth that life is not free of pain and suffering, however much we might hope that this wasn't so.

Note

1 On 28 August 2012, I emailed Knowlson to ask him whether Beckett ever told him what happened at the Forty-Foot when he was six years

old. 'Did he jump? Did he freeze? I know he dived and swam a great deal in his life, and was wondering what was the result of this particular event'. Knowlson replied 'As far as I was aware, he just jumped in as a little boy and learned to swim there with his father. Be a brave boy therefore comes from his initial fear of the deepish water. He loved diving afterwards. Don't really know any more than you do though.'

References

Bair, Deirdre (1980). *Samuel Beckett: A Biography*. London: Pan Books.
Beckett, Samuel (1963). *Watt*. London: Calder.
Beckett, Samuel (1980). *Company*. London: Calder.
Beckett, Samuel (1987). *Proust and Three Dialogues with Georges Duthuit*. London: Calder.
Beckett, Samuel (1990). *The Complete Dramatic Works*. London: Faber and Faber.
Beckett, Samuel (1993). *Dream of Fair to middling Women*. London: Calder.
Beckett, Samuel (1996). *Eleutheria*. Trans. Barbara Wright. London: Faber and Faber.
Beckett, Samuel (2009). *The Letters of Samuel Beckett: 1929–1940*. Ed. Martha Dow Fehsenfeld and Lois More Overbeck. Cambridge: Cambridge University Press.
Beckett, Samuel (2012). *The Collected Poems of Samuel Beckett*. Ed. Seán Lawlor and John Pilling. London: Faber and Faber.
Boulter, Jonathan (2004). 'Does Mourning Require a Subject? Samuel Beckett's *Texts for Nothing*', *Modern Fiction Studies* 50.2, 332–50.
Boulter, Jonathan (2011). *Melancholy and the Archive: Trauma, Memory and History in the Contemporary Novel*. London: Continuum.
Bracken, Patrick (2002). *Trauma: Culture, Meaning and Philosophy*. London: Whurr.
Cohn, Ruby (2001). *A Beckett Canon*. Ann Arbor, MI: University of Michigan Press.
Freud, Sigmund (1991). *On Metapsychology: The Theory of Psychoanalysis*. Trans. James Strachey. London: Penguin.
Harvey, John H. (2002). *Perspectives on Loss and Trauma: Assaults on the Self*. London: Sage.
Harvey, Lawrence E. (1970). *Samuel Beckett: Poet and Critic*. Princeton, NJ: Princeton University Press.
Horowitz, Mardi (1986). *Stress Response Syndromes*. Northvale, NJ: Jason Aronson.

Janoff-Bulman, Ronnie (1992). *Shattered Assumptions: Towards a New Psychology of Trauma*. New York: The Free Press.

Knowlson, James (1996). *Damned to Fame: The Life of Samuel Beckett*. London: Bloomsbury.

Marlowe, Christopher (1990). *Doctor Faustus*. Ed. John D. Jump. Manchester: Manchester University Press.

O'Brien, Eoin (1986). *The Beckett Country: Samuel Beckett's Ireland*. London: The Black Cat Press.

Parkes, Colin Murray (1972). *Bereavement: Studies of Grief in Adult Life*. London: Tavistock.

Pilling, John (1976). *Samuel Beckett*. London: Routledge & Kegan Paul.

Robinson, Lawrence, Melinda Smith and Jeanne Segal. 'Emotional and Psychological Trauma: Causes, Symptoms, Help', www.helpguide.org/mental/emotional_psychological_trauma.htm. Accessed 6 August 2012.

Scaer, Robert (2005). *The Trauma Spectrum: Hidden Wounds and Human Resiliency*. New York: Norton.

Shainberg, Lawrence (1987). 'Exorcising Beckett', *Paris Review* 104, 100–36.

Shakespeare, William (1987). *The Tempest*. Ed. Frank Kermode. London: Methuen.

Stolorow, Robert D. (2008). 'The Contextuality and Existentiality of Emotional Trauma', *Psychoanalytic Dialogues: The International Journal of Relational Perspectives* 18.1, 113–23.

Worth, Katharine (1981). 'Beckett and the Radio Medium'. In John Drakakis (ed.), *British Radio Drama*. Cambridge: Cambridge University Press, pp. 191–217.

Žižek, Slavoj (2000). 'Melancholy and the Act', *Critical Inquiry* 26.4, 657–81.

2

'Void cannot go': trauma and actor process in the theatre of Samuel Beckett

Nicholas E. Johnson

Acting on stage, both as an activity and as a career choice, has intrinsic challenges and certain structures that theoretically could contribute to, or even engender, trauma in those who undertake it. Many theatre projects involve stringent physical demands, intense emotional engagement, pressured time constraints, financial precarity and repetition. Due to the difficulty and duress inherent in certain of his plays, Samuel Beckett has been pressed into service as an emblematic example in the discourse around trauma and the actor. This conjunction arises understandably, perhaps, from the subject matter in his fiction and drama, especially after the Second World War; from his biography, rich with psychological stress and strain; and simply from his overall cultural significance in the twentieth century, manifested by the expansive body of criticism around his work (of which this volume is a part). There is also no doubt that certain symptoms associated with trauma have been reported among the makers associated with Beckett's drama. The most famous and widely known instance of this is the testimony of Billie Whitelaw about performing *Not I*. Her similes and metaphors, used across various published interviews and cited with great frequency in both scholarship and media, include descriptions of 'an opened wound ... all that pain ... torture' (Ben-Zvi, 1990: 9), 'falling backwards into hell' (Gussow, 1996: 85), and 'an astronaut tumbling out into space' (Knowlson and Knowlson, 2006: 169). Beckett, also famously, asked 'what have I done to you?' (Knowlson and Knowlson, 2006: 169) when

Whitelaw's vertigo overcame her at one point in rehearsal. It seems that he was conscious of the unusual demands his theatre placed on both practitioners and audiences. Contemporary approaches to Beckett in performance have not left this legacy behind, to the point that the emotional and physical demands of acting Beckett have become a form of advertising.[1]

This discourse is worthy of further analysis for several reasons. First, Beckett studies has tended to focus on trauma in terms of the characters of his fictions and dramas, rather than the material circumstances of enacting Beckett, in particular the actual people who are tasked with making these characters come to life. Second, while *Not I* is a notable exception (in that analysis frequently addresses the testimony of performers), it is far from the only case in which traumatic paradigms might arise in Beckett's drama, with other pieces (*Play* and *Endgame*, to name only two) having equally demanding physicalities and alarming subject matter. It is the goal of this chapter to move beyond the presently available, most frequently cited and limited testimonies of trauma, and indeed to question the centrality of trauma in the discourse of performing Beckett. In parallel, this chapter develops the Beckettian notion of the 'void' – elaborated in his prose and embodied in his theatre – as an alternative model for acting as such. After first exploring the relevant actor theories in their historical contexts, this research will draw on interviews collected from noted 'Beckett actors' with both historical and contemporary relevance to the field, as well as some students and amateurs engaging with Beckett for the first time. These qualitative data illuminate a more fluid and complex relation between trauma and actor process, verifying that Beckett's drama is not necessarily traumatic. By connecting Beckett's theatre to pragmatic and psychophysical theories of acting, this contribution seeks to develop a theatrical praxis for the philosophical concept of the void, and then to show how the difficulty and duress organic to any acting process can be worked through, supported and survived.

The actor's task

First, the establishment of a foundation for how to understand the concept of 'acting' is required, since the actor has been a highly variable category across histories and cultures. Further, since live theatre (like all media) is affected by the rapid revolutionary shift in recent history brought on by digital culture, whatever was once certain about theatrical acting cannot be relied upon any longer. Thus, rather than assuming a shared basis for discussion, and rather than seeking to offer any comprehensive picture of a hugely diverse set of practices, this chapter will begin by outlining my own perspective – conceptual, material and social – on the nature of the theatre actor today.

A potent and flexible model of general artistic practice emerges in *Holy the Firm*, a poetic work of philosophy by the American essayist Annie Dillard. Dillard models the artist as a figure bridging between the human and what she calls the 'divine'.[2] The artist has a vision of some eternal truth (or fragment of a whole) within that greater source, and then has an ethical and practical challenge to pivot and express this vision to the human (or, again, to a portion or fragment of a greater humanity). There are, then, two burdens or obligations that any artist bears: first that of witnessing, and subsequently that of communication. At both moments, there is the possibility – indeed the likelihood – of failure or disaster, and with this moment of burden or difficulty there is the possibility of trauma in its original Greek sense. That is to say, seeing and speaking can both wound.

It seems at first that Dillard's structure prioritises the work of art considered as an object (something fixed in space but unbounded in time), rather than the event (something durational but ephemeral and intangible in space). Where objects of art are concerned, the model works as articulated, and the artist appears to be a kind of sole mediator. A painter can view a vista of exceptional beauty or terror, produce a canvas, and immediately deliver this to the viewer (bracketing, of course, those agents of the culture industry who mediate through galleries and auction houses). A poet or novelist appears to be similarly equipped with the means to communicate with minimal collaboration (excepting, again, agents, editors, publishers and booksellers). Where events of art are concerned, however, relative solitude is not an option. A composer cannot bring an orchestra piece or an opera directly to the audience without interpersonal *artistic* mediation. A playwright depends on a series of collaborators, each recognised as an artist in their own right, to make a production occur. While a person could purchase and read a score or a play, the mode of reception is not in its intended form. So the aesthetic model for the event – in this case theatre – is somewhat more complex. A playwright is actually addressing collaborators, instead of the audience directly. A theatre director sees the vision not unmediated, but *through* a playwright's eyes. The director also cannot communicate directly with the public, but generally requires actors and designers to create and deliver the message. The actor represents the final term in the chain on Dillard's bridge, a figure both dependent and independent, and nearest to the 'human' side. Fixed on the director as the immediate authority, representing the playwright, whose script represents one vision of the divine, the actor is an artist who has to witness in order to then speak. Naturally, the larger the number of relations in this chain, the greater the possibility for friction, for stress, for difficulty, and perhaps for the wound. The presence of producers, technicians, Estates and reviewers in bringing a project to life complicates the picture still further.

If this is a conceptual model of the challenge inherent in the actor's position, it would not be complete without a material analysis as well. The working actor who does not become her own playwright and director is always in a situation of seeking to please others, frequently being judged on characteristics both beyond and within her control: physical appearance, vocal sound, collaborative qualities, prior success and the all-important 'who one knows'. In countries where the theatre model is not generally salaried, such as the United States or Ireland, job security and financial issues around wages are foremost in generating stress for actors and in causing people to leave the profession. The United States Bureau of Labor Statistics defines the occupation of the actor without reference to either the human or the divine: 'play parts in stage, television, radio, video, motion picture production, or other settings for entertainment, information, or instruction. Interpret serious or comic role by speech, gesture, and body movement to entertain or inform audience. May dance or sing' (Bureau of Labor Statistics, 2015). The national employment estimate in 2014 for this occupation was 50,570 people. The median hourly wage for this group in 2015 was $18.80, and the percentage of industry employment for both film and theatre sectors was only 8% (Bureau of Labor Statistics, 2016). In the very few places in the US where one can be a working actor, the supply is enormous, the demand is low, and when an actor does what might be called by an outsider 'succeed', this means that one has work that pays highly enough to get one through the remainder of the year. In Ireland, which has about 4,000 actors, the majority earn less than €12,000 per year from acting (Sheridan, 2012). Such statistics provide some support for the contention that as a career choice in highly developed economies, acting is stressful in comparison to other careers; indeed, the necessity of actors to have non-acting work in order to survive raises the question of whether this is a career at all.

The social history of the actor includes contradictory periods when the role was of religious significance or fundamental to civil society, as well as periods when the dominant associations were with the occult, with prostitution, or otherwise outside the realm of respectability. The cultural valuation of the acting profession today reflects that historical split, especially in the Anglo-American context. Huge numbers of people are attracted to a celebrity culture that often rests on actors portraying people other than themselves, but that interest coexists with a certain reluctance for families to let their children grow up to be actors, usually on grounds of fiscal security. What also prevails today in popular discourse is a misunderstanding of the relation between actors and their emotions. The following sections explore this by addressing theories of acting in the context of embodiment.

Representation as revolution

The majority of the Western theatre tradition from the Greeks until the late nineteenth century has been what might be called 'presentational' in form: the actor's duty was solely to communicate or to entertain, and the urge to replicate life as lived offstage accurately was largely absent. Forms as diverse as Roman tragedy, medieval mystery plays, Elizabethan tragedy, commedia dell'arte, Racinian tragedy, Restoration comedy and melodrama did not put weight on verisimilitude in scene or naturalism in playing style, and a historical review of these aesthetics will show that they did not seek to present real life, but rather a formal model. Training for such a theatre was therefore composed of a sequence of physical activities that prepared the voice to be heard and the body to be seen. The range of human emotions was presented largely through gesture, and the recognition of gestures on the part of the audience carried the meaning. Denis Diderot, who wrote *The Paradox of the Actor* in dialogue form in 1770, is probably the most famous figure to codify the idea that in order to move the audience, the actor must remain unmoved.[3] It is not an accident that this follows an understanding of perception and phenomenology rooted in the thinking of René Descartes, whose dualism would permit such a separation between what the body is feeling and what that same body is thinking. There is a clear line from Diderot to Vsevolod Meyerhold (1874–1940), whose system of 'biomechanics' treats acting largely as an athletic task, in service of a non-naturalistic theatre.

The turn towards the contemporary understanding of actors and emotions is relatively recent, and can be traced to Konstantin Stanislavski, probably the major figure in acting theory to this day, though his influence has been processed through translation, via disciples, and often taken out of context and misunderstood.[4] Stanislavski was working and writing at a time of huge development in the natural sciences, and a Darwinian model based on meticulous observation of exterior qualities, together with a Freudian model that posited a natural existence for the unconscious, could be seen to have upended many of the principles of the more theoretical Cartesian model of embodiment. Ulrika Maude refers to this moment in her writing on 'Beckett, Body and Mind' in the *New Cambridge Companion to Samuel Beckett*:

> Beckett's writing captures a paradigm shift in our understanding of subjectivity, for since the second half of the nineteenth century, Darwinian thought, neurology, behaviourism and even some

aspects of psychoanalysis had pointed to a biomechanical rather than conceptual understanding of the self. (Maude, 2015: 181)

What Maude summarises here illuminates both the revolutionary quality of Stanislavski in his time, as well as the limitations of the model for a theatre of today. The canonical European theatre of the 1880s and 1890s that is studied today as 'Naturalism' – figures such as Henrik Ibsen, Anton Chekhov, Gerhart Hauptmann and George Bernard Shaw – was actually a rebellious innovation at the time, linked to political movements and explicitly rooted in the scientific principle of the period: namely, improvement through observation. This is the period when scenography and plots were actively designed to mirror the minute activities, problems, rooms and costumes of its audience. Stanislavski writes in the midst of this milieu:

> Our experience has led to a firm belief that only our kind of art, soaked in the living experiences of human beings, can artistically reproduce the implacable shadings and depths of life. Only such art can completely absorb the spectator and make both understand and also inwardly experience the happenings on the stage, enriching his inner life, and leaving impressions which will not fade with time. (Stanislavski, 2003: 17)

He refers to the previous 'presentational' school of acting, which he also acknowledges as an art, but distinguishes his system explicitly:

> [In the other school, the actor's] objective is different. He lives his part as a preparation for perfecting an external form. Once that is determined to his satisfaction he reproduces that form through the aid of mechanically trained muscles. Therefore, in this other school, living your role is not the chief moment of creation as it is with us, but one of the preparatory stages for future artistic work. (20)

Stanislavski's ideas were communicated in the United States during the great theatrical churn of the 1930s, first by the influential Group Theatre in New York, and later in studios set up by Lee Strasberg and Sanford Meisner, two figures sometimes identified as the source of what is now known simply as the 'Method' or 'Method Acting'.[5] By this declension, a limited reading of the first part of Stanislavski's writing on acting, in a translation which was questionable, has now been transmitted into innumerable schools of training focused on creating 'truth' on stage – not the eternal and abstract truths of Greek tragedy, but rather truth in the sense of verisimilitude, where an actor can say 'I really cried', and where an audience can say 'I found that believable'. Indeed, believability in the sense of a credible emotional landscape remains one of the dominant criteria commonly taken for success in the theatre. This model is laden with presumptions which do not apply well to Beckett. Many of Beckett's plays do not arise out of situations that are believable in the sense of being familiar or routine in daily experience: people live in ashcans and urns, or are buried to their neck in earth, or body parts float in midair. More problematically for the Method actor, the people placed in these uncommon situations do not express the emotions that might arise organically, were an actor to seek to find 'rational' responses or 'sensible' backgrounds for each predicament. The pursuit of truth on stage, in such a context, has more to do with commitment to the task and fulfilment of the image, even where it is not aligned with everyday experience.

A further legacy of Stanislavski's tradition in actor training is actively dangerous, and reflects its distortion through what is called affective memory, or emotion memory. As to whether the actor must truly feel what is represented on stage or whether genuine emotion may arise during the course of performance, Stanislavski is relatively cautious, since in his view emotions cannot be controlled.[6] In Hollywood, as might be predicted, this has been taken rather further by assorted salespeople. Ivana Chubbuck, whose technique promises to teach 'actors how *to win*' (Chubbuck, 2004: 1), inverts the discourse of self-help to encourage actors to self-harm. She proposes a model whereby 'your dark side, your traumas, your beliefs, your priorities, your fears, what drives your ego, what makes you feel shame and what initiates your pride are your colors, your paints to draw with as an actor' (2). Addressing aspirants in the imperative, her various formulas for creating chemistry between actors suggest that an actor should, as a first step, 'identify the trauma or insecurity that most defines you' (230) and then 'be very specific and detailed as you viscerally relive the horrible event' (258).[7] Actors are rewarded with Oscars, it seems, when they actually lose or gain weight to play a role, or alter their appearance to become truly one with their subject, particularly an ugly one; actors are rewarded with immortality when their intensity of dedication to a particular role or their immersion in a dark character leads to an overdose, a psychological break, or even a suicide. This valorisation of illness is an extremely harmful myth, and a distortion of the craft. The culture retains, through this fascination with the fatality of 'true acting', the memory of the actor as an occult figure or a necromancer, and it has developed a hunger for assessing that intensity by counting the cost to the performer. This creates a market for unsustainable acting, and incentivises actors to self-promote by selectively framing and exposing their on-the-job pain.

Such models of acting not only run counter to wellness; they also reject the development of artistic practice that is one legacy of Beckett's theatre over the past century, not to mention that of Brecht and Artaud.[8] Realism and verisimilitude belong to a period of history, and in all other art forms naturalism is gone; this attraction to the theatre as the site of reflective truth is anomalous.[9] It seems likely that this ongoing interest relates partly to the rise of film, for which Method acting is relatively well suited, because in a recorded medium an extreme emotion only needs to happen once. Theatre acting is distinguished not only by repetition, but also by the central role of physical presence with others. The embodied skills of physical control, emotion regulation, flexibility and empathy are simply the tools of the craft, whereby the actor can meet the obligations of crossing a bridge towards the human. The actor's interior state is interesting, from that task-focused perspective, only insofar as it either enhances or disrupts that transaction with the collaborators and the audiences. The priority here can be summarised in a comment by Simon Munnery: 'Many are willing to suffer for their art. Few are willing to learn to draw' (2001).

Pragmatic acting and the cognitive turn

The debate and controversy surrounding Stanislavski's definition of acting actually mirrors the competing definitions of trauma, namely the extension during the nineteenth century from the use of the word 'trauma' to refer to a physical wound in medicine, as in the usage 'trauma centre' at a hospital, and the idea of trauma as a psychological wound, as in 'post-traumatic stress'.[10] This recently evolved conflation of body and mind is precisely the point, in that these can no longer be disentangled or spoken of as wholly separate. The so-called 'cognitive turn' in literary studies and critical theory has begun to take account of advances in neuroscience, and to explore them in relation to cultural production. This nexus was of great interest to Beckett, whose entire oeuvre grapples with the question of body and mind via figures such as René Descartes, Henri Bergson and Samuel Johnson. However, the process of enactment and embodiment of his plays disrupts a binary view of acting. Due to the plays' phenomenological demands on actors and audiences, Beckett's treatment of form troubles the separation between psychological and biomechanical approaches, perhaps offering a 'third way' to think through performance itself.[11]

The most famous polemic against Stanislavski in recent years is probably *True and False* by David Mamet, in which he inaugurates a 'pragmatic' or 'practical' school of acting, a kind of anti-technique. Mamet privileges a physical art of acting that he likens to swimming, as a task that one can only learn 'in the water' or 'in the arena', and he belittles emotion memory and sense memory as 'paint-by-numbers' (Mamet, 1999: 80). He calls Stanislavski a 'technique based on luck … a superstition, an investment in self-consciousness, in introversion', writing that this 'spares us from the horrible necessity of living in a theatre world for which we are totally unprepared', and he goes so far as to call the technique of schools derived from Stanislavski 'nonsense' and 'a cult' (6). Though his tone in the book is aggressive and at times problematic as a result, it nonetheless raises provocative questions. His ideas about an irreducible risk to which actors must grow accustomed has much in common with what this essay will later theorise as the 'void'. Mamet sees emotional memory as a form of extortion, an attempt to 'buy off the audience'. He writes:

For craftspeople in the theatre to set out to manipulate the emotions of others is misguided, abusive, and useless. In the theatre, as outside it, we resent those who smile too warmly, who act overly friendly, or overly sad, or overly happy, who, in effect, *narrate* their own supposed emotional state ... The addition of 'emotion' to a situation which does not organically create it is a lie. First of all, it is not emotion. It is a counterfeit of emotion, and it is cheap. (77–8)

In rejecting artificially generated emotions, ancillary character stories and the entire 'academic' approach to acting, Mamet seems to echo the theatrical preferences of Beckett. When Mamet writes that the actor should 'say the words as simply as possible, in an attempt to accomplish a goal like that delineated by the author' (81), it sounds for all the world as if Beckett is directing.

An even more significant challenge to established models of actor training is the growing understanding in the sciences of the psychophysical link, for which acting provides a compelling case study. Writing from within these sciences, Thalia R. Goldstein and Paul Bloom have begun analysis of acting through its cognitive and psychological dimensions. They seem aware of the relatively recent rise of naturalism, though their research continues a bias towards this expectation of verisimilitude from a successful actor.[12] Their branch of psychology identifies the variance in techniques of acting as relating to three fundamental cognitive tasks: theory of mind, empathy and emotion regulation. There are additional skills involved, such as memorisation, physical behaviour, imagination and attention span, but the first three are critical. Actors, psychologists, avid fiction writers or readers and teachers who 'practice' theory of mind, Goldstein writes, can increase their ability to understand what others are thinking, believing, feeling or desiring. The work of acting actually expands one form of social intelligence, and this can be taught and trained (Goldstein, 2012).

From within the discipline of theatre studies, a rich exploration of the implications and applications of cognitive theory has been underway for a decade. Recent key works by Bruce McConachie, F. Elizabeth Hart, Jonathan Pitches and Rhonda Blair (among others) have created a sub-field that continues to percolate, although it has not yet found substantial traction in actor-training conservatories.[13] Phillip Zarrilli, a key interlocutor in this discourse through his monograph *Psychophysical Acting* (2009) and as editor of the volume *Acting (Re)Considered* (2002), is also linked strongly to the work of Beckett, as both practitioner and theorist. Several of the projects anthologised in *Acting (Re) Considered* represent an effort to codify a new actor training. Two are of particular interest in the present narrative: the 'BOS method' and the 'task-based perspective'.

'BOS' is the acronym used to stand for the surnames of Susana Bloch, Pedro Orthous and Guy Santibañez-H., whose work explicitly introduces a method they call 'psychophysiological' (Bloch et al., 1987: 1–19). The group notes first that 'while the gnostic-verbal (literary) and the body-expressive (physical) aspects of acting behaviour are quite well covered pedagogically [in acting schools], the emotional-expressive (psychophysiological) are almost entirely left to the intuition, life experience, or "emotional memory" of the student actor, with little or no technical support' (Bloch et al. in Zarrilli, 2002: 220). By addressing the role of breathing pattern, muscular/postural embodiment and facial mimicry in the creation and reception of emotions, Bloch and her colleagues attempt to create a system for learning to express emotion at a physiological level. They identify two axes on which they map six basic emotions: the parameters of 'tension/relaxation' and 'avoidance/approach' in embodied postures. After developing their subjects' skills at generating these emotions seemingly 'at will' via embodiment, in situations with no plot or character development, the group noted both that such emotions were immediately legible by others, not necessarily felt subjectively by the actors, and that the activity itself had therapeutic side-effects. Their conclusion seems to vindicate Diderot, though two centuries later:

> This is quite good evidence that in order to appear 'natural' or 'true' on the stage, actors do not need to 'feel' the emotion they are playing but must produce the correct effector-expressive output of the emotional behavior. If anything, in our opinion, subjective involvement and identification with the emotions may hinder the theatrical performance. In fact, it is possible that actors often confuse the unspecific excitation they feel during acting with the

belief that they are truly 'feeling' the emotion that they portray. (Bloch et al. in Zarrilli, 2002: 234)

The 'task-emotion' theory of acting inaugurated in the work of Elly Konijn shares many of the same presumptions about the nature of cognition with the above method. After narrating the 'actor's dilemma' of whether emotions should or should not be truly felt on stage along binary lines, Konijn proposes a third stream that she calls the 'self-expressive' approach, in which self-expression will naturally be authentic (an approach she associates with Jerzy Grotowski and Peter Brook). Konijn's main contribution is to isolate the emotions associated with the different levels of 'task' at which all actors must operate. She distinguishes four layers which correspond to four different emotional landscapes at any given moment:

> The actor (1) acts on stage as a private person with his daily life affairs; (2) works on stage as a craftsman, trying to perform his acting tasks, or job, as well as possible; (3) operates on the level of the inner model of the character to be performed in the actor's imagination; and (4) behaves on the level of the realised character performed on stage. (Konijn, 2002: 64)

The inputs of the actor's task-concerns, together with the aesthetic demands of the performance, generate the output of 'task-emotions' in the actor. The logical conclusion, which Konijn subsequently supports through survey data and empirical physiological testing, is that 'the actual context of the performance situation *in itself* is a source of intense emotions for the actor as a craftsman' (68). These task-emotions tend to dominate the actor's physiology, whether or not they align with the emotions the actor is seeking to create (or perhaps believes have been created) on stage.

Practitioner testimonies

The reason that these findings are so significant for acting in Beckett – or any strand of theatre-making that has followed the path of his late dramas – is Beckett's deployment of stage situations and 'theatre machines' that generate emotional landscapes in the actor not because of underlying 'character emotions' to be mapped or understood, but rather because they represent a specific task to be performed. The clearest example of this is Beckett's *Play*, which offers an almost flawless minimal model of the general task of the actor: arrive, get in position, when the light is on speak, when the light is off no longer speak, then repeat. If an actor were to focus on the characteristics of M, W1 and W2, as a character-based or internal approach might suggest, one does not have to look very far to find the pain. There is strong textual evidence that M has committed suicide prior to the play. Is it thus required, to succeed at the delivery of *Play*, that the actor seek the emotional depths of suicidal depression? Or is there, as in *The Unnamable*, simply that 'strange notion' of 'a task to be performed, before one can be at rest' (Beckett, 2009b: 22)? The actor occupies the constrained space of the urn, perhaps for twenty to thirty minutes; if one follows the specifications of the urns in the stage directions to the letter, unless the stage is outfitted with trapdoors, the actor is probably kneeling, which is a stress position; the actor is then under a strict system in which silence, in the face of the light, would be a visible failure, and in which speech, in short bursts of rapid-fire sprints, may lead to hyperventilation. Should this be considered traumatic? Should the conflation of the idea of difficulty and the idea of torture be allowed here? Or should *Play* be considered, instead, a kind of challenge or game, a set of parameters for an event, in which merely by participating authentically, the actor will organically produce the state – in themselves and in the audience – that the text is designed to generate?

In the direction of *Play* for the *Ethica* project in 2012 and 2013, rehearsals were structured in line with the system of the play.[14] Rather than actors learning rapid-fire cues off one another, they were instructed to learn monologues – the complete texts of W1, W2 and M – as continuous statements. In rehearsal actors were then not allowed to perform these monologues continuously, but instead were prompted by an active interrogator, who would sometimes hold a flashlight or a pointed object, or who might even touch the actor as a cue. For weeks this process was not conducted in the sequence of the texts as written, but rather improvised by the prompter, to prevent actors learning the lines as cues and to acclimatise actors to the nature of the stage task and its inherent hierarchies of power. Such a model seeks to scaffold and prepare the actor for the actual risk they will undertake during performance. When the final cues are put into the hands of an operator who will toggle between faces, the actors are prepared for anything that might change, and it makes mistakes recoverable. The play becomes, in this way, a living system, an enactment of the event itself.

The actors who went through this experience were either in education or recently out of education, and the majority did not have any prior exposure to Beckett. Data collection following the process verified that moments of difficulty did indeed arise, but that they did not rise to the traumatic level; compensatory and preparatory strategies that were integrated into the process by the ensemble, including habits of mindfulness, rituals of physical and vocal warm-ups, consideration of the project as a 'game' or 'challenge' in which actors were competing with Beckett and themselves, and an atmosphere of mutual support all contributed to the sustainability of their work. A digital analysis of the qualitative survey data pulled out certain terms that arose most frequently in their descriptions: 'physical' and 'body' were the top keywords, arising significantly more than 'emotion' or 'emotional' in survey answers about their experience of the project and their answers about compensation strategies that helped them. The most persistent term used in relation to their learning was 'work', reflecting the task-orientation organic to such a process.[15] One actor added, following the formal survey questions about the presence of trauma in their process, a useful distinction: 'My experience of working on Beckett felt more like trauma control … not so much experiencing trauma as working in the trauma department. Like an athlete might describe their training as trauma, in the long run it only makes them better and stronger.'[16]

Athleticism may indeed provide one key to moving beyond the traumatic model. The BOS system described above takes its cue from an aphorism found in the writings of Antonin Artaud: 'The actor is an athlete of the heart' (Artaud, 1958: 133). In the focus on the task to be achieved in sport, and the rigorous measurements taken of its comparative difficulty for other humans, there is a notable lack of fetishisation of the physical pain, difficulty or emotional struggle that it certainly takes to get there. This leads to its own difficulties in sport, of course – the problem of repression – but the evidence of this difficulty bursts out through the seams of media stories, rather than being routinely placed front and centre in the way, for example, that Lisa Dwan has done in media interviews:

> It looks like torture, and it is … I had no idea what I was taking on, how rarely performed this was. Many people have tried to do it and given up; the text is almost unlearnable, the physical stress is unbearable, the mental stress even worse. I meditate three times a day, I run, I am seeing a chiropractor, I have a hernia from pushing the sound out, my digestive system is affected. It has really taken its toll, but the rewards of speaking that gorgeous text are very great. (Sulcas, 2014)

For a contrasting 'athletic' model that shows the role of the pragmatic, task-oriented approach, an emblematic actor might be Barry McGovern, who responded as follows:

> Your question about the relationship between working on Beckett's theatre and trauma somewhat baffles me. You mention extreme states of physical or emotional duress. The only plays I can think of where there might be a lot of duress in the playing of them are *Play* and *Not I*. Not having played in either (and it wouldn't apply to Auditor in *Not I*) I can't speak from personal experience. I do know that having seen many productions of both plays and spoken to actors who were in them that they both require huge degrees of concentration and focus, mainly because they both require very fast delivery and, in the case of *Play*, a need to come in on cue immediately the spot hits the face. But this hardly amounts to trauma. It's what we do. I've experienced far more nervous anxiety playing, say, Miller or Sondheim than playing Beckett. *The Unnamable* section of my *I'll Go On* and Lucky in *Waiting for Godot* are the most physically and vocally demanding pieces of Beckett I've done, but they're not traumatic! They are technically difficult, but you train/ rehearse to cope with that. That's an actor's job.[17]

The actor and the void

The title of this chapter takes its cue from Beckett's prose, rather than his theatre, drawing on a resonant statement put forward in *Worstward Ho:* 'Void cannot go' (Beckett, 2009a: 87). This gemlike ontology exploits a line of thinking about the fundamental nature of the negative that extends from the sixth century BCE to the present day, via the pre-Socratics, the *Tao Te Ching*, Meister Eckhart and Theodor Adorno, among many others. As Maurice Blanchot writes in the author's introduction to 'From Anguish to Language', 'the world, things, knowledge, are to [the writer] only landmarks across the void. And he himself is already reduced to nothing. Nothingness is his material' (2001: 3). These terms resonate strongly with Beckett's own pronouncements in the 'Three Dialogues' with Georges Duthuit and in the widely cited 1937 'German Letter'. In Beckett's prose, as in his criticism, 'nothing' is substantive; silence and stillness, analogously, form a fundamental substrate of Beckett's theatre. Is it possible for an actor to embrace the philosophical and practical dimensions of the performance task through a reflection on the 'void'? Can Beckett's own ethic of witnessing and speaking – his self-suspension as a courageous pivot on the bridge between the void and the human – apply to the performer? Can an awareness of this fundamental negative ontology at least assist an actor in the performance of tasks, duties, obscure obligations? Might the recognition of such a substrate normalise difficulty and perseverance, instead of trauma?

In contemporary capitalism, absence is coded as a threat, as emotionally negative, as a lack needing to be filled. But this negativity is both fundamental and unavoidable in the condition of being, especially of being an actor: the nature of the task, its inherent stressors, its precarity and its ontology make it a terrain largely defined and framed by absences. Avoiding this, or repressing this, cuts off the actor working in such a culture from the actual skills of applying silence, stillness, or performing 'nothing' as a precise and meaningful action, which is more integral to physically based training methods of earlier centuries and of Asian performance approaches, such as Noh. Indeed, training for 'acting' at all seems to emphasise that one should be 'doing' something on stage, as opposed to creating spaces for others – audiences or scene partners – to imagine and to feel.

Others have invoked the term 'void' in relation to the Beckett actor. In *Theatre of Shadows*, Rosemary Pountney writes:

There is thus nothing left to the Beckett actor but to master the notation of action allotted to him and then reach beyond his normal creation of an identity. He must first attempt to make himself a void, to create an inner space or channel, and then allow this to fill with Beckett's speech rhythms and repetitions until gradually an identification with the creative consciousness behind the lines takes place. The actor in fact 'tunes in' to Beckett rather than creating his own character. At best his imaginative identification is so strong that a fusion of actor and author takes place, which in turn creates the extraordinary impact Beckett's plays often have on audiences. (1998: 184–5)

Though her focus on authorial fidelity (and surprisingly gendered prose) may be questionable, Pountney is at least half right. Like a musical instrument, the actor is indeed a vessel defined – made useful – in part through strategic voids. Current practice would suggest that this vessel is, in fact, a conduit between an author and an audience, rather than a one-way channel.

Rethinking the actor in terms of the void opens up several pathways for further exploration. The testimonies presented here highlight the Beckett actor as emblematic of innumerable acts of local courage in confronting, framing and using the void, which is one way to understand the work that is required of all actors. Though narratives constructed in the press or in public perception might emphasise the difficulty of performing Beckett's plays, especially those with heightened physical demands, trauma is not a necessary trope to 'normalise' in the discourse surrounding Beckettian performance, and it would be excessive to argue that bodily pain is 'indispensable for the realization of [Beckett's] art' (Hori Tanaka et al., 2012: 16) – at least, not in any sense greater than the inevitability of pain in the human condition.

The void need not be traumatic. When Beckett's plays demand physical stillness or constraint, or include stances that operate as 'stress positions' when sustained over time – as in *Endgame*, *Happy Days*, *Play*, *That Time*, *A Piece of Monologue*, the mimes and *Catastrophe* – the question must be about what is required for repetition, for sustainability and for survival. If an actor reports traumatic symptoms such as panic, fear, anxiety and nightmare, scholars and practitioners must be careful to disentangle the overdetermined origins of these feelings: are they ingrained in the source material, individual to the actor's process, specific to the performance context and material circumstances, or simply authentic physiological responses to the physical demands that can be understood, engaged and managed through that same lens? Beckett is, ultimately, an artist who can lead us to develop a more unified theory of acting that takes account of the 'cognitive turn' and the integration that characterises embodiment. He can perhaps help us to see how it is not with resignation, nor with fear and trembling, but rather with profound bravery, that actors can say, 'the show must go on'.

Acknowledgements

The research for this chapter was partly funded by Enterprise Ireland (Project CS20151382E), and I am indebted to Burç İdem Dinçel for research assistance. In addition to the artists and sources identified in the bibliography and notes, I drew on numerous experiences in theatres and classrooms, observing and collaborating with many artists and teachers, indeed more than it would be possible to list here. Although the written work is of sole authorship, I wish to acknowledge the following theatre artists who provided interviews or testimonies in response to specific questions during the research: Marc Atkinson, Peter Corboy, Siobhán Cullen, Lisa Dwan, Hannah Grady, Katherine Graham, Judy Hegarty-Lovett, Jonathan Heron, Conor Lovett, Nichola MacEvilly, Matthew Malone, Barry McGovern, Maeve O'Mahony, Ellen Patterson, Cathal Quinn and Sarah Jane Scaife.

Notes

1 An extensive media campaign around Lisa Dwan, related to her world tour of the Walter Asmus/Royal Court production of 'The Beckett Trilogy', comprising *Not I* / *Footfalls* / *Rockaby*, emphasised the physical demands on the Beckett performer, while making explicit reference to the Whitelaw legacy.

2 This 'bridge' model is extrapolated from Dillard's essays, which are

imagistic and often oblique, rather than stated explicitly. See Dillard, 1977: 68–72.

3 'If the actor were full, really full, of feeling, how could he play the same part twice running with the same spirit and success?' See Diderot, 1883: 8.

4 See Benedetti, 2008: xvi–xvii. This section will consciously draw on the 1948 American edition of Stanislavski, as the earlier version was the influential one in terms of forming the divisions discussed here.

5 The most famous anecdote surrounding the Method is an exchange between Dustin Hoffman and Laurence Olivier on the set of *Marathon Man*. After seeing Hoffman utterly exhausted, having driven his body to the limit for the sake of one shot in the film, Olivier is said to have remarked: 'Why don't you try acting, my boy?' Though apocryphal, this is a lucid statement of the Diderot school's riposte to the American interpretation of Stanislavski.

6 Stanislavski writes about emotions being truly felt on stage: 'the unfortunate part about them is that we cannot control them. They control us. Therefore we have no choice but to leave it to nature and say: "If they will come, let them come. We will only hope that they will work with the part and not at cross purposes to it"' (2003: 190).

7 Laughably, Chubbuck's exercises always end with the admonition: 'Let it go'.

8 For the rich alternatives afforded by assessing the Beckett actor and psychology in relation to Brecht, see Rokem, 1987: 175–84; Brater, 1975: 195–205.

9 It is important to note here that the Anglo-American sphere remains the focus in this particular argument; many European theatre cultures have moved beyond default naturalism, and for many Asian theatre cultures it has always been and remains a minority in practice.

10 For a study of this progression and its relation to early modern distinctions between soul and body, see Long, 2012: 49–72.

11 There is a long history of explorations of Beckett acting, but this argument is particularly indebted to Kalb (1989) and McMullan (2010). Most recently, Andrew Head has specifically explored this post-Stanislavski Beckett actor in his PhD research on the subject and in several conference papers; see Head, 2015.

12 See Goldstein and Bloom, 2011: 141–2.

13 These works include McConachie and Hart (2006), Pitches (2006) and Blair (2008).

14 Though I led the rehearsals for *Play*, I collaborated with Marc

Atkinson as a co-director of the overall *Ethica* project, which collected four Beckett shorts as a single production: *Play, Come and Go, Catastrophe* and *What Where*. These were performed in Bulgaria, Ireland and Northern Ireland over a two-year period.

15 Analysis of transcribed interviews with all participants in the project, as well as email survey answers, was conducted using the Voyant digital text-analysis package.

16 Maeve O'Mahony, email correspondence, 1 March 2015.

17 Barry McGovern, email correspondence, 22 February 2015.

References

Artaud, Antonin (1958). 'An Affective Athleticism'. In Antonin Artaud (ed.), *The Theatre and Its Double*. Trans. Mary Caroline Richards. New York: Grove Press, pp. 133–41.

Beckett, Samuel (2009a). *Company / Ill Seen Ill Said / Worstward Ho / Stirrings Still*. Ed. Dirk Van Hulle. London: Faber and Faber.

Beckett, Samuel (2009b). *The Unnamable*. Ed. Steven Connor. London: Faber and Faber.

Benedetti, Jean (2008). 'Translator's Foreword'. In Konstantin Stanislavski, *An Actor's Work*. London: Routledge, pp. xv–xxii.

Ben-Zvi, Linda (1990). 'Billie Whitelaw: Interviewed by Linda Ben-Zvi'. In Linda Ben-Zvi (ed.), *Women in Beckett: Performance and Critical Perspectives*. Urbana, IL: University of Illinois Press, pp. 3–10.

Blair, Rhonda (2008). *The Actor, Image, and Action: Acting and Cognitive Neuroscience*. London: Routledge.

Blanchot, Maurice (2001). *Faux Pas*. Trans. Charlotte Mandell. Stanford, CA: Stanford University Press.

Bloch, Susana, Pedro Orthous and Guy Santibañez-H. (1987). 'Effector Patterns of Basic Emotions: A Psychophysiological Method for Training Actors', *Journal of Social Biological Structures* 10.1, 1–19. Reprinted in Phillip B. Zarrilli (ed.), *Acting (Re)Considered: A Theoretical and Practical Guide*. 2nd edn. London: Routledge, 2002, pp. 219–38.

Brater, Enoch (1975). 'Brecht's Alienated Actor in Beckett's Theatre', *Comparative Drama* 9.3, 195–205.

Bureau of Labor Statistics, U.S. Department of Labor (2015). 'Occupational Employment Statistics, May 2015', www.bls.gov/oes/current/oes272011. Accessed 15 July 2016.

Bureau of Labor Statistics, U.S. Department of Labor (2016). 'Actors'. In

Occupational Outlook Handbook 2016–17 Edition, www.bls.gov/ooh/entertainment-and-sports/actors.htm. Accessed 15 July 2016.

Chubbuck, Ivana (2004). *The Power of the Actor: The Chubbuck Technique*. New York: Gotham Books.

Diderot, Denis (1883). *The Paradox of Acting*. Trans. Walter Herries Pollock. London: Chatto & Windus.

Dillard, Annie (1977). *Holy the Firm*. New York: Harper & Row.

Goldstein, Thalia R. (2012). 'What, Cognitively, Does an Actor Actually Do?', *Psychology Today* 19, www.psychologytoday.com/blog/the-mind-stage/201201/what-cognitively-does-actor-actually-do. Accessed 7 April 2015.

Goldstein, Thalia R., and Paul Bloom (2011). 'The Mind on Stage: Why Cognitive Scientists Should Study Acting', *Trends in Cognitive Sciences* 15.4, 141–2.

Gussow, Mel (ed.) (1996). *Conversations with and about Beckett*. New York: Grove Press.

Head, Andrew (2015). 'Beckett's Implied Actor: Debts, Legacies and a Contemporary Performance Culture'. Paper given at the 'Staging Beckett' conference, University of Reading, 9 April 2015.

Hori Tanaka, Mariko, Yoshiki Tajiri and Michiko Tsushima (eds) (2012). *Samuel Beckett and Pain*. Amsterdam: Rodopi.

Kalb, Jonathan (1989). *Beckett in Performance*. Cambridge: Cambridge University Press.

Knowlson, James, and Elizabeth Knowlson (eds) (2006). *Beckett Remembering/Remembering Beckett*. London: Bloomsbury.

Konijn, Elly (2002). 'The Actor's Emotions Reconsidered: A Psychological Task-based Perspective'. In Phillip B. Zarrilli (ed.), *Acting (Re)Considered: A Theoretical and Practical Guide*. 2nd edn. London: Routledge, pp. 62–81.

Long, Zackariah C. (2012). 'Toward an Early Modern Theory of Trauma: Conscience in *Richard III*', *Journal of Literature and Trauma Studies* 1.1, 49–72.

Mamet, David (1999). *True and False*. New York: Vintage.

Maude, Ulrika (2015). 'Beckett, Body and Mind'. In Dirk Van Hulle (ed.), *The New Cambridge Companion to Samuel Beckett*. Cambridge: Cambridge University Press, pp. 170–84.

McConachie, Bruce, and F. Elizabeth Hart (eds) (2006). *Performance and Cognition: Theatre Studies and the Cognitive Turn*. London: Routledge.

McMullan, Anna (2010). *Performing Embodiment in Samuel Beckett's Drama*. London: Routledge.

Munnery, Simon (2001). *Attention Scum*. Series 1. BBC2 television.

Pitches, Jonathan (2006). *Science and the Stanislavski Tradition of Acting.* London: Routledge.

Pountney, Rosemary (1998). *Theatre of Shadows: Samuel Beckett's Drama 1956–76.* London: Colin Smythe.

Rokem, Freddie (1987). 'Acting and Psychoanalysis: Street Scenes, Private Scenes, and Transference', *Theatre Journal* 39.2, 175–84.

Sheridan, Colette (2012). 'The Pay's the Thing', *Irish Examiner*, 24 November 2012.

Stanislavski, Konstantin (2003 [1948]). *An Actor Prepares.* Trans. Elizabeth Reynolds Hapgood. London: Routledge.

Sulcas, Roslyn (2014). 'Suffering for Her Art, and Beckett: Lisa Dwan Performs Solo at BAM in 3 Beckett Plays', *New York Times*, 24 September 2014.

Whitelaw, Billie (1995). *Billie Whitelaw … Who He?* New York: St. Martin's Press.

Zarrilli, Phillip B. (ed.) (2002). *Acting (Re)Considered: A Theoretical and Practical Guide.* 2nd edn. London: Routledge.

Zarrilli, Phillip B. (2008). *Psychophysical Acting: An Intercultural Approach after Stanislavski.* London: Routledge.

Part II

Body and subjectivity

3

Insignificant residues: trauma, face and *figure* in Samuel Beckett

David Houston Jones

> But the faces of the living, all grimace and flush, can they be described as objects?
>
> Samuel Beckett, *First Love*

A number of important contributions to trauma theory position Samuel Beckett's work as a privileged point of reference. For Robert Eaglestone, the ethical necessity of 'an ongoing conversation about the Holocaust' results in 'a conversation which, Beckett-like, can't go on, but must go on' (2000: 105). Jonathan Boulter goes further, arguing in 2004 that this troubled dialogue is part of a 'larger recognition' that Beckett's work, 'in its continual interrogation of the workability of the concepts of trauma and mourning, may in fact be read as a generalised critique of the use of trauma and mourning as interpretive tropes' (2004: 345; see also Smith, 2007). Thomas Elsaesser's classic account of the response of the moving image to trauma, meanwhile, mobilises Beckett's work, with its ambivalent determination 'to name the unnamable', in order to link the problematic of unrepresentability to those of belatedness, latency and the prospect of agency in narrative cinema (2001: 195). Elsaesser returns to Beckett in his 2013 *German Cinema: Terror and Trauma*, where the possibility of expressing trauma is twice linked to Beckett's 'obligation to express' dictum.[1] Despite Beckett's periodic appearance in trauma theory and visual culture studies, few critical accounts have offered sustained consideration of all three (see Jones, 2011).

In what follows, I consider the visual dimension of the
'obligation' dictum, which itself originates in Beckett's 'Three
Dialogues', a text concerned with the visual arts, as an indirect
response to trauma (Beckett, 1983). The visual constitutes both
a key context for recent debates on testimony (including the
notorious iconophilia controversy) and the sphere in which
Beckett's standpoint to unspeakability takes on certain key forms.
In particular, I analyse the face, which, as *la figure*, aligns facial
features and the wider problem of expression in the francophone
aspect of Beckett's work. The face is seen here as the visual
figure that best illuminates the interface between Beckett's work
and trauma theory and, equally, in Beckett, as a visually coded
response to unspeakability. If the face operates as a cipher of
the expressive, it also initiates an important dialogue between
the apparently inexpressive ends to which it is put in Beckett
and assumptions concerning facial expression which go back to
Duchenne de Boulogne's pioneering work on facial musculature
in the 1860s.

In his 1995 text 'The Face', Giorgio Agamben comments on
what he calls the face's 'pure communicability':

> Inasmuch as it is nothing but pure communicability, every human
> face, even the most noble and beautiful, is always suspended on the
> edge of an abyss. This is precisely why the most delicate and grace-
> ful faces sometimes look as if they might suddenly decompose,
> thus letting the shapeless and bottomless background that threat-
> ens them emerge. But this amorphous background is nothing else
> than the opening itself and communicability itself inasmuch as
> they are constituted as their own presuppositions as if they were
> a thing. The only face to remain uninjured is the one capable of
> taking the abyss of its own communicability upon itself and of
> exposing it without fear or complacency. (2000: 95)

Agamben casts a long shadow over this essay as a thinker of trauma:
in particular, I have in mind the theory of testimony in *Remnants
of Auschwitz* as a form of impossible speech which, as an 'essential
lacuna' within testimony, issues from its own impossibility (2002:
13). In itself this is a reframing of the problem of unspeakability
which subtends Beckett's work and trauma theory alike. I retain
it here, however, both because of its implication in the liminal

status of the face in Agamben's later work and because of the visual forms which that liminal presence suggests. Agamben did not subsequently develop the essay entitled 'The Face', collected in *Means Without End*; the essay, though, both implicitly links the face to trauma theory due to its resonances with Agamben's theory of testimony, and addresses unrepresentability in ways that chime with Beckett's own formulation of the question.

Agamben's face is concerned with the idea of 'communicability': for Agamben, 'there is a face wherever something reaches the level of exposition and tries to grasp its own being exposed'. The face is associated with the act of expression, as in the literary trope of prosopopoeia, where 'art can give a face even to an inanimate object, to a still nature' (2000: 91). The face, for Agamben, is equivalent to this act of naming, a creative gesture that confers meaning upon a thing, and is conceived of in both lyrical and visual terms. In *Remnants of Auschwitz*, the impossible speech attributed to the dead entails both the lyrical restoration of 'face' and the visual encounter with the Gorgon's impossible face, the face that cannot be seen. What is striking is the precarious account Agamben gives of facial expression: the face is always on the verge of lapsing into the troubled 'shapeless and bottomless' background that surrounds it. Clearly it is not exactly the physical make-up of the face that is at stake here, nor its 'real' background, but the threat to its intelligibility, which Agamben argues is always present. The threat can only be surmounted by 'taking the abyss of [the face's] own communicability upon itself and of exposing it without fear or complacency'. The failure to do so, for Agamben, is strikingly and somewhat incongruously cast as a form of facial injury, a claim that remains entirely undeveloped in his work.

The second highly provocative element of Agamben's account is the description of what happens when the face realises its communicability:

> As soon as the face realises that communicability is all that it is and hence that it has nothing to express – thus withdrawing silently behind itself, inside its own mute identity – it turns into a grimace, which is what one calls character. Character is the constitutive reticence that human beings retain in the word; but what one has to take possession of here is only a nonlatency, a pure visibility:

simply a visage. The face is not something that transcends the
visage: it is the exposition of the visage in all its nudity, it is a
victory over character – it is word. (2000: 96)

In contrast to the latency that is elsewhere associated with
testimony (both in Agamben's work and that of others such
as Elsaesser), the face is now associated with 'non-latency'. In
contrast to the common view of the face as 'expressive', in particular as expressive of readily recognisable affects, the face is
now associated with a 'pure visibility'. Pure visibility, in turn, is
deemed to be equivalent to 'non-latency', suggesting that rather
than concealing hidden depths of meaning, the face is ultimately
an empty cipher. Such a suggestion, of course, is not the same as
a simple statement of the face's emptiness. Instead, it arrives at
that conclusion in a rhetorically painstaking manner, labouring,
like Beckett, the statement of expression's absence. The grimace is
associated with this expression of a 'mute identity' or, to put it in
familiar terms, of the expression of the inability to express.

I want to draw attention to two aspects of Agamben's treatment
of the face: the ambiguous status of the grimace and the role of
background in consideration of the face's visual form. The latter
preoccupation, I suggest, is cognate with Beckett's treatment of
the face, in particular in facially framed responses to trauma that
appeal to visual traditions. While some of those responses down-
grade the expressive capabilities of the face while maintaining
its integrity, in other cases the face is reduced to its constituent
parts, disaggregated into a limited range of facial components
(*Not I*), or elided with the machinery of language (*Watt*). The
threat of facial decomposition, in Beckett, always accompanies
facial expression, and attains prominence in the works for theatre
and television, where the illuminated face literally fades into a
dark background. It is rooted, however, in the verbal deployment
of facial disappearance in Beckett's early prose.

The face and the grimace

The grimace enjoys a special status in foundational accounts
of the expressive face, chief among which is that in Duchenne

de Boulogne's *Mécanisme de la physionomie humaine* (1862). Duchenne's work offered a new understanding of facial musculature, and its experimental basis consisted of stimulating different areas of the face with an electric scalpel or 'excitateur' in order to simulate facial expressions. As a result, the idea of the 'language of the passions' could be rethought, as François Delaporte has shown, in terms of concrete physiological evidence: 'the study of the language of the passions rests on the knowledge of the mechanisms of expression. But the perception of the signs of this language in action carries a symptomatology of the passions and a new profile of what can be perceived and enunciated' (Delaporte, 2008: 4). The 'language of the passions' shapes the background of my argument, from the uncontextualised reference to the 'face of God' in Agamben's 'The Face' (2000: 98) to the strand of Christian imagery that runs through Beckett's visually inflected works.

Following Duchenne, instead of ascribing different 'passions' to the heart, the liver or the nervous system and imagining a facial 'ensemble' resembling a mask, the observer of facial expressions could now empirically relate them to the sets of muscles in which they originated. Duchenne's experiments were made possible by the discovery of an elderly shoemaker whose facial nerves, as a result of an earlier illness, were largely insensitive to pain: the man's facial muscles could thus be exposed to electrical stimulation and the resulting 'expressions' photographed.[2] For Duchenne's predecessor Condillac, the language of facial expression begins as a series of grimaces and contortions, which subsequently develops into a range of signifiers of emotion. In Duchenne, the grimace stands for inexpressive muscular movements, including those provoked by electrical stimulation of multiple facial muscles:

> It often happens in these delicate experiments that the electrode meets a nerve trunk that sets off a large number of muscles. The 'en masse' contraction that results never produces anything but a grimace that resembles no expression. This 'en masse' contraction mimics the convulsive spasms one sees in a chronic nervous affliction called *tic indolent de la face*. (1990: 17)

Here, the grimace is understood simply as a muscular contraction that does not recall the conventional language of facial expression. The grimace, then, is positioned as the obverse of facial expression, a gesture that, because it does not correspond to the repertoire of recognised expressions, signifies the inexpressive. Indeed, in François Delaporte's suggestive phrase, 'les grimaces ne sont pas le matériau donné pour l'élaboration des signes, mais des résidus *insignifiants*' ('grimaces [in Duchenne] are not the material given for the elaboration of signs, but the *insignificant* residues') (2008: 89). Such a view of the grimace raises epistemological questions: the observer's interpretation of it is entirely determined by a pre-defined range of expressions and emotions; when something outside of these categories is encountered, it cannot be accommodated, and is relegated to a position of meaninglessness. The grimace stands outside of the conventional language of the passions, and to encounter it is to address an intransigent discursive residue. The grimace, then, is associated with narratorial reflexivity and epistemological breakdown, two of the key features of the traumatic sub-texts of Beckett's work. There, the problematisation of the face as a vector of the affect comes to the fore in uniquely distressed forms.

From facial mechanics to facial avoidance: *Not I* and *Film*

In Beckett's most extreme staging of the face, *Not I*, we see the frenzied spectacle of a mouth that emits a torrent of words, and periodically laughs and screams. The actor's body is completely invisible, on a platform '8 feet above stage level', and the face appears suspended in mid-air above the blacked-out stage (Beckett, 1990: 376). The incessant babble of Mouth contrasts with another faceless figure, the Auditor, 'downstage audience left, tall standing figure, sex undeterminable, enveloped from head to foot in loose black djellaba, with hood' (376), and the gesture of helplessness and incomprehension periodically made by this figure creates an analogue to that of the audience, faced with what has been described as the 'unnamable trauma' at the heart of the play (Herren, 2007: 70). In Laura Salisbury's reading, Mouth is 'not only a subject dislocated from herself by trauma, she also seems to be a creaking mechanical system placed under the obligations and demands of experimental tests on the limits of language' (2009:

97). As well as the linguistic system, I suggest, *Not I* engages with another mechanical system: that of facial expression.

The provisional desubjectification wrought by language in the play is complemented by the subversion of the face, as Mouth performs the untenable strain placed upon the system of facial expression by traumatic experience. Indeed, it is well nigh impossible to speak of facial expressions here: this is a disembodied mouth, separated from the contextual framing of the face and of the facial muscles identified by Duchenne, resulting in a speaking object that is not quite a face and that interrogates the expressive capabilities of the face. Language and laughter, too, are radically defamiliarised, and the play contrasts the periodic 'brief laugh' with the even rarer 'good laugh' (Beckett, 1990: 377). A very similar opposition occurs in Duchenne between the 'joie fausse' and 'rire ironique' on the one hand, and the 'rire naturel vrai' on the other (1862: 55–69). Duchenne comments in these terms upon the figure of the old shoemaker in figure 32 of the *Mécanisme de la physionomie humaine*, in which he claims to be spontaneously causing laughter in the subject, stimulating laughter which is 'franc et communicatif' ('frank and communicative') (61). Despite the emphasis on the *orbicularis oculi* as the muscle characterising what has become known as the 'Duchenne' smile, denoting genuine positive emotion, a remarkable slippage in Duchenne's account positions laughter as the index of the affective state, in preference to the movements of the face.[3]

In Beckett, then, the face poses a dilemma of intelligibility. On the verge of disappearing, it is a shape we glimpse against a dark background, and which hovers on the edge of our field of vision, as in the Süddeutscher Rundfunk production of *…but the clouds…*[4] Beckett's work makes the face operate at the limit of its expressive capabilities, as in *Not I* and the television plays, while relying at other times, in works such as *Eh Joe, En attendant Godot* and *Fin de partie* on actors with what we habitually call 'expressive' faces. Here, a key example is Beckett's *Film*, in which the male character, 'O', played by Buster Keaton, is in flight from an entity named 'E', who turns out to be the camera eye: 'the protagonist is sundered into object (O) and eye (E), the former in flight, the latter in pursuit. It will not be clear until end of film that pursuing perceiver is not extraneous, but self'; 'search of non-being in flight from extraneous perception breaking down in inescapability of self-perception' (1990: 323). *Film* is thus thought of as an allegory of Berkeley's doctrine of the implication of consciousness in perceivedness, or '*esse* is *percipi*'.[5]

The drama of the gaze in *Film* is bound up with Beckett's long-standing fascination with silent film and the film theory of the 1920s. That interest is seen in Beckett's letter to Eisenstein in 1936, more than twenty-five years before writing *Film*, requesting admission to the Moscow State School of Cinematography (Leyda, 1988: 59). It is also seen in the strong convergence between Beckett's interests and those of Rudolf Arnheim as demonstrated by Matthijs Engelberts, in particular the danger of silent film being swamped by the emerging 'industrial film' of the 1930s, with its 'stereoscopic colour and gramophonic sound' (Engelberts, 2008: 154). The film is set 'about 1929', anchoring it in the era of silent film, and its facial drama recalls the prominent role played in 1920s cinema by facial close-ups. The avoidance of the facial close-up until the end of *Film* itself reads as homage or critique of the role, in Joe Kember's analysis, of the 'magnified, mobile human face as a kind of spectacle in itself' in the facial expressions genre (2009: 165; see also Kember, 2001).

The avoidance of the gaze in Beckett is further contextualised by a filmic analysis that pursues the implications of the 'averted look' in a quite different context: that of Noa Steimatsky on the films of Robert Bresson. In a process compared by Steimatsky to autism for its radical avoidance of the visual markers of social interaction, the actor's avoidance of the camera eye and the broader 'movements of withdrawal' (Steimatsky, 2012: 164) of the face within Bresson's cinematography contribute to a fundamental change in the status of the face in the visual field:

> This levelling of persons and objects, of anthropomorphic and aniconic forms, challenges our intuitive response to the human face as standing out in the visual field and, from that privileged position, endowing it at will with order and with expressivity. In the cinema the human face is a traditional measure of the shot: the range of close-up, medium close-up, medium shot, and so on is firstly defined by the face. For the face is positioned high in a hierarchy

of attention and meaning that routinely follows anthropomorphic projection and identification – with regard to figure and ground, orientation, narrative focalization and other varieties of relations unfolding within and across shots. What does it mean, then, to disrupt or even reverse this hierarchy, to pull the face effectively downward to a world of inert matter where other objects would seem to await the human glance to endow them, too, with a face? (166)

The reconfiguration of the visual attention accorded the face, then, amounts to a redefinition of the face's relation to the non-human objects that surround it: to embed the face in a dynamic of invisibility or avoidance is to suggest its visual equivalence to the 'world of inert matter'. Steimatsky's important insight recalls the work of another early film theorist, Béla Balázs, and the idea of 'the living physiognomy that all things possess' (Balázs, 2011: 46). Balázs's conceptual 'levelling' both demotes the human and institutes a fraternal cohabitation with the 'pleasant and lovable faces' (46) of everyday objects, recalling the 'old trusty things' of *First Love* or, equally, *Happy Days* (Beckett, 1995: 39). Beckett's disturbance of the visual hierarchies in which the face is conventionally placed, I suggest, manifests itself as both avoidance (in *Film*) and a critique of the smile rooted in facial iconicity. The largely impassive face in the Süddeutscher Rundfunk *Eh Joe*, for instance, with its post-publication transition to a brief uncontextualised smile, may be seen as an example of what Kember has recently termed the 'weakly expressive' face in cinema.[6] The 'designedly vacant thematics' observed by Kember in the face of the silent film actor Harry Langdon (seen by Beckett in Dublin in the 1920s) may be seen as a precursor to the radically indeterminate faces of Beckett's own film, theatre and television plays (Kember, 2018).[7]

The aniconic smile

As Steimatsky notes, the hierarchy of anthropomorphic and aniconic forms is imbued with religious meaning: '"Aniconic" means basically "non-iconic," in the sense of non-anthropomorphic, non-figurative. The term is used broadly in theological and anthropological discussions of religions or cultures that

forbid the representation of god, or even any image making'
(2012: 176, n. 23). The idea of iconophilia, meanwhile, has been
negatively applied to the insistence of thinkers such as Georges
Didi-Huberman on the primacy of the tortured phenomenology
of Holocaust images. For Didi-Huberman, images such as the
clandestine photographs of Auschwitz gas chambers taken by
members of the *Sonderkommando* in 1944 can only be apprehended in the plenitude of their covert, chaotic composition. The
effort to make the images presentable, by contrast (as has been
repeatedly attempted) is the sign of the 'urgent desire to *give a
face* to that which, in the image itself, is no more than movement, blur and event' (2008: 34). The reparative instinct by which
viewing tries to mitigate the roughness and blurred movement of
the images means that they are frequently 'ill seen' (67).[8]

I extend Steimatsky's account of the aniconic in order to take
account of its ambiguous status in Beckett's faces, in particular
the making of face in conditions that apparently preclude image-
making, and the implication of the face in iconographic accounts
of the Passion. Engelberts's brief history of Beckett's engagement
with early film theory aptly foregrounds the troubled iconicity of
the face, casting the struggle of the early theorists of 'film as art'
as 'a hymn to the camera and a song of praise of moving images
projected on the big screen' (2008: 162), a song to which *Film*
belatedly lends it voice:

> *Film* is clearly a *lamento* on the gaze, and the cinematographic aes-
> thetic here gives way on the screen to the theory of self-perception
> and being. End of the celebration of the gaze. In the face of the
> suffering that identifies him with a Christ, eyewitness to his own
> passion, what else is the figure to do but flee before the camera?
> Finally, what is there to do except for this gesture of O, so charac-
> teristic of the Beckettian universe and so *little* characteristic of early
> cinema theory: 'He covers his face with his hands'. (Engelberts,
> 2008: 162)

Engelberts's identification of a *Passion* of viewing embeds
Beckett's investment in early cinema in facial iconicity in a highly
revealing way. The Passion as traumatic sub-text durably influences Beckett's representation of the face: the face's impossible

address is bound up with the 'Passion' of Beckett's *Film*, and ultimately connects with the coded implication of the iconic and the Passional in Beckett's theory of expression. Despite his well-known dismissal of Christianity as a 'mythology with which I am perfectly familiar', Beckett mobilises iconic pre-texts (iconographic sources and their textual mediation) in order to exploit their ambiguous treatment of the human (Duckworth, 1972: 18). I consider briefly two types of iconic reference: those that exploit a sense of iconicity beyond and in contradiction to specific reference points, and those that tap directly into the iconographic traditions surrounding the Passion.

Neary's reference in *Murphy* to 'Luke's portrait of Matthew, with the angel perched like a parrot on his shoulder', for all its plausibility, refers not to a specific work but to the reader's willingness to believe that such a portrait must exist. As Brigitte Le Juez argues, 'the confusion of the religious image – a form of revelation – springs from Neary's mingling of religiously themed paintings, which might include, for example, *Saint Matthew and the Angel* by Rembrandt and *Saint Luke Drawing the Virgin* by Rogier van der Weyden' (2013: 214). Rather like the elusive image of the face dissolving into darkness, seen so often in Beckett, the icon acts as a lure, resulting in an indeterminate mode of visual reference. As Le Juez further notes, the parrot on Mary's shoulder symbolises the Annunciation, whose depiction by Antonello da Messina is echoed, as James Knowlson argues, in Beckett's *Footfalls* (Haynes and Knowlson, 2003: 75). Beckett's view of the Annunciation may also have been shaped by his contemplation of the sculptures in Bamberg cathedral, in particular the juxtaposition of Elizabeth, Mary and the Laughing Angel. Beckett's humorous admission of his own inability to 'keep a laughing angel in an Annunciation' links iconicity as a mode of reference to the problematic of facial expression once more, and to the particular indeterminacies of the smile (Knowlson, 2008: 25).[9] The Annunciation, meanwhile, is the privileged figure of Didi-Huberman's analysis of the 'ill-seeing', which he argues has traditionally afflicted art historical constructions of legibility. The curious strategy of facial highlighting and apparent neglect of detail in Fra Angelico, by contrast, is born of an engagement with the inexpressible in religious iconography (Didi-Huberman, 2009: 15).

In the television play *Nacht und Träume*, we encounter a seam of references that concretely evoke the iconography of Christ's Passion. The ghostly face of the protagonist is raised towards a cup offered to him by an unseen hand. When the hand reaches down to wipe perspiration from the protagonist's face, the work implicitly evokes the tradition of the 'vera icon' and the legend that Christ's face is imprinted on the cloth.[10] The wider resonance of the cup, meanwhile, extends from the bitter cup of the garden of Gethsemane to the Last Supper.[11] The idea of the imprint of Christ's face famously recurs in *Endgame* when Hamm, in a moment of facial avoidance that recalls *Film*, covers his face with the 'old stancher' (Beckett, 1990: 134). In the French *Fin de partie*, the 'vieux linge' further recalls the Veronica cloth, and, for Ruby Cohn, the cloth used to wrap Christ's body following the crucifixion.[12] A similar cloth in Beckett's novel *Watt* is instrumental in the association of facial avoidance with the Passional sub-text. Watt is periodically compared to Christ, including in the garden scene in which his painful progress towards the narrator is compared to Bosch's *Christ Mocked (The Crowning with Thorns)*: 'His face was bloody, his hand also, and thorns were in his scalp'. Watt's hands are later anointed by the character Sam (Beckett, 1978: 157, 161). In another incident, Watt suffers an unprovoked attack, and responds with Christ-like forebearance:

> Watt found this was the wisest attitude, to staunch, if necessary, inconspicuously, with the little red sudarium that he always carried in his pocket, the flow of blood, to pick up what had fallen, and to continue, as soon as possible, on his way or in his station, like a victim of mere mischance. (Beckett, 1978: 30)

In the English, the Latin *sudarium* (a vestment worn during Mass) aligns Watt's sufferings once more with those of Christ, an association reinforced by the reference to the 'station[s]' of his journey, recalling the Stations of the Cross.[13] Although the latter association is lost in the French translation, the connection to the Veronica cloth is reinforced in the reference to the 'petit linge' (Beckett, 2007: 34).

Well-known as Beckett's religious preoccupations may be, their incursion into the character of Watt returns us to Beckett's concern with facial expression, and with the extraordinary inhibition of the communicability of the affect that takes place in the text's account of Watt's smile:

> Watt had watched people smile and thought he understood how it was done. And it was true that Watt's smile, when he smiled, resembled more a smile than a sneer, for example, or a yawn. But there was something wanting to Watt's smile, some little thing was lacking, and people who saw it for the first time, and most people who saw it saw it for the first time, were sometimes in doubt as to what expression exactly was intended. To many it seemed a simple sucking of the teeth.
> Watt used this smile sparingly. (Beckett, 1978: 23)

Watt's smile is a failed facial expression: as the undercutting narrative voice indicates, those who see it are in doubt as to the signified emotion. The statement is followed up by the brutal reference to the 'sucking of the teeth', an expression with no affective connotation, and the even more sardonic 'Watt used this smile sparingly'. The suggestion is that Watt proceeds by simple mimicry, without experiencing the affects he attempts to imitate. On closer examination, though, the process that Watt follows, if not its outcome, may in fact converge with 'normal' facial activity. In the psychology of facial expression, smiling is primarily a social activity, and its performance is conventionally situated in relation to the other's gaze (Provine, 1997: 160). In situating Watt outside of the normative dynamics of the face, and instead producing a residual facial discourse, Beckett shows a deep fascination with the instability of discourses of facial expression and the power of the iconic to provoke such instabilities. Like an imprint or after-image, the face of the icon is embedded in the text and disrupts, as in Steimatsky, the order of representation in which it is placed. The smile is the vehicle, here, of that disruption.

The dilemma of face in *Watt* is embedded in the extraordinary problematic of naming that pervades the text. Watt's struggle to perform facial expressions recalls the act of making face in Agamben, or of conferring identity upon a thing. Watt agonises over common objects such as the cooking pot that he uses in the course of his duties in Mr Knott's house:

> For Watt now found himself in the midst of things which, if they consented to be named, did so as it were with reluctance. And the state in which Watt found himself resisted formulation in a way no state had ever done, in which Watt had ever found himself, and Watt had found himself in a great many states, in his day. Looking at a pot, for example, or thinking of a pot, at one of Mr. Knott's pots, of one of Mr. Knott's pots, it was in vain that Watt said, Pot, pot. (Beckett, 1978: 78)

The indeterminacy that emanates from the struggle to name issues both from linguistic alienation and from a range of visual sources that further problematise facial expressivity.

The final sections of *Watt* extend the novel's facial problematics to include an increasingly ambiguous facial figure. As the other characters bend over Watt in the station waiting room, he is treated as an object of uncertain origin whose identification becomes a pressing concern: 'The clothes seem to me the same, said Mr Case. He went to the window and turned over, with his boot, the hat. I recognise the hat, he said. He rejoined Mr Gorman and Mr Nolan in the doorway. I see the bags, he said, but I cannot say that I recognise the face' (Beckett, 1978: 241–2). The scene sees a literal demotion of the human face to the world of objects and, after the passages on the enigmatic 'figure' which, following its gradual approach, 'without any interruption of its motions, grew fainter and fainter, and finally disappeared' (227), produces the arresting image at the end of the book of Watt's own face illuminated by the sun: 'The sun had not yet risen, above the sea. It had not yet risen, but it was rising fast. As he watched, it rose, and shone, with its faint morning shining, on his face' (243). The laboured production of the image recalls that in *How It Is*, where the protagonist's agonising progress through a landscape of inert matter is bound up both with the encounter with self-image and a specifically visual form of expression: 'my tongue comes out again lolls in the mud I stay there no more thirst the tongue goes in the mouth closes it must be a straight line now it's over, it's done, I've had the image' (Beckett, 1996:

34). Prostrate like Watt in the station waiting room, the speaker filters the mud through his mouth like a worm. At the same time, he is concerned with his progress from an external vantage point: only this non-existent perspective can produce the figure of the straight line that is equated with expression. Though no such observer is present, the narrator's preoccupation with his own image in the gaze of the observer once more produces an unlikely figure, that of the smile: 'I realise I'm still smiling there's no sense in that now' (34).

Facial decomposition and the word

Beckett's illuminated faces prove to be deeply implicated in iconographical traditions that scrutinise the expressive face. As Angela Moorjani has shown, the spotlit faces of *Play* are rooted in paintings of upturned faces such as Elsheimer's *The Flight into Egypt*: Beckett's interest in artists such as Elsheimer was partly prompted by his reading of R. H. Wilenski's *Introduction to Dutch Painting*, and the 'spotlight effects' of both *Play* and *Film* are in part a technological literalisation of 'spotlight painting' techniques (Moorjani, 2008).[14] Following Moorjani and Knowlson and Haynes, Joanne Shaw argues that the related light effects in Caravaggio and in Rembrandt's portraits can be applied to the articulation of character in Beckett's prose works, in a 'limitless recession where not only the landscape recedes but [also] the figures in it' (2012: 223).[15] I turn now to a facial recession that contextualises the apparently self-defeating narrative strategies of *Watt* and *How It Is* seen above: that in Beckett's *Dream of Fair to middling Women*. Here, the making of face is aligned with the verbal aspect seen in Agamben, where the 'exposition of the visage' is termed 'word' (2000: 96); the making of the word takes place through recession or, as Beckett termed it in his observation of Giorgione's *Self-Portrait* (c.1510), 'reticence' (Nixon, 2011: 143). Face, in *Dream*, is closely associated with the act of expression and with Beckett's evolving theory of novelistic form. In this early work, the character of Lucien is imagined by reference to 'Rembrandt's portrait of his brother', which proves to constitute another productively unstable pictorial source:

He was [...] an efflorescence at every moment, his contours in perpetual erosion. Formidable. Looking at his face, you saw the features bloom, as in Rembrandt's portrait of his brother. (Mem: develop). His face surged at you, coming unstuck, coming to pieces, invading the airs, a red dehiscence of flesh in action [...]. Jesus, you thought, it wants to dissolve. Then the gestures [...] unfolding and flowering into nothingness, his whole person a stew of disruption and flux. And that from the fresh miracle of coherence that he presented every time he turned up. How he kept himself together is one of those mysteries [...]. He should have become a mist of dust in the airs. He was disintegrating bric-à-brac. (Beckett, 1993: 116–17)

Like an image in which figure and ground simultaneously recede, or the figure in *Watt* that disappears as it approaches, Lucien's character is articulated by means of an efflorescence that is also a 'dehiscence': his features bloom precisely as they disintegrate. The dissolving facial image is bound up with Beckett's vision of an art that wrests expression from unspeakability, and with the strong echo of the Lucien passage in the later remarks in *Dream* on the book Belacqua wants to write. The 'unspeakable trajectory' of the reader is famously located, here, 'in the silence, communicated by the intervals, not the terms, of the statement' (138), and once again abuts the pictorial source of the 'portrait of Rembrandt's brother':

I shall state silences more competently than ever a better man spangled the butterflies of vertigo. I think now [...] of the dehiscing, the dynamic décousu of a Rembrandt, the implication lurking behind the pictorial pretext threatening to invade pigment and oscuro; I think of the Selbstbildnis, in the toque and the golden chain, of his portrait of his brother, of the cute little Matthew angel that I swear van Ryn never saw the day he painted, in all of which canvases during lunch on many a Sunday I have discerned a disfaction, a désuni, an Ungebund, a flottement, a tremblement, a tremor, a tremolo, a disaggregating, a disintegrating, an efflorescence, a breaking down and multiplication of tissue, the corrosive groundswell of Art. (138–9)

There are two potential sources here: the *Portrait of Rembrandt's Brother* in the Louvre, which is in fact attributed to Charles

Waltner, and the portrait seen by Beckett in the Gemäldegalerie in Kassel.[16] Not only do Rembrandt and Elsheimer inform *Play* and *Film*, then, but Rembrandt's faces enjoy a special position in Beckett's thinking on artistic expression. As Eoin O'Brien notes, furthermore, Beckett's 'introduction to Rembrandt' may well have come in the National Gallery of Ireland via the *Rest on the Flight into Egypt*, the subject famously depicted by Elsheimer, whose own *Flight into Egypt* Beckett saw in Munich's Alte Pinakothek in 1937, and whose shadow belatedly surfaces in *Play*.[17]

Beckett's evolving manifesto for a form of artistic expression implicated in the inexpressive is further contextualised by the programmatic statement in *Dream*, of 'a punctuation of dehiscence, flottements, the coherence gone to pieces, the continuity bitched to hell because the units of continuity have abdicated their unity, they have gone multiple, they fall apart'. The facial implosions that Beckett derives in part from Rembrandt are implicated in a view of novelistic form rooted in literary modernism. As John Bolin demonstrates, Lucien's face is part of a modernist dissolution of character exemplified by Gide and Dostoevsky. Working from the notes on Beckett's lectures at Trinity College Dublin made by two of his students, Bolin links the 'complexity and irresolution' of character in Gide's *Dostoevsky* to that in Beckett's aesthetics. As Bolin argues, in his 1930 lectures on the novel Beckett paraphrased or quoted the following passage from Gide's *Dostoevsky* in which the process of disintegration in modernist characterisation is linked to the interplay of light and shadow in Rembrandt's portraits:

> Between [Dostoevsky's] novels and those of the authors quoted above [Stendhal, Tolstoy, Voltaire, Fielding, Smollett, Lesage, etc.] there is all the difference possible between a picture and a panorama. Dostoevsky composes a picture in which the most important consideration is the question of light. The light proceeds from but one source. In one of Stendhal's novels, the light is constant, steady and well-diffused. Every object is lit up in the same way, and is visible equally well from all angles; there are no shadow effects. But in Dostoevsky's books, as in a Rembrandt portrait, the shadows are the essential. Dostoevsky groups his characters and happenings, plays a brilliant light upon them, illuminating one aspect only.

Each of these characters has a deep setting of shadow, reposes on
its own shadow almost. (Gide, 1949: 99, quoted in Bolin, 2009:
519)[18]

Instead of continuity, here there is multiplicity, so that *all* the
features bloom simultaneously and the figure cannot be separated from its shadow, nor figure from ground. The distinction of
the object from 'the immeasurable background of space or time
which is not it' is drastically undercut (Joyce, 1992: 178, quoted
in Bolin, 2009: 528). The 'cosmic' or 'limitless space' which
Moorjani argues that Beckett derives from Elsheimer threatens to
overwhelm the object (whether an individual character in a novel
or one of the figures in the urns in *Play*); the figure can only be
apprehended in the profusion of its aspects, simultaneously image
and shadow, image and word, expression and non-expression.
These, then, are the troubled roots of Beckett's later faces, whose
dynamics of avoidance and recession are forever associated with
the early encounter with Rembrandt's 'spotlight' portraits. If, for
Agamben, the grimace is 'the constitutive reticence that human
beings retain in the word' (2000: 96), the faces of *Film* and the
television plays articulate a facial reticence that casts into doubt
both the visual representation of the icon and the category of the
human that the face exemplifies. This aniconic face undermines
the place of the human face atop a hierarchy of order and representation in which the material, non-human landscape is forever
subordinate. Instead, the face occupies a position of intractable
residuality, almost a non-object, ready to collapse once more into
the shadow of its making.

Notes

1 Elsaesser applies Beckett's 'dictum' to post-war German film about
   the recent past, 'by varying Samuel Beckett's dictum: "it can't be represented, it must be represented"'. Later on, Elsaesser takes Beckett's
   and Pinter's 'compressed, uncommunicative monologues' as exem-
   plifying post-Holocaust communication between 'Germans and
   Jews' (Elsaesser, 2013: 11, 29).
2 On the significance of Duchenne's work for the evolving field of
   photography, see also Elkins 2013: 35, 252–4.

3 On the legacy of Duchenne's observation on the role of the *orbicularis oculi*, see Ekman and Rosenberg, 2005: 217.

4 *...nur noch Gewolk...*, directed by Samuel Beckett with Klaus Herm and Kornelia Bose, June 1977, Süddeutscher Rundfunk, Stuttgart.

5 The phrase is often quoted as 'esse est percipi', including by Beckett in *Film* (Beckett, 1990: 323). See Berkeley, 1901: 259.

6 Beckett added the smile in rehearsal, as his correspondence with Alan Schneider on the text and its direction indicates: 'I asked in London and Stuttgart for a smile at the end (oh not a real smile). He "wins" again. So ignore direction "Image fades, voice as before." Face still fully present till last "Eh Joe." Then smile and slow fade.' Beckett to Alan Schneider, 7 April 1966, reprinted in Harmon, 1998: 202.

7 On Beckett's familiarity with Langdon, see Knowlson, 1996: 377.

8 See also the analysis of the visual coding of Beckettian testimony in *Ill Seen Ill Said* in Jones, 2011: 73–106.

9 On sculpture and the facial expressions 'beyond words' of the TV plays, see Nixon, 2011: 151.

10 During the filming of *Nacht und Träume*, according to cameraman Jim Lewis, 'at the moment when the drops of perspiration are wiped from the brow of the character, Beckett simply said that the cloth alluded to the veil that Veronica used to wipe the brow of Jesus on the Way of the Cross. The imprint of Christ's face remains on the cloth.' Jim Lewis, quoted in Knowlson, 1996: 682.

11 In this context, see Herren, 2007; McTighe, 2013: 146.

12 See Cohn, 2001: 226. See also Ackerley, 2009.

13 The sudarium or maniple also refers to a vestment worn during Mass. See Braun, 1910. On the parallel use of a cloth in the crucifixion scene in Beckett's *Ernest et Alice*, see also Hulle and Nixon, 2013: 186.

14 On the 'spotlight painting' techniques, see Haynes and Knowlson, 2003: 77–80, quoted in Moorjani, 2008: 134.

15 The reference is from Wilenski, 1929: 63, quoted in Beckett, 1930s. See also Knowlson, 2009; Shaw, 2012: 223.

16 On the former, as John Pilling notes, 'SB seems (for once) happy enough with the received wisdom' (Pilling, 2004: 240). On the Kassel portrait, see Nixon, 2011: 216.

17 Haynes and Knowlson, 2003: 79–80, quoted in Moorjani, 2008: 131. For a detailed reading of the Louvre portrait of Rembrandt's brother, see McQueen, 2003: 272–4. On Beckett's first encounter with Rembrandt, see O'Brien, 1993: 146.

18 For a compelling reading of the later dialogue between the faces of
    Molloy and Sartre's *La Nausée*, see Bolin, 2012: 138–50.

References

Ackerley, Chris J. (2009). '"Ever Know What Happened?": Shades and
    Echoes in Samuel Beckett's Television Plays', *Journal of Beckett Studies*
    8.1–2, 136–64.
Agamben, Giorgio (2000). *Means Without End: Notes on Politics.*
    Minneapolis, MN: University of Minnesota Press.
Agamben, Giorgio (2002). *Remnants of Auschwitz: The Witness and the
    Archive.* New York: Zone.
Balázs, Béla (2011). *Béla Balázs: Early Film Theory: Visible Man and the
    Spirit of Film.* Ed. Erica Carter. New York: Berghahn Books.
Beckett, Samuel (1930s). 'Notes on Art'. Beckett International Foundation,
    University of Reading, UoR MS 5001.
Beckett, Samuel (1978 [1953]). *Watt.* London: Calder.
Beckett, Samuel (1983). 'Three Dialogues'. In Ruby Cohn (ed.), *Disjecta:
    Miscellaneous Writings and a Dramatic Fragment.* London: Calder,
    pp. 138–45.
Beckett, Samuel (1990). *The Complete Dramatic Works.* London: Faber
    and Faber.
Beckett, Samuel (1993). *Dream of Fair to middling Women.* New York:
    Arcade Publishing.
Beckett, Samuel (1995). *Samuel Beckett: The Complete Short Prose,
    1929–1989.* Ed. Stanley E. Gontarski. New York: Grove Press.
Beckett, Samuel (1996). *How It Is.* London: Calder.
Beckett, Samuel (2007). *Watt.* Paris: Editions de Minuit.
Berkeley, George (1901). *The Works of George Berkeley. Vol. 1 of 4.* Oxford:
    Clarendon Press. www.gutenberg.org/files/39746/39746-h/39746-h.
    html. Accessed 27 February 2017
Bolin, John (2009). '"Preserving the Integrity of Incoherence"?:
    Dostoevsky, Gide and the Novel in Beckett's 1930 Lectures and
    Dream of Fair to middling Women', *Review of English Studies* 60.246,
    515–37.
Bolin, John (2012). *Beckett and the Modern Novel.* Cambridge: Cambridge
    University Press.
Boulter, Jonathan (2004). 'Does Mourning Require a Subject? Samuel
    Beckett's *Texts for Nothing*', *Modern Fiction Studies* 50.2, 332–50.
Braun, Joseph (1910). 'Maniple'. In *The Catholic Encyclopedia.* New
    York: Robert Appleton.

Cohn, Ruby (2001). *A Beckett Canon*. Ann Arbor, MI: University of Michigan Press.

Delaporte, François (2008). *Anatomy of the Passions*. Stanford, CA: Stanford University Press.

Didi-Huberman, Georges (2008). *Images in Spite of All: Four Photographs from Auschwitz*. Chicago: University of Chicago Press.

Didi-Huberman, Georges (2009). *Confronting Images: Questioning the Ends of a Certain History of Art*. University Park, PA: Penn State University Press.

Duchenne, Guillaume-Benjamin-Amand (1862). *Mécanisme de la physionomie humaine, ou analyse electro-physiologique de l'expression des passions*. Paris: Renouard.

Duchenne, Guillaume-Benjamin-Amand (1990) [1862]). *The Mechanism of Human Facial Expression*. Trans. R. Andrew Cuthbertson. Cambridge: Cambridge University Press.

Duckworth, Colin (1972). *Angels of Darkness: Dramatic Effect in Samuel Beckett with Special Reference to Eugène Ionesco*. London: Allen and Unwin.

Eaglestone, Robert (2000). 'From Behind the Bars of Quotation Marks: Emmanuel Levinas's (non)-representation of the Holocaust'. In George Paizis and Andrew Leak (eds), *The Holocaust and the Text*. London: Macmillan, pp. 97–108.

Ekman, Paul, and Erika L. Rosenberg (eds) (2005). *What the Face Reveals: Basic and Applied Studies of Spontaneous Expression Using the Facial Action Coding System (FACS)*. Oxford: Oxford University Press.

Elkins, James (2013). *Photography Theory*. London: Routledge.

Elsaesser, Thomas (2001). 'Postmodernism as Mourning Work', *Screen* 42.2, 193–201.

Elsaesser, Thomas (2013). *German Cinema – Terror and Trauma: Cultural Memory Since 1945*. London: Routledge.

Engelberts, Matthijs (2008). '*Film* and *Film*: Beckett and Early Film Theory'. In Linda Ben-Zvi and Angela Moorjani (eds), *Beckett At 100: Revolving It All*. New York: Oxford University Press, pp. 152–65.

Gide, André (1949). *Dostoevsky*. London: Secker and Warburg.

Harmon, Maurice (ed.) (1998). *No Author Better Served: The Correspondence of Samuel Beckett and Alan Schneider*. Cambridge, MA: Harvard University Press.

Haynes, John, and James Knowlson (2003). *Images of Beckett*. Cambridge: Cambridge University Press.

Herren, Graley (2007). *Samuel Beckett's Plays on Film and Television*. Basingstoke: Palgrave.

Hulle, Dirk Van, and Mark Nixon (2013). *Samuel Beckett's Library*. Cambridge: Cambridge University Press.

Jones, David Houston (2011). *Samuel Beckett and Testimony*. Basingstoke: Palgrave Macmillan.

Joyce, James (1992). *A Portrait of the Artist as a Young Man*. Harmondsworth: Penguin.

Kember, Joe (2001). 'Face-to-Face: The Facial Expressions Genre in Early British Film'. In Alan Burton and Laraine Porter (eds), *The Showman, the Spectacle and the Two-Minute Silence*. Trowbridge: Flicks Books, pp. 28–39.

Kember, Joe (2009). *Marketing Modernity: Victorian Popular Shows and Early Cinema*. Exeter: University of Exeter Press.

Kember, Joe (2018). 'The Strong Man'. In Steve Neale (ed.), *Silent Features*. Exeter: University of Exeter Press.

Knowlson, James (1996). *Damned to Fame: The Life of Samuel Beckett*. London: Bloomsbury.

Knowlson, James (2008). 'Beckett the Tourist: Bamberg and Würzburg'. In Linda Ben-Zvi and Angela Moorjani (eds), *Beckett at 100: Revolving It All*. New York: Oxford University Press, pp. 21–34.

Knowlson, James (2009). 'Beckett and Seventeenth-Century Dutch and Flemish Art', *Samuel Beckett Today/Aujourd'hui* 21, 27–44.

Le Juez, Brigitte (2013). 'Words without Acts: Beckett's Parrots'. In Mary Bryden (ed.), *Beckett and Animals*. Cambridge: Cambridge University Press, pp. 212–24.

Leyda, Jay (1988). *A Premature Celebration of Eisenstein's Centenary*. London: Methuen.

McQueen, Alison (2003). *The Rise of the Cult of Rembrandt: Reinventing an Old Master in Nineteenth-Century France*. Amsterdam: Amsterdam University Press.

McTighe, Trish (2013). *The Haptic Aesthetic in Samuel Beckett's Drama*. Basingstoke: Palgrave Macmillan.

Moorjani, Angela (2008). '"Just Looking": Ne(i)ther-World Icons, Elsheimer Nocturnes, and Other Simultaneities in Beckett's *Play*'. In Linda Ben-Zvi and Angela Moorjani (eds), *Beckett at 100: Revolving It All*. New York: Oxford University Press, pp. 123–38.

Nixon, Mark (2011). *Samuel Beckett's German Diaries 1936–1937*. London: Continuum.

O'Brien, Eoin (1993). *The Beckett Country: Samuel Beckett's Ireland*. New York: Arcade Publishing.

Pilling, John (2004). *A Companion to Dream of Fair to middling Women*. Tallahassee, FL: Journal of Beckett Studies Books.

Provine, Robert R. (1997). 'Yawns, Laughs, Smiles, Tickles, and Talking: Naturalistic and Laboratory Studies of Facial Action and Social Communication'. In James A Russell and José-Miguel Fernández-Dols (eds), *The Psychology of Facial Expression*. Cambridge: Cambridge University Press, pp. 158–75.

Salisbury, Laura (2009). '"What Is the Word": Beckett's Aphasic Modernism', *Journal of Beckett Studies* 17.1–2, 78–126.

Shaw, Joanne (2012). 'Light and Darkness in Elsheimer, Caravaggio, Rembrandt and Beckett', *Samuel Beckett Today/Aujourd'hui* 24, 219–31.

Smith, Russell (2007). '*Endgame*'s Remainders'. In Mark S. Byron (ed.), *Samuel Beckett's* Endgame. Amsterdam: Rodopi, pp. 99–120.

Steimatsky, Noa (2012). 'Of the Face, in Reticence'. In Angela Dalle Vacche (ed.), *Film, Art, New Media: Museum Without Walls?* Basingstoke: Palgrave Macmillan, pp. 159–77.

Wilenski, Reginald H. (1929). *An Introduction to Dutch Art.* London: Faber.

4

'The skin of words': trauma and skin in *Watt*

Michiko Tsushima

Skin as the site of trauma

In medical and psychiatric literature, especially in Freud's work, the term 'trauma' is used to describe 'a wound inflicted not upon the body but upon the mind' (Caruth, 1996: 3). However, trauma originally meant 'wound' in Greek, 'an injury inflicted on the body' (Caruth, 1996: 3), implying that something from the outside tears, cuts or wounds the skin. The relation between trauma and skin has become an important theme in various fields. For example, in contemporary art, skin is often shown as 'a place of wounds and stigmatization'. Claudia Benthien, referring to the performances of the artists Gina Pane and Marina Abramović, observes that '[t]he display of female skin, in particular, often involves violence or self-inflicted wounds, cuts, and burns' (2002: 3).

This chapter tries to return to the original relationship between trauma and skin and understand that relationship as it is presented in Beckett's novel, *Watt*. First, what did it mean for Beckett to write *Watt* during the Second World War? With the help of Didier Anzieu's concept of 'the Skin Ego', I explore the possibility that in *Watt* Beckett was attempting to 'weave a symbolic skin' (1989: 230) and 're-establish a temporarily faltering Skin Ego' (231). If Beckett's act of writing *Watt* can be considered an attempt to recover the psychic skin by weaving a 'skin of words' (204), we might think that this act of writing has a therapeutic aspect: by writing *Watt* Beckett tried to overcome his traumatic experiences and mental crisis. In 'Life as Trauma, Art as Mastery: Samuel Beckett and the Urgency of Writing', Lois Oppenheim identifies the therapeutic value of Beckett's writing: 'writing served to transcend, or at least temporarily to quell, the suffering that was his experience of the human condition' (2008: 419). Of 'the urgency writing had for Beckett', she writes, 'his creative use of words ... served as tangible evidence of being alive and as a means of protection against his fears of separation, alienation, and death. In this respect it helped him to master his severe anxiety' (438). From this therapeutic perspective, we might suggest that writing *Watt* may have been necessary for Beckett as a means for him to come to terms with his wartime traumatic experiences. Beckett was desperately in need of a protective skin.

Yet at the same time, we should note that reading *Watt* only from a therapeutic perspective disregards 'the force and truth' (Caruth, 1995: vii) of traumatic reality. Cathy Caruth points out that the study of trauma faces the crucial problem of 'how to help relieve suffering, and how to understand the nature of the suffering, without eliminating the force and truth of the reality that trauma survivors face and quite often try to transmit to us'. And she holds that we need to 'listen to trauma beyond its pathology for the truth it tells us' (1995: vii–viii). Relating this view to Holocaust testimonies, Robert Eaglestone writes, 'to respond to the "force and truth" of testimony is one needful thing, to respond to the pain of survivors is another, equally needful thing' (2004: 33), and he points out the importance of 'respond[ing] to the "force and truth" of testimony' without resolving, assimilating or normalising it through the clinical formula of trauma. This chapter tries to understand *Watt*, 'the skin of words' that Beckett tried to weave, as something that expresses the 'force and truth' of a trauma that cannot be resolved or assimilated. Reading *Watt*, we will see how the 'force and truth' of trauma is revealed by the subject possessed by the traumatic experience and how it manifests itself as a force that dissolves the apparatus of figuration, including the system of linguistic representation.

Weaving 'the skin of words'

Most of *Watt* was written during the Second World War in Roussillon, where Beckett and his partner Suzanne Deschevaux-Dumesnil had taken refuge from the Gestapo. They stayed in Roussillon from October 1942 until early 1945. When they arrived in Roussillon, they were 'subject to feelings of deep depression' (Knowlson, 1997: 294), having experienced a variety of traumatic events since hearing of the arrest of their friend Alfred Péron. But after a while they settled in a house that they rented for the duration of the war, and Beckett took up *Watt*, the novel that he had begun to write in Paris in February 1941.[1] Beckett spent his days working in the fields in exchange for farm produce: it was hard manual labour that numbed and exhausted his body. However, for Beckett, it was much better than merely waiting for the end of the war. He spent his evenings writing *Watt*. But nobody in Roussillon knew about his writing except Suzanne. Although Beckett and Suzanne had relative security in Roussillon, they were 'virtual prisoners': since there was the risk of arrest, they could not go outside of the immediate area. For them Roussillon 'came to feel claustrophobic' (Knowlson, 1997: 301). Beckett also felt horror at the thought of a totalitarian bureaucracy: hearing the news of Marcel Lob, the grammarian-turned-farmer in Roussillon who had been arrested in Apt for being a Jew, and seeing Lob's wife's all-out efforts to prove that she was the wife of an Aryan, Beckett recoiled at the 'rationalistic barbarism' (Knowlson, 1997: 306) in the bureaucracy which could decide whether a human being would survive or not according to the existence of a certificate of baptism. Beckett was powerless and exposed to the terror and anxiety caused by the war.

Beckett's state of mind during this period could be understood in light of Didier Anzieu's concept of 'the Skin Ego'. Anzieu defines 'the Skin Ego' as 'a mental image of which the Ego of the child makes use during the early phases of its development to represent itself as an Ego containing psychical contents, on the basis of its experience of the surface of the body' (1989: 40). This mental image of the skin as a surface is acquired 'on the basis of the mutually inclusive relation of the bodies of mother and child', in other words, as the child 'experiences the contact of its body with that of the mother, and within the framework of a secure relation of attachment to her' (38). And the impairment of this Skin Ego causes certain psychic weaknesses.

According to Anzieu, for the patient whose Skin Ego is temporarily faltering, spoken and written words provide a substitute: 'The spoken word, and even more, the written word, has the power to function as a skin' (231). And this he terms the 'skin of words' (204). For example, he speaks of the case of a patient who had suffered serious burns and was experiencing acute pain. He explains how lively conversation with his female research student enabled this patient to 'reconstitute a Skin Ego sufficient for his skin to be able, in spite of physical injury, to perform its functions as a protective shield against external aggression and a container of painful affects' (203).[2] Thus the 'skin of words' could alleviate the pain of the burn victim. Anzieu contends that the origin of the 'skin of words' is found in 'the "bath of words" of the infant to whom those around him speak or sing' (203–4). He also shows that writing ('a speech addressed to oneself') fulfils the 'reconstituting function after an intense emotional upset, a tension in relations with those around one or an inner crisis', and that 'this is true not only of many writers ... but also of many who simply write (without aiming at aesthetic effect or seeking an audience)' (230–1). He mentions the case of Micheline Enriquez's patient Fanchon, who secured her standpoint in relation to the world by writing word by word the spatio-temporal frame in which she was situated, her concrete acts and perceptions. This activity is described as 'representational writing' by Enriquez. Anzieu also speaks of the similar case of Doris Lessing's character in *The Golden Notebook* who resorts to her Blue Notebook to combat depression: in the notebook she kept a record of facts by writing down what she did every day, feeling as if she 'had saved that day from chaos' (231).

Perhaps the same is true of Beckett, who experienced traumatic events during wartime. We might suggest that his traumatic experiences produced 'the rupture of the Skin Ego' or 'holes in the Skin Ego' (Anzieu, 1989: 213–14), and that by writing *Watt* Beckett tried to 'weave a symbolic skin' and 're-establish a temporarily faltering Skin Ego'. In this sense, the act of writing *Watt* could be considered his attempt to recover the psychic skin that functions to contain painful affects and protect against unbearable external stimuli. Beckett himself said later that he had written *Watt* 'as a stylistic exercise and in order to stay sane, "in order to keep in touch"' (Knowlson, 1997: 303). However, this does not mean that he succeeded in this attempt. *Watt*, 'the skin of words' that Beckett tried to weave, rather shows the failure to acquire a protective skin.

An open wound in the skin

It is possible to see a parallel between the psychic condition of Beckett in wartime and that of the protagonist in *Watt*. *Watt* tells the story of a man called Watt who arrives at the house of Mr Knott to replace a servant called Arsene. First Watt serves Mr Knott as a downstairs servant, and later he takes the place, upstairs, of Erskine, a servant whose service comes to an end. Finally, Watt's duties end and he leaves the house of Mr Knott, though knowing nothing of him. Later he stays in a lunatic asylum where he meets a fellow inmate called Sam (the narrator of this story) and tells him about his experiences in Mr Knott's house. In this novel, like Beckett himself, Watt is presented as a vulnerable subject who is powerlessly exposed to traumatic situations and cannot feel peace of mind.

There are various images of open wounds in the skin in *Watt*. Even before Watt arrives at Mr Knott's house, he is already depicted as a vulnerable subject, and this vulnerability is shown through descriptions of his skin. One scene depicts Watt, just off the train, walking toward Mr Knott's house like 'a headlong tardigrade' or with 'a funambulistic stagger' (Beckett, 2009: 24). Coming behind him, Lady McCann throws a stone at him.

> [S]he picked up a stone and threw it, with all her might ... at Watt ... the stone fell on Watt's hat and struck it from his head, to the ground. This was indeed a providential escape, for had the stone fallen on an ear, or on the back of the neck, as it might so easily have done, as it so nearly did, why then a wound had perhaps been opened, never again to close, never, never again to close, for

> Watt had a poor healing skin, and perhaps his blood was deficient
> in? [*sic*] And he still carried, after five or six years, and though he
> dressed it in a mirror night and morning, on his right ischium a
> running sore of traumatic origin. (25)

Thus Watt is attacked by Lady McCann and barely escapes disaster, but he is saved by his hat, functioning here as a protective shield. In Part 1 Beckett describes Watt as someone who
has already been wounded and has 'a poor healing skin'. He has
'a running sore of traumatic origin' on his right ischium (25).
Watt's 'poor healing skin' is a memory of a forgotten original
trauma, and he has not recovered from it. His wound has not
healed over. It is still exuding pus.[3]
The image of a wound is also seen in Watt's bloody face, wit-
nessed by the narrator, Sam, in the garden of the asylum in Part 3:

> I saw his face, and the rest of his front. His face was bloody, his
> hands also, and thorns were in his scalp. (His resemblance, at that
> moment, to the Christ believed by Bosch, then hanging in Trafalgar
> Square, was so striking, that I remarked it.) And at the same instant
> suddenly I felt as though I were standing before a great mirror ...
> so that I looked at my hands, and felt my face, and glossy skull, with
> an anxiety as real as unfounded. (136)

Watt's face covered with wounds is compared to the face of
Christ. And in witnessing Watt's bloody face, Sam witnesses his
own mirror image; in other words, he witnesses himself, which
arouses 'real' anxiety within him.
The various images of an open wound show the condition
of the powerless subject who is exposed to what wounds it. In
light of Anzieu's theory, we could say that these images indicate
a psychic wound or a traumatised psychic condition. In these
images we recognise his idea of 'a perforable envelope' (Anzieu,
1989: 38). Anzieu holds that 'a perforable envelope' involves the
anxiety of 'a flowing away of vital substance through holes, an
anxiety not of fragmentation but of emptying, well expressed
metaphorically by certain patients who describe themselves as
an egg with a broken shell being emptied of its white (actually of
its yolk)' (38–9). This anxiety shows that the patient experiences
'the dangers of depersonalization' (38). This view suggests that

the psychic wound involves the anxiety of 'a flowing away of vital substance through holes'.

Indeed *Watt* presents images of open wounds together with images of the porous body from which liquid flows out spontaneously.[4] For example, we can think of the image of tears flowing from Watt's eyes. In one scene, he sheds tears after departing from Mr Knott's house:

> [W]hen the time came for Watt to depart, he walked to the gate with the utmost serenity. But he was no sooner in the public road than he burst into tears. He stood there, he remembered, with bowed head, and a bag in each hand, and his tears fell, a slow minute rain, to the ground, which had recently been repaired. (Beckett, 2009: 180)

Another striking image is that of food overflowing from a woman's mouth. In his speech Arsene talks about a woman in a brothel named Mary who has an exceptional appetite and eats all day without resting. And it is said that 'at no moment of Mary's waking hours was Mary's mouth more than half empty', and it was, 'nine times out of ten, full to overflowing' (45). Arsene explains:

> I assert ... that it was so full, nine tenths of the time, that it did overflow, all over this ill-fated interior, and traces of this exuberance, in the form of partially masticated morcels of meat, fruit, bread, vegetables, nuts and pastry I have frequently found in places as remote in space, and distinct in purpose. (45)

Here we find the image of masticated food in a thick liquid state overflowing from a mouth.

From the viewpoint of Western cultural history, one notices that these images of skin in *Watt* differ from 'a masculine body image of armored, thickened skin' found in the myth of Achilles and the legend of the armoured Siegfried: the motif of 'armored skin' is 'scattered throughout Western literature and cultural history' and involves 'the narcissistic male fantasy of an invulnerable, impenetrable, phallic body' (Benthien, 2002: 133–6, 238). The images of skin presented in *Watt* are also different from 'the modern notion of skin as a closure and boundary surface' (Benthien, 2002: 38). Alluding to Bakhtin, Benthien explains how a new bodily canon that conceived of the body as 'a strictly demarcated entity with an impenetrable, smooth facade' took the place of 'the body notion that dominated European popular culture from the Middle Ages to the Baroque', the conception of the grotesque body (37–9). The new, later image is described by Bakhtin as 'an entirely finished, completed, strictly limited body, which is shown from the outside as something individual', and 'that which protrudes, bulges, sprouts, or branches off … is eliminated, hidden, or moderated. All orifices of the body are closed' (Bakhtin, 1984: 320). In contrast, the older image of the body makes use of an artistic logic that 'ignores the closed, smooth, and impenetrable surface of the body and retains only its excrescences (sprouts, buds) and orifices, only that which leads beyond the body's limited space or into the body's depths' (Bakhtin, 1984: 317–18). 'Eating, drinking, defecation and other elimination … as well as copulation, pregnancy, dismemberment, swallowing up by another body' are the main events in the sphere of the grotesque body (Bakhtin, 1984: 317). The images of the porous bodily surfaces shown in *Watt* are evocative of the grotesque body described by Bakhtin.[5] They are also suggestive of the pre-Enlightenment conception, described by Duden, of the skin as a porous surface. The skin was considered an impermeable surface that 'can open or be induced to open anywhere' (Duden, 1991: 121). Instead of being 'a material seal shutting the inside off from the outside', the skin was 'a collection of real, minute orifices – the pores – and potential larger openings' (121) that functioned as exits that could emit body fluids, including 'blood, milk, excrement, sweat, humidity, scorbutic and impure matter' (124).

Watt presents various images of a wound in the skin along with images of fluids that flow out from the bodily orifices. Seen in light of Anzieu's theory, we can understand these images of skin as indicative of the vulnerability of the subject who is exposed to traumatic situations. In other words, this novel represents trauma through the image of an open wound in the skin or 'a perforable envelope'.

In need of an acoustic-tactile envelope

In *Watt* Beckett stresses that Watt, who is in a traumatised state, feels a desperate need for peace of mind. We could say that this is a reflection of Beckett's psychic condition as well. Watt tries to find a psychic envelope that could surround him to give him security and rest. This can be thought of as a return to the archaic topology that prefigures Anzieu's idea of the Skin Ego. According to Anzieu, 'the Skin Ego is based upon an envelope that is primarily tactile and acoustic in origin' (1989: 181). The young child establishes its Skin Ego on the basis of its pre-verbal experience of the bodily surface. When the mother takes care of the child, her care 'produces involuntary stimulation of the epidermis as she bathes, washes, strokes, picks up and hugs the baby' (39). Through her care, which involves touching the bodily surface, the 'tactile envelope' is formed for the child's psyche. Before the establishment of this 'tactile envelope', the 'sound envelope' is formed. Anzieu writes, 'Even earlier, the Self forms as a sound envelope through the experience of a bath of sounds (concomitant with the experience of nursing). This sound-bath prefigures the Skin Ego' (167). This universe of sound is 'the first psychical space' for the child. Being surrounded by musical sounds, the child experiences 'a first harmony' and 'a first enchantment' (170–1).

Often in the novel Watt tries to reach peacefulness by placing himself in a situation where he is surrounded by a kind of 'sound envelope' or 'tactile envelope'. This can be thought of as an attempt to return to the prenatal state of being enclosed in a womb or the early phase of the original communication between the mother and the child. For example, after the scene in which Watt has a stone thrown at him by Lady McCann, there is a scene in which he feels weak and sits down on the path in a foetus-like posture. He takes a rest beside a ditch and listens to 'the little nightsounds in the hedge behind him, in the hedge outside him' with pleasure. He hears 'other distant nightsounds too, such as dogs make, on bright nights, at the ends of their chains, and bats, with their little wings, and the heavy daybirds changing to a more comfortable position, and the leaves that are never still' (Beckett, 2009: 26). After a short time, he rolls himself over into the ditch and hears the voices of a mixed choir coming from afar. This passage evokes the image of a foetus hearing various outside sounds from inside an enclosed womb. Another 'sound envelope'-like experience occurs when Watt thinks of the lock and key for Erskine's room and says, 'Obscure keys may open simple locks, but simple keys obscure locks never' (106). Soon after he says these words, he regrets having done so. But gradually he begins to feel pleased by these words: 'And a little later they pleased him again, no less than when they had first sounded, so gentle, so cajoling, in his skull' (106). This scene shows how Watt is pleased by the audio-phonic aspect of language, while the resonating sounds in his skull evoke a 'sound envelope'. Later, Watt hears Mr Knott's voice as his stay at the house draws to a close. Watt has the pleasurable experience of being surrounded by meaningless noises like 'a wild dim chatter' and the sound of rain and waves (180–1). The novel has other descriptions of little and meaningless sounds which give Watt pleasure. They indicate Watt's experience of a 'sound envelope'. Anzieu explains that this psychic sound space is 'shaped like a cavern': 'It is a hollow space like the breast or the bucco-pharyngeal cavity, a sheltered, but not hermetically sealed, space. It is a volume within which there are rumblings, echoes and resonances' (1989: 171). Thus Watt tries to reach temporary peace of mind by placing himself in the space of acoustical resonance.

The experience of a 'tactile envelope' is found in the description of Watt's amorous dealings with Mrs Gorman. Every Thursday Mrs Gorman calls on Watt. Watt lets her enter the kitchen and opens a bottle of stout for her. Every Thursday they 'sit on each other, turn about, kissing, resting, kissing again and resting again' (Beckett, 2009: 122). Watt would 'set her on his knee, and wrap his right arm about her waist, and lean his head upon her right breast … and in this position remain, without stirring, or stirring the least possible, forgetful of his troubles, for as long as ten minutes, or a quarter of an hour' (120). This is described as 'his post-crucified position' (120). Thus Watt wraps Mrs Gorman and is wrapped by her, and feels relief from his troubles. It is as if he shares a skin with her. This evokes what Anzieu calls 'the phantasy of a common skin': it is 'the symbiotic union with the mother'

represented by 'a tactile ... image in which the two bodies of child
and mother have a common surface' (1989: 42). Moreover, in the
novel Watt's hat (a hat that belonged to his grandfather) and coat
(a greatcoat that belonged to his father) can also be thought of as a
part of his skin or 'tactile envelope'. These exemplary scenes show
that Watt is desperately in search of temporary peace of mind,
in need of a psychic skin made of a 'sound envelope' or a 'tactile
envelope'.

Being possessed

We have seen how *Watt* represents trauma through the vulnerable image of holes in the skin or 'a perforable envelope', and how
it describes the traumatised subject who is in need of a protective
skin. Now we shall look at what causes Watt's traumatic experience in this novel. As Boulter sees the trauma presented in this
novel in Watt's encounter with Mr Knott, who represents 'the
event of incomprehensibility or unknowability' (2008: 97), we
could suggest that Watt's traumatic experience is caused by his
encounter with the incomprehensible and unnarratable event in
Mr Knott's house (which is inseparable from the existence of Mr
Knott). Boulter writes, 'It is not simply that Watt is called upon
to witness the event of unknowability: it is that this experience of
impossible witnessing itself cannot be known, or narrated, despite
Watt's – and his narrator's – best attempts to do so' (2008: 97).
Boulter also holds that the trauma in this novel involves Watt's
impossible relation to Mr Knott, that is, 'the call, the *obligation*, to
witness the unwitnessable, as it were, to bear *unbearable* witness'
(100).

   Watt's traumatic encounter with the unwitnessable event is
seen particularly when the Galls, the piano tuner and his son,
visit: it is 'the principal incident of Watt's early days in Mr Knott's
house' (Beckett, 2009: 59), in which these two men come to the
house to tune a piano, exchange a few words and leave. For Watt
this incident of the Galls father and son is not something that can
be grasped at the narrative level. The incident ceases to signify
anything. It has 'gradually lost, in the nice processes of its light,
its sound, its impacts and its rhythm, all meaning' (60). And it

becomes 'a mere example of light commenting bodies, and still-ness motion, and silence sound, and comment comment' (60). Only 'a purely plastic content' (59–60) remains in his mind. The incident is experienced as something that discloses 'the fragility of the outer meaning' (60). And this incomprehensible incident that cannot be transformed into narrative language comes back repeatedly into Watt's mind and possesses him, giving him great distress.

> What distressed Watt … was not so much that he did not know what happened, for he did not care what had happened, as that nothing had happened, that a thing that was nothing had happened, with the utmost formal distinctness, and that it continued to happen, in his mind, he supposed, though he did not know exactly what that meant, and though it seemed to be outside him, before him, about him, and so on, inexorably to unroll its phases, beginning with the first (the knock that was not a knock) and ending with the last (the door closing that was not a door closing), and omitting none, uninvoked, at the most unexpected moments, and the most inopportune. (62–3)

Watt is possessed by this incident, described as 'a thing that was nothing had happened'. It continues to haunt him and does not stop tormenting him, for he cannot accept that 'a thing that was nothing had happened'. The incident 'revisited him in such a way that he was forced to submit to it all over again, to hear the same sounds, see the same lights, touch the same surfaces, and so on, as when they had first involved him in their unintelligible intrica-cies' (63). This haunting experience recalls Caruth's description of the phenomenon of trauma. She holds that 'the *structure of its experience* or reception' is important in understanding the experi-ence of trauma: 'the event is not assimilated or experienced fully at the time, but only belatedly, in its repeated *possession* of the one who experiences it. To be traumatised is precisely to be pos-sessed by an image or event' (1995: 4–5). Trauma is considered not as 'mere repression or defense' but as 'a temporal delay that carries the individual beyond the shock of the first moment', as 'a repeated suffering of the event' (1995: 10).

The traumatic event that possesses Watt cannot be integrated into the existing schemes of knowledge or transformed into a narrative memory. As Caruth writes, alluding to Pierre Janet in her edited collection *Trauma: Explorations in Memory*, the traumatic recall has no place 'within the schemes of prior knowledge' in that it 'has never, from the beginning, been fully integrated into understanding'. So the traumatic event cannot become 'a "narrative memory" that is integrated into a completed story of the past' (Caruth, 1995: 153). In the same volume van der Kolk and van der Hart also point out the importance of Janet's work and observe that traumatic memories are 'the unassimilated scraps of overwhelming experiences, which need to be integrated with existing mental schemes, and be transformed into narrative language' (1995: 176).[6] In *Watt* it is suggested that if this event could be integrated into a narrative memory, Watt's suffering would stop. '[I]f he could say … Yes, I remember, that is what happened then, if then he could say that, then he thought that then the scene would end, and trouble him no more' (Beckett, 2009: 63). To explain the event means to exorcise it. '[T]o explain had always been to exorcise, for Watt' (64).

The novel emphasises that this tormenting experience of the unwitnessable event at Mr Knott's house gradually alienates Watt from the existing linguistic scheme shared by everyone else, one where everyone believes that a thing and a word coincide with each other. In other words, Watt's words begin to fail him and his world becomes incapable of being verbally expressed; he begins to suffer a condition where a thing and a word become non-coincident. This non-coincidence is revealed, for example, in his experience with a pot.

> Looking at a pot … or thinking of a pot, at one of Mr Knott's pots, of one of Mr Knott's pots, it was in vain, that Watt said, Pot, pot. Well, perhaps not quite in vain, but very nearly … And it was just this hairbreadth departure from the nature of a true pot that so excruciated Watt. (67)

Watt agonises over this extremely small difference.

> Watt was greatly troubled by this tiny little thing, more troubled perhaps than he had ever been by anything, and Watt had been frequently and exceedingly troubled, in his time, by this imperceptible, no, hardly imperceptible, since he perceived it, by this indefinable thing that prevented him from saying, with conviction,

and to his relief, of the object that was so like a pot, that it was a
pot. (68)

'This tiny little thing' and 'this imperceptible, no, hardly
imperceptible … thing' indicate that the non-coincidence between
a thing and a word is imperceptible to everyone except Watt. 'The
pot remained a pot, Watt felt sure of that, for everyone but Watt.
For Watt alone it was not a pot, any more' (68). Thus 'this hair-
breadth departure from the nature of a true pot' is imperceptible to
everyone else. This means that Watt's experience of witnessing this
incomprehensible incident cannot be shared with other people.

In *Watt* the experience of the traumatic event is revealed as
its effects. Watt, possessed by the traumatic event and alienated
by the existing linguistic system, becomes a subject whose existence has the force to disrupt existing institutions or traditions.
The novel presents not only the image of a wound inflicted upon
Watt but also the image of a wound that Watt inflicts. In one
passage Watt is depicted as a lawbreaker who damages the existing order at its core. One of Watt's duties at Mr Knott's house is
to give Mr Knott's leftover food to the dog and 'witness the dog's
eating the food' (96). But after the first few weeks, Watt abruptly
stops doing so. 'This refusal … by Watt, to assist at the eating,
by the dog, of Mr Knott's remains, might have been supposed to
have the gravest consequences, both for Watt and for Mr Knott's
establishment' (98). However, there is no punishment for Watt,
and 'Mr Knott's establishment swam on … with all its customary
serenity' (98). This refusal by Watt is described as a violation of
'such a venerable tradition, or institution', that it is tantamount
to violence. And in Watt's mind this transgression is grasped as
an image of damage being inflicted on the skin. He reflects that
'if the hurt to Mr Knott's establishment did not at once appear, it
would perhaps one day appear, a little bruise at first, and then a
bigger, and then a bigger still, until, growing, growing, it black-
ened the entire body' (98). Watt, subjected to a traumatic event
and obsessed with the non-coincidence of a thing and a word,
becomes a figure who embodies a force that refuses and violates
the existing institution, power or tradition and gradually destroys
it insidiously.

Violence to the surface of language

Later in the novel we learn that the experience of the traumatic event at Mr Knott's house mentally deranges Watt and compels him to use language that deviates from the ordinary, thereby disrupting the existing system of linguistic representation. In particular, Watt adopts a manner of speaking 'back to front' (Beckett, 2009: 140) in Part 3, and in Part 3 (and partly in Part 2) it is revealed that the text of *Watt* is a 'little notebook' in which Sam, a fellow inmate in the lunatic asylum, has recorded what Watt has told him in the asylum. When Watt speaks to Sam, he speaks in a low and rapid voice, 'with scant regard for grammar, for syntax, for pronunciation, for enunciation, and very likely, if the truth were known, for spelling too, as these are generally received' (133). And Watt talks 'back to front', the same way that he walks. At first he starts inverting the order of the words only in sentences. He then begins to invert the order of the letters in the word, not that of the words in the sentence. He continues to invert the elements of his language in an ever newer and more complex manner, which also involves permutation, and the madness of his language increases. We could say that Watt's way of speaking does violence to the surface of language or the scheme of linguistic representation by confusing and disrupting the way letters, words and sentences are joined together.

In addition, Watt's way of explaining external phenomena around him by exhaustively listing all possibilities and combinations of possibilities seems to involve the undoing of the world of signification based on language. For example, he goes through all possible combinations of how Mr Knott moves around his room or how the furniture in his room changes position every day. The permutations and combinations, or the exhaustive series that prevail in the novel, are concerned with, to borrow Deleuze's words, 'exhausting the possible', exhausting the dimension of the possible itself. According to Deleuze, in the dimension of the possible a person tries to realise the possible 'according to certain goals, plans, and preferences', and this realisation 'always proceeds through exclusion, because it presupposes preferences and goals that vary' (1997: 152–3). Thus 'the combinatorial' in *Watt* exhausts the possible by 'forming exhaustive series of things' (161). Deleuze aptly says, 'The combinatorial is the art or science of exhausting the possible through inclusive disjunctions. But only an exhausted person can exhaust the possible, because he has renounced all need, preference, goal, or signification' (154).

These characteristics of Watt's language may be also understood in light of Connor's idea of 'an assault upon the skin' (2001: 45). Connor sees a longing for 'an assault upon the skin', for example, in Artaud, who 'mistrusting his own body, colonised and infected as he felt it to be by God, language, and history ... sought a body remade in the immediacy of cry and gesture, a body mutilated into clamorous muteness' (45). And Connor considers this mutilation as 'a blow against articulation' (45). He continues:

> The sacrifier, the lacerator, the self-abuser, the piercer, all seek, like Artaud, to do violence to the primary violence that deprives me of my body, the violence of representation, naming, abstraction, the alienation of the body into significance. There is an assault that goes beyond the attempt to efface and rewrite what is written on the skin: it is an assault upon the skin as the bearer or scene of meaning. It is an assault upon the apparatus of figuration, of which the skin is the privileged sign or locale. (45)

Thus an assault upon the skin does not merely mean 'the attempt to efface and rewrite what is written on the skin': it is also an assault upon 'the skin as the bearer or scene of meaning' or 'the apparatus of figuration' itself. What takes place in *Watt* seems to be related to this assault. We find Watt 'do[ing] violence to the primary violence', 'the violence of representation, naming, abstraction'. Watt's manner of speaking 'back to front' assails the apparatus of figuration by undoing the way linguistic elements are joined together, by thus giving 'a blow against articulation'. Watt's urge to produce permutation can also be thought of as an assault upon 'the skin as the bearer or scene of meaning': by going through all combinations of possibilities, the world of signification is dissolved. As Connor describes this assault as 'a disfiguration that will erase – but visibly erase – the apparatus of figurality itself' (2001: 44), the permutation *visibly erases* 'the skin as the bearer or scene of meaning'. Further we should note that *Watt* presents itself as an incomplete text or a mere draft, in which we find, for example, a number of question marks, missing or illegible parts (marked 'Hiatus in MS' and 'MS illegible'), and a list of 'Addenda' whose incorporation was prevented by 'only fatigue and disgust' (Beckett, 2009: 215). In these explicit textual violations, or the self-conscious incompleteness of the text, we see an assault upon 'the skin as the bearer or scene of meaning'.

In a letter, his artistic manifesto, written in 1937, a younger Beckett posited that literature should move towards what he calls a 'literature of the unword' (1984: 173). It is an attempt, through language, to 'bore one hole after another in it [language], until what lurks behind it – be it something or nothing – begins to seep through' (172). He writes, 'Is there any reason why that terrible materiality of the word surface should not be capable of being dissolved, like for example the sound surface, torn by enormous pauses, of Beethoven's seventh Symphony …?' (172). Whereas in this letter the violence to the surface of language or 'an assault upon the skin' was an artistic goal, in *Watt* it can be considered the effect of Watt's experience as someone going through a traumatic event. In other words, the traumatic encounter with an incomprehensible and unwitnessable event is revealed in its effects, and the madness of language seen in *Watt* is the effect of that traumatic encounter.

However, we cannot say that there is an essential inconsistency between this letter and *Watt*. We might be able to relate these two by considering that *Watt*, a novel written in the context of the historical catastrophe of the Second World War, discloses what was not clearly presented in Beckett's earlier work. *Watt* indicates the possibility that behind Beckett's critique of language and his assault upon the surface of language there is a traumatic encounter with the incomprehensible and unwitnessable event – the event in which 'a thing that was nothing had happened'.

The 'force and truth' of trauma

As I suggested in the early part of this chapter, *Watt* can be regarded as 'the skin of words' – a psychic envelope that Beckett tried to weave. This does not mean that by writing *Watt* he suc-

ceeded in making a protective skin and healed his psychological
wounds. Rather, I would like to suggest that having been exposed
to the extreme terror and anxiety caused by the war, Beckett had a
desperate need for a protective skin, though ironically 'the skin of
words' that he tried to weave shows the impossibility of obtaining
such a skin. At the same time, this 'skin of words' reflects the
'force and truth' of a traumatic reality that cannot be resolved.
We have seen how in *Watt* this force manifests itself as violence
to the surface of language, as a force that disrupts the apparatus of
linguistic representation.

In *Watt* the 'force and truth' of trauma also appears as the
force that deprives a human being of all senses and emotions and
thereby of his or her humanity. In Part 3 we see how in the closing
period of his stay at Mr Knott's house, Watt is gradually deprived
of human senses, emotions and his existence. 'What little there
was to see, to hear, to smell, to taste, to touch, like a man in a man
in a stupor he saw it, heard it, tasted it, touched it' (Beckett, 2009:
172). Watt becomes 'weak now of eye, hard of hearing, and with
even the more intimate senses greatly below par' (175). And he
eventually reaches a state of ataraxy and utmost serenity. Behind
all these exists the ambience around Mr Knott that benumbs
all senses and emotions. Mr Knott is the enigmatic force that is
'dimming all, dulling all, stilling all, numbing all' (173). And this
ambience possesses Watt. This is why in Part 4 Micks, a servant
who has just arrived at the house to take over Watt's position, is
said to be unusually repelled as he witnesses Watt who, just before
his departure, is standing in the kitchen with his facial expression
becoming 'gradually of such vacancy' (190). Micks,

> raising in amaze an astonished hand to a thunderstruck mouth,
> recoiled to the wall, and there stood, in a crouching posture, his
> back pressed against the wall, and the back of the one hand pressed
> against his parted lips, and the back of the other pressed against the
> palm of the one. (190)

But we are told that it was not Watt's face but 'something that
was not Watt, nor of Watt, but behind Watt, or beside Watt, or
before Watt, or beneath Watt, or above Watt, or about Watt,
a shade uncast, a light unshed, or the grey air aswirl with vain

entelechies' that caused Micks to recoil in this way (190). And this 'something' that surrounds Watt corresponds to the ambience around Mr Knott mentioned above. We could say that Micks is presented as a witness of the 'force and truth' of trauma, the force that benumbs all and deprives Watt of his humanity completely.

To put it in another way, Watt's traumatic encounter with Mr Knott and the incomprehensible incident at his house in which 'a thing that was nothing had happened' means, metaphorically, the experience of 'touching' or 'being touched by' the dimension of nothing. To return to Connor's idea of 'an assault upon the skin', this dimension of nothing evokes what he calls 'the unfigurable support of figurality' (2001: 44). He suggests that an assault upon the skin as 'the bearer or scene of meaning' (45) reveals skin as 'the unfigurable support of figurality' which is reserved before or underneath it. He writes, 'Before, or underneath, the skin there must be a skin, to bear the mark of the first infliction' (50). Watt's traumatic experience points to this duplicity of skin.

In this sense, we could say that in *Watt* a force that disrupts the apparatus of representation is revealed in what can be called the duplicity of skin. Indeed in the following fragment in the addenda that Beckett describes as a 'soul-landscape' we find this duplicity.

> on the waste, beneath the sky, distinguished by Watt as being, the one above, the other beneath, Watt. That before him, behind him, on all sides of him, there was something else, neither sky nor waste, was not felt by Watt. And it was always their long dark flowing away together towards the mirage of union that lay before him … Indeed the sky and the waste were of the same dark colour, which is hardly to be wondered at. Watt also was very naturally of the same dark colour. This dark colour was so dark that the colour could not be identified with certainty. Sometimes it seemed a dark absence of colour, a dark mixture of all colours, a dark white. But Watt did not like the words dark white, so he continued to call his darkness a dark colour plain and simple, which strictly speaking it was not, seeing that the colour was so dark as to defy identification as such. (Beckett, 2009: 217–18)

In this landscape Watt's body is situated at the point where duplicity discloses itself. Watt stands in the dimension where the sky above him and the waste beneath him are differentiated. But

it is indicated that there is another dimension that lacks differentiation. It is the dimension of the 'dark colour' which is also
'a dark absence of colour, a dark mixture of all colours', where
the sky, the waste and Watt are not distinguished. And it is said
that this singular dark colour 'def[ies] identification as such'.[7] In
light of Connor's conception of the skin, we could suggest that
the dimension where the sky, the waste and Watt are distinguished
corresponds to the skin as 'the bearer or scene of meaning' or 'the
apparatus of figuration'. And the unfigurable dimension of the
'dark colour' evokes skin as 'the unfigurable support of figurality'
which corresponds to the dimension of nothing. This fragment
in the addenda, depicted as 'precious and illuminating material'
(Beckett, 2009: 215), imparts to us a secret about the 'force and
truth' of traumatic reality in *Watt*: it shows itself in the duplicity
of skin.

Notes

1 Beckett started writing *Watt* in Paris in February 1941 and finished it
   in Roussillon in December 1944. But he 'tinkered with' it over the next
   few months after he left Roussillon for Paris early in 1945 (Knowlson,
   1997: 303–10).
2 These two functions of 'the Skin Ego' belong to the nine functions
   that Anzieu explains in *The Skin Ego*. His understanding of the former
   function is based on Freud's observation that 'the Ego has a parallel
   function as a *protective shield against stimulation*', with the surface
   layer of the epidermis which 'protects the sensitive layer beneath …
   and shields the organism in general against physical attack, some
   forms of radiation and an excess of stimuli' (1989: 102). The containing function means that the young child has a mental representation
   of itself as a psychic container, a psychic envelope. The container
   forms 'a passive receptacle where the baby may store its sensations/
   images/affects, which in this way, are neutralized and preserved'. It
   also has an active aspect: it 'elaborates, transforms and restores to the
   child his sensation/images/affects in a representable form' (101).
3 We find other images of 'a poor healing skin' in Beckett's description
   of the Lynch family in *Watt*. See Beckett, 2009: 85–7.
4 For a discussion of the orifices of the body in Beckett, see Tajiri, 2007:
   47–63. Tajiri shows how in the Beckettian prosthetic body, confusion
   of the bodily orifices and their flows occurs. And alluding to Anzieu's

notion of the Skin Ego and the image of 'a perforable envelope', he discusses how the orifices and their flows are highlighted as prosthetic parts, as 'the locus of interaction between the inside and the outside' (56).

5 Knowlson sees 'a wonderful example of the grotesque in literature' in Beckett's description of the Lynch family (1997: 303).

6 For a discussion of traumatic memory and narrative memory, see van der Kolk and van der Hart, 1995: 158–82.

7 This dimension of the 'dark colour' that defies identification reminds us of a force that deprives things of their colours and identities in *Watt*. For example, in Part 4 the narrator describes the process by which with time the colours of Watt's coat and hat gradually change, and both lose not only their colours but their contours and identities (Beckett, 2009: 189). It is the process in which 'identification as such' is being dissolved.

References

Anzieu, Didier (1989). *The Skin Ego*. Trans. Chris Turner. New Haven, CT: Yale University Press.

Bakhtin, Mikhail (1984). *Rabelais and His World*. trans. Helene Iswolsky. Bloomington, IN: Indiana University Press.

Beckett, Samuel (1984). *Disjecta: Miscellaneous Writings and a Dramatic Fragment*. Ed. Ruby Cohn. New York: Grove Press.

Beckett, Samuel (2009). *Watt*. Ed. Chris J. Ackerley. London: Faber and Faber.

Benthien, Claudia (2002). *Skin: On the Cultural Border between Self and the World*. Trans. Thomas Dunlap. New York: Columbia University Press.

Boulter, Jonathan (2008). *Beckett: A Guide for the Perplexed*. London: Continuum.

Caruth, Cathy (ed.) (1995). *Trauma: Explorations in Memory*. Baltimore, MD: Johns Hopkins University Press.

Caruth, Cathy (1996). *Unclaimed Experience: Trauma, Narrative, and History*. Baltimore, MD: Johns Hopkins University Press.

Connor, Steven (2001). 'Mortification'. In Sara Ahmed and Jackie Stacey (eds), *Thinking Through the Skin*. London: Routledge, pp. 36–51.

Deleuze, Gilles (1997). 'The Exhausted'. Trans. Anthony Uhlmann. In Daniel W. Smith and Michael A. Greco (eds), *Essays Critical and Clinical*. Minneapolis, MN: University of Minnesota Press, pp. 152–74.

Duden, Barbara (1991). *The Woman beneath the Skin: A Doctor's Patients in Eighteenth-Century Germany*. Trans. Thomas Dunlap. Cambridge, MA: Harvard University Press.

Eaglestone, Robert (2004). *The Holocaust and the Postmodern*. Oxford: Oxford University Press.

Knowlson, James (1997). *Damned to Fame: The Life of Samuel Beckett*. New York: Touchstone.

Oppenheim, Lois (2008). 'Life as Trauma, Art as Mastery: Samuel Beckett and the Urgency of Writing', *Contemporary Psychoanalysis* 44.3, 419–42.

Tajiri, Yoshiki (2007). *Samuel Beckett and the Prosthetic Body: The Organs and Senses in Modernism*. Basingstoke: Palgrave Macmillan.

van der Kolk, Bessel A., and Onno van der Hart (1995). 'The Intrusive Past: The Flexibility of Memory and the Engraving of Trauma'. In Cathy Caruth (ed.), *Trauma: Explorations in Memory*. Baltimore, MD: Johns Hopkins University Press, pp. 158–82.

5

Bodily object voices in *Embers*

Anna Sigg

In Beckett's memory plays, such as *Krapp's Last Tape*, *Not I*, *Footfalls*, *Rockaby*, *Ohio Impromptu* and *Embers*, the characters make an almost mechanical effort to rework their traumatic pasts. Although Jonathan Boulter's articles, such as 'Does Mourning Require a Subject?' (2004), and Russell Smith's article (2007) on Beckett's *Endgame* stress the importance of attending to the concept of trauma in Beckett's plays, critics find it generally difficult to relate Beckett's minimalist works to trauma theory, because, in his plays, the categories of memory, self and the past, on which the mechanism of trauma is based, have become unknowable. However, as Cathy Caruth points out, the concrete source of the primary trauma can generally rarely be located and grasped. She explains that trauma is based on a temporal delay, suggesting that 'the event is not assimilated or experienced fully at the time, but only belatedly, in its repeated possession of the one who experiences it' (1996: 4). Although the concrete origin of the trauma is sometimes only located off-stage and thus not always accessible, it haunts the characters from a distance and speaks through their bodies. Beckett's plays stage the condition of trauma rather than the primary traumatic event itself.

Beckett was adamant that *Embers*, like his other radio plays, not be performed on stage: it was meant to be broadcast as a one-time event. As a radio play, *Embers* effectively 'blinds' its listener and places him or her in a mental cave, a ghostly place of darkness from which the memories of traumatic loss depicted in the play emerge. Donald McWhinnie points out the 'intimacy of radio' (1959: 57), and indeed, the radio play's intimate, ghostly atmosphere serves to create a close connection between the character and the witnessing listener of the traumatic stories. Agency is located within the lack of distance between listener and character. In a radio play the 'theatre', the 'representation' or 'performance' is much more obviously inside the listener's head than in regular theatre. Therefore, the protagonist Henry's commands to listen to his inner voices are most of all directed at the listener off-stage during the moment when he or she is listening to the radio play. When Henry commands: 'you needn't speak. Just listen' (Beckett, 2006a: 209) or repeatedly utters the persistent phrase 'white world. Not a sound. Listen to it!' (200), the 'you' is also directed at the listener off-stage. The listener takes on an active role as he or she cannot escape into the passive realm of silence.

Embers focuses on the character Henry, who finds himself in a cycle of traumatic repetition. Boulter points out that, for Henry, 'mourning [becomes] the inevitable continuation of Being' (2004: 336). Throughout the play, he is tortured by a roaring, internal sea-like sound, a form of 'tinnitus' – a ringing in the ears – which reminds him of his dead father and his own mortality. He describes his memories as 'some old grave [he] cannot tear [him] self away from' (Beckett, 2006a: 203). Henry re-enacts the stories of his past, but is unable to finish them with the use of words. However, they can be completed by listening to the internal sea sound – his ringing in the ears – which, in the BBC production, can be heard during the pauses.

The connection between Henry's traumas and the listener's perception of the tinnitus can be illuminated by drawing on Mladen Dolar's idea of the acousmatic voice and Jacques Lacan's concept of the *objet (petit) a*, which is often referred to as 'object-cause of desire' (Žižek, 1989: 53). The *objet a* is described as a leftover or placeholder, which also carries elements of wholeness. Slavoj Žižek argues that it is 'objectively nothing, though, viewed from a certain perspective, it assumes the shape of something' (1991: 12). Lacan explains that '*objet a* is something from which the subject, in order to constitute itself, has separated itself off as organ' (1977: 103). More specifically, he relates the *objet a* to the drives, such as 'the anal level (the faeces)' (103–4) and the invocatory drive (the ears and the voice). Due to its chameleon-like characteristics, it always remains somewhat distant and inaccessible. Despite its elusiveness, it is the avatar of traumatic loss, which is exactly why it appears so disturbing. It represents a confrontation with the loss, and the limits of its own representation. According to Dolar and Žižek, the object voice is essentially a manifestation of Lacan's *objet a*. It is 'a voice whose source one cannot see … [i]t is a voice in search of an origin, in search of a body' (Dolar, 2006: 60). I would like to suggest that the broadcast, internal sound of the sea is an uncanny intimation of the unconscious – a manifestation of both Dolar's object voice and the Lacanian *objet a*. The ringing in the ears expresses Henry's mourning and his traumatic confrontation with mortality, but it also speaks back to the loss and redirects it. I, thus, read Henry's tinnitus as a bodily countervoice – it screams back to the disturbing memories, releasing, redirecting and modifying them. It is a counter-voice of agency and resistance. Dolar points out that the acousmatic object voice is not attached to a subject, but emerges from a traumatic place of otherness: it 'does not go up in smoke in the conveyance of meaning … [it] functions as a blind spot' (2006: 4). I suggest that Henry's object voice originates from this blind spot. Salecl and Žižek describe the estrangement, which this voice generates, as 'adding a soundtrack to a silent film' (1996: 92) – a soundtrack of bodily countermelodies to the trauma that Henry and the listener initially refuse, but ultimately seem to accept as their own. Inside the listener's head – due to the intimacy of the radio performance – Henry's tinnitus may re-enact, speak back to and destabilise the original malleable sonic sound memories.

Hugh Kenner conceived of *Embers* as 'Beckett's most difficult work' (1962: 174). This difficulty may partly arise from the fact that critics, such as Louise O. Cleveland (1968), Katharine Worth (1981), Clas Zilliacus (1976) and David J. Alpaugh (1973), simply disagree on the number of characters in the play. Anna McMullan wonders: 'Is his wife Ada actually present with Henry on the seashore, or does their dialogue take place in Henry's mind?' (2010: 74). While some critics claim that Henry engages in real conversations with his dead wife Ada, and listens to an actual sound of the ocean, others, such as Zilliacus, suggest that Henry simply interacts with the various imaginary voices of his mind. He states: '[t]he universe which the radio audience is confronted with … is a totally subjective one … The interplay between Henry and other characters takes place in Henry's mind' (1976: 82). Likewise, Jonathan Kalb claims that '*Embers* has no surface narrative other than that of a haunted man talking about talking to himself' (1994: 130). Based on textual evidence and the BBC performance, which was first broadcast on 24 June 1959 and directed by Donald McWhinnie, my own interpretation is closest to Zilliacus's and Kalb's ideas. As Zilliacus points out, the unnatural sea sound of the BBC performance, which Henry even describes in the text itself as a 'sound … so strange, so unlike the sound of the sea' (Beckett, 2006a: 197), suggests that the sound we hear is not the real sea, but an internal object voice – *objet a*. This voice may simply be an internal sea-like roaring tinnitus, a medical, physical condition, which developed as a response to his traumatic loss.

The intensive use of pauses in the play, followed by the roaring sea sounds, suggests that 'Not a sound. [*Pause.*]' (Beckett, 2006a: 207) is simply Henry's tinnitus that emerges within, through and in response to silence. Worth aptly argues that there is 'one sound he cannot suppress, the sound of the sea. It is heard in every pause' (1981: 204). Indeed, Henry repeatedly demands to hear silence: 'White world. Not a sound. Listen to it!' (Beckett, 2006a: 200). Kevin Branigan points out that 'silence appears to be the desired endpoint of his radio aesthetic, and silence has the effect of purifying the sounds and voices which are suspended in it' (2008: 81). I read Henry's roaring ringing in the ears as both a manifestation of repressed memories, but also an active response to them. This tinnitus turns into an object voice, a Lacanian *objet a*, which manages to displace the original trauma and affirms this displacement through the psychological and emotional distance and processes of depersonalisation and de-realisation that it generates. His tinnitus will always resemble a slightly different sound – it will never become the actual sound associated with the original loss. In fact, the tinnitus – as object voice – modifies and redirects the sound and the disturbing, traumatic memories. Henry states:

That sound you hear is the sea. [*Pause. Louder.*] I say that sound
you hear is the sea, we are sitting on the strand. [*Pause.*] I mention
it because the sound is so strange, so unlike the sound of the sea,
that if you didn't see what it was you wouldn't know what it was.
[*Pause.*] (Beckett, 2006a: 197)

The BBC production's sound of the ocean is very unnatural, which
implies that perhaps the production never intended to convey the
idea of the sound as resembling the actual sound of the ocean.
Nevertheless, Henry repeats the phrase 'the sound you hear is the
sea' in an attempt to convince himself. Further on, he makes clear
that it is indeed impossible that the sound we hear is the sound of
the sea, because the roaring waves follow him wherever he goes.
He explains: 'I once went to Switzerland to get away from the
cursed thing and never stopped all the time I was there' (198).
Moreover, in the following passage, he states: 'Today it's calm, but
I often hear it above in the house and walking the roads and start
talking, oh just loud enough to drown it, nobody notices' (198).
McMullan quite accurately claims that 'the entire soundscape of
the play may be seen as a defiant sonic struggle against the sea'
(2010: 74). However, it is important to understand that the sea
sound is simply an internal voice.

Rather than introducing a dialogue, the play opens with Henry's
'sea' tinnitus: '*Sea scarcely audible. Henry's boots on shingle. He
halts. Sea a little louder*' (Beckett, 2006a: 197). The BBC production accurately follows these stage directions by playing with the
dynamics of the bodily sounds. The production begins with the
roaring sea sound and Henry's '*boots on shingle*', his footsteps.
Only the '*hooves*' (198) are temporarily able to stop his tinnitus.
However, the rhythmic sound of the hooves simply instigates
another form of ringing in the ears. It seems as if Henry is talking
directly back to his memories through the internal voice of the
sea, thus entering into a musical conversation with it:

HENRY: On. [*Sea. Voice louder.*] On! [*He moves on. Boots on
shingle. As he goes.*] Stop. [*Boots on shingle. As he goes, louder.*] Stop!
[*He halts. Sea a little louder.*] Down. [*Sea. Voice louder.*] Down!
[*Slither of shingle as he sits. Sea, still faint, audible throughout what
follows whenever pause indicated.*] Who is beside me now? [*Pause.*]

… My father, back from the dead, to be with me. [*Pause.*] As if he
hadn't died. [*Pause.*] … Can he hear me? [*Pause.*] Yes, he must
hear me. [*Pause.*] Just be with me. [*Pause.*] That sound you hear is
the sea. [*Pause. Louder.*] (197)

There is a cyclical rhythm to this object voice. Henry wishes to
escape from it, but he is strangely fascinated by it and refuses to
ignore it. The internal sound of the sea is as close and as distant as
Henry can get to his traumatic memories.

Only the 'Ada' voice (in the BBC production staged as very
monotonous and calming) of Henry's character clearly and
directly affirms the roaring internal sea sound. She states:

I don't think you are hearing it. And if you are what's wrong with
it, it's a lovely peaceful gentle soothing sound, why do you hate it?
[*Pause.*] And if you hate it why don't you keep away from it? Why
are you always coming down here? (206)

Perceiving it as a 'peaceful gentle soothing sound', the 'Ada' part
in Henry's character affirms the memories through the bodily
sound of tinnitus, whereas the other voice of his personality is
still resistant to giving up language as a means to represent loss.
While Henry expresses his wish to drown out the voice through
the sound of hooves or his various stories, his inner voice of Ada
affirms the sound, and thus also the traumatic past. She claims:
'There is no sense in that. [*Pause.*] There is no sense in trying to
drown it' (207). The inner voice of Ada is clearly one that advocates the healing and acceptance of trauma through acknowledg-
ing the truth. It is a voice of agency, which at times struggles to
be heard.

The Bolton–Holloway exchange conveys the positive aspects
of Henry's tinnitus. Beckett describes the ringing in the ears as an
object voice with direction and purpose rather than an accidental
sound, or a manifestation of an illness. In the Bolton–Holloway
exchange, his ringing in the ears most of all signifies the body's
refusal to be silenced and the insistence on being heard:

[W]hite world, not a sound. [*Pause.*] Listen to it! [*Pause.*] Close
your eyes and listen to it, what would you think it was? [*Pause.
Vehement.*] A drip! A drip! [*Sound of drip, rapidly amplified, suddenly cut off.*] Again! [*Drip again. Amplification begins.*] No! [*Drip*

cut off. Pause.] Father! [*Pause. Agitated.*] Stories, stories, years and
years of stories. (200)

The idea of the drip recalls the line from *Endgame* when Hamm
complains: 'there is something dripping in my head' (Beckett,
2006a: 104). I read this passage as a striking description of pul-
satile tinnitus – the idea of hearing one's blood flow through
one's body, which conjures up the idea of the body demanding
to be heard. In the BBC production, the drip is very amplified,
and appears extremely traumatising. It also sounds very regular
and rhythmic, and resembles another form of tinnitus. Most of
all, the drip suggests that silence, for Beckett, is essentially the
continuous bodily voices of one's body. I argue that for Henry,
trauma can arguably be represented and reworked through the
affirmation of the object voice – *objet a* – through which his
trauma manifests itself. However, it is also a traumatising, 'dreadful' (200) disturbing head noise, a sound of 'dying glow' (200) that
continually reminds him of his transience and mortality.

Placing Henry's experience of loss and drowning in the context
of trauma theory is fitting, because Henry shows all the signs of
acoustic trauma. His ringing in the ears may be both a psychoso-
matic result of a too close confrontation with trauma and a way
to overcome the disturbing experience through the distance and
displacement of the original trauma, which the tinnitus creates.
In other words, the internal roaring sound of the ocean 'composes' various counter-voices in response to all these primary
and secondary sonic traumas. Since trauma is unrepresentable,
it cannot be accurately represented, which the BBC production
conveys through the purposeful artificiality of the sea sound. The
avatar of trauma (Henry's tinnitus as *objet a*) reminds him of
the fact that there is always something missing in the symbolic
order, because the symbolic order is the register of consciousness
engendered by the abstractions of language. Henry's self constantly desires a sense of wholeness through the realm of symbolic
representation and his constant talking, but his incomplete stories
demonstrate that wholeness can never be regained. His trauma is
not an event that occurred at a certain point in time – it turns into
a timeless condition. Through his constant oscillation between

remembering and forgetting, Henry simultaneously gets close to and distances himself from 'some old grave' (203), which most of all represents his relationship to mortality. He is fascinated and attracted by it, but tries to push it away at the same time.

Henry's words have become meaningless and arbitrary. Unlike the sound of the ocean in his head, his language is too close to him to represent trauma accurately. His verbal response to this (missed) traumatic encounter is silence. However, since silence itself and the sounds generated around moments of silence speak back through his object voice, agency can be located within the realm of the body. The ocean-like object voice is certainly a destructive sound, and a form of acoustic torture, but also a possibility for Henry to rework his confrontation with the trauma through affirmation. He needs the mediation, a sound that creates distance and manages to represent and transcend trauma through that distance and depersonalisation. Zilliacus aptly points out that 'whenever words fail him, Henry is exposed to the sea-sound in his brain' (1976: 201). Words simply generate an auditory 'hell', which Henry describes as 'small chat to the babbling of Lethe about the good old days when we wished we were dead' (Beckett, 2006a: 201). Language generates an infinite continuum of trauma, in which the traumatic memories can neither be grasped nor transcended. Incapable of finishing a single sentence, Henry has become one of those traumatised 'people [who] always stop in the middle of what they are saying' (208). He complains to the voice of his dead wife Ada that his father no longer answers him; she, in turn, responds: 'the time comes when one cannot speak to you any more' (207). Agency can thus only lie within the more distant bodily object voice – his ringing in the ears – which is heard after and during every pause.

The fact that the father's voice is neither included in the play nor the performance suggests that even the dead father figure may simply be a voice in Henry's head, and thus a way for Henry to comprehend his own trauma of having drowned in the ocean through objectification and externalisation. Instead of reading Henry as an orphan, reworking the loss of his father, it is tenable to assume that father and Henry are the same person. Possibly the father side of his psyche attempted to commit suicide by drowning in the sea. Henry clearly explains his similarities to his father: 'I'm like you in that, can't stay away from it, but I never go in, no, I think the last time I went in was with you. [*Pause.*]' (198). Perhaps the reason why he appears so scared of the sea is that he himself lived a traumatic near-death experience 'the last time [he] went in' (198). This idea is supported by the fact that Henry describes his physical appearance as resembling his father's, which Ada also claims: 'I never forgot his posture. And yet it was a common one. You used to have it sometimes' (208). Moreover, in his conversation with his father voice, he expresses his difficulty in remembering: 'Never met Ada, did you, or did you, I can't remember, I can't remember, no matter, no one'd know her now' (201). And later on, he realises: 'I have forgotten almost everything connected with you' (208). Caruth explains that 'the historical power of the trauma is not just that the experience is repeated after its forgetting, but that it is only in and through its inherent forgetting that it is first experienced at all' (1996: 8). It is quite possible that Beckett conceived of the mechanism of trauma by creating Henry as a character, who tries to forget his own trauma of drowning by attributing it to his father.

Henry seems to acknowledge the fragility of his own illusion: the illusion that the sound he hears is the external sound of the ocean of another person's (his father's) trauma. The following exchange between Ada and Henry strongly conjures up a traumatising experience at the sea involving Henry himself, and possibly the experience of drowning:

> HENRY: I thought I might try and get as far as the water's edge …
> ADA: Well, why don't you? … [… *He goes towards the sea* …]
> HENRY: Don't, don't …
> [*Sea suddenly rough.*]
> ADA: [*twenty years earlier, imploring.*] Don't! Don't!
> HENRY: [*ditto, urgent.*] Darling!
> …
> [*Rough sea. Ada cries out. Cry and sea amplified* …] (205)

The horrifying sound of the cry and the amplified sea sound, which resound together as a forceful object voice, demonstrate that Beckett represents trauma most of all through bodily internal sea sounds. This fragmented memory clearly conjures up the idea of Henry's own drowning in the ocean. It is interesting that the memories are represented through a very visceral cry, thus rendering the trauma primarily an acoustic one. Since Ada, too, is clearly just imaginary and simply another part of his psyche, I believe that there is only one character in the play: Henry, who suffers from a traumatising type of tinnitus – a bodily object voice. More specifically, he oscillates between two different auditory hallucinations, suggesting two different approaches to his trauma: the inner voice of Ada – the voice of affirmation – and the inner voice of the father and storyteller – the voice of death, language, resistance and defiance. Both propose ways to deal with his confrontation with trauma.

This idea of displacing the trauma and reliving it through his father is supported by the fact that Henry sees himself as both a detached narrator of his own trauma of drowning and a storyteller. He self-consciously starts various stories, which he does not finish. He explains: 'I never finished it, I never finished any of them, I never finished anything, everything always went on for ever. [*Pause.*]' (198). Inventing various stories, such as his father's drowning, allows him to be in control and to safely distance himself from the trauma by becoming the detached observer figure of his 'father's' trauma. Like Mouth in *Not I*, 'he' approaches the trauma, but not 'I'. He refuses to accept that the traumatic story he tells is not just a story, but *his* story. Henry attributes the trauma to his father, thereby remaining safely 'distanced' and 'elsewhere'. Trauma theorist Charles E. Scott describes this phenomenon clearly:

> [T]hose who have undergone intense trauma speak of watching it happen to them as though they were outside of it – safely distanced – and as though they were articulating a vast indifference to themselves in the traumatic occurrence. That occurrence is there – I see it (strangely, it's happening to my body but not to me-seeing-it-happen. Who is that man drowning? Looks like me. I believe he's stopped breathing.) But that occurrence is not I. I'm elsewhere. There is something beautiful in the indifference of drowning. But now imagine a dark figure plunging in the water. Something jarring happens. Like a rude awakening. The distance collapses into

terrible chest pain, heaving effort to cough ... Unbearable pressure
in my head. Agonizing light. I, having drowned, am now here.
(Scott, 2009: 119–20)

Given Henry's constant attempts at storytelling, this apt
description of the distressing experience of drowning can be
applied to the illustration of the traumatic memories in *Embers*.
There is not necessarily something beautiful, but certainly something beautifully tragic in the idea of watching his father drown
himself from a distance. Imagining his own trauma as something
similar to the previous description of a 'dark figure plunging in
the water ... collapsing into terrible chest pain, heaving effort to
cough' is simply unbearable, but watching his father drown from
the edge of the cliff becomes tolerable. The memories remain
traumatic, but they now become transformed and approachable
through a 'gentle soothing' (Beckett, 2006a: 206) sea sound, as the
Ada voice in him explains. In order to communicate the trauma
and to communicate with the trauma, Henry needs to objectify
it by delegating it to the various voices in his head. When Henry
approaches the traumatic memories too closely, he experiences
them as a horrifying auditory hell, but the traumatic object voice
resounds as *objet a* when he tries to access them from a distance
through the voice of his father. This object voice can be affirmed
through the inner voice of Ada, through which it can become a
meaningful echo voice of the original one, which makes symboli-
sation possible.

The various psychological secondary effects of trauma are
clearly described in the text and displayed in the BBC performance. Although Henry primarily seems to be suffering from the
experience of drowning, which is made clear through the omni-
presence of the sea motif, he is also tortured by sonic memories
of his dysfunctional family relationships. The death-like experience of drowning seems to have instigated a traumatic cycle of
chain reactions and acoustic displacements, which led him to
focus on these other secondary traumas. He conjures up various
traumatising memories: his relationship with his father and his
relationship with his daughter, whom he seems unable to love.
These memories distract from the primary trauma: his confronta-

tion with his mortality by drowning. Although it remains unclear whether his actual father is alive or dead, since he explains that 'we never found your body' (198), it can be assumed that he abandoned Henry. Henry tells the imaginary voice of his dead wife Ada again and again: 'I was trying to be with my father … I mean I was trying to get him to be with me' (207). Henry communicates with the object voice of his dead father by re-enacting their complicated traumatic relationship during his lifetime: 'You wouldn't know me now, you'd be sorry you ever had me, but you were that already, a washout, that's the last I heard from you, a washout' (201). It is striking that the *'violent slam of door'* (201), which follows this exchange, does not sound in the BBC production like a door at all, but like the sound of a body being beaten, thus again imbuing the idea of trauma with sounds generated by or through the body. And later, he explains: 'that was always the way, walk all over the mountains with you talking … and then suddenly … not a word to a soul for weeks, sulky little bastard, better off dead. [*Long pause.*]' (201). As I have mentioned before, given the fact that the father has no actual voice in the play, it may very well be that his father is simply Henry's *internal* voice of self-hatred, a part of himself, which he wishes 'was better off dead' (201). This again reinforces his confrontation with mortality, which his tinnitus – as object voice and counter-voice – represents. This distressing experience instigates a cycle of secondary traumas, which manifests itself in his own relationship with his daughter:

> Horrid little creature, wish to God we'd never had her, I used to walk with her in the fields, Jesus that was awful, she wouldn't let go my hand and I mad to talk … [*Addie's loud wail …*] (201)

Considering that the disturbing description of Henry's relationship with his daughter calls for a 'loud wail' reveals Beckett's attempts to convey suffering through bodily object voices rather than language. The BBC performance underlines this interpretation, because this moment is staged as one of the most horrifying traumatic object voices in the play.

These voices of suffering in performance, like the loud wail discussed above, may appeal to the listener in a very visceral way due to their intensity. The performance truly achieves what Beckett

meant by 'a work designed so that, first and foremost, it will
"work on the nerves of the audience, not its intellect"' (Hutchings,
1986: 87). The trauma literally hurts the listener's ears, thus insti-
gating another small, secondary acoustic trauma. Considering
that Addie is not a simple character in the play, but an internal
voice in Henry's mind, this sound can be taken as an instance
of Henry's body demanding to be heard, calling out his lack of
responsibility and denouncing his inability to love his daughter.
Moreover, Henry's body seems to oscillate between two different
counter-voices. On the one hand, Henry perceives his tinnitus
as a recurring murmur that haunts him and that needs to be
'drowned out' (the storyteller voice) through a 'gramophone'
(Beckett, 2006a: 207). On the other hand, it carries a potentially
healing 'countermelody' – one that serves to modify, objectify and
redirect the original traumatic scream of despair of a drowning
subject into a calming and roaring sea sound of affirmation (the
Ada voice). Since the trauma cannot be integrated into Henry's
self through the realm of language, his body speaks back to it to
compensate for the impotency of language. It either 'drowns out'
the voice of silence emanating from the trauma or manages to
affirm it.

I believe that both voices have potential for agency, resistance
and possibly even healing. Both ideas – to drown out or to affirm
– suggest a refusal to be silenced and victimised. *Embers* is certainly not a play that can be laughed at – quite literally. In fact, it
dramatises the refusal to laugh. Henry's refusal and inability to
laugh at his trauma may be an attempt to reach out to the listener,
indirectly asking him or her to 'intervene' and become an auditory witness to the traumatic events. The BBC production stages
this refusal most clearly through awkward silences, and several
failed attempts at laughter. When Ada insists that he laugh, he
first refuses, and then he repeatedly produces several horrifying,
broken, bodily sounds that resemble the sound of a person vomit-
ing. Each laugh becomes more unfinished and broken, and in
the BBC production, the listener gets the sense that the laughter
emerges from elsewhere, a place that is 'not I'. Henry's attempts
at laughing can be best explained through Beckett's important
statement: 'Try again. Fail again. Fail better' (Beckett, 1983: 7).

Indeed, the BBC performance demonstrates that Henry does just that: his attempts to laugh at trauma may be seen as an acoustic gesture of refusal and defiance.

The BBC production strengthens my interpretation of the play as a whole. My argument that the conception of silence in the play is an engaged, active silence, and essentially the bodily object voice of traumatised suffering, is supported by the fact that the director chose to ignore the '*pauses*' in Beckett's stage directions. Every time a pause is written in the stage directions, McWhinnie plays the roaring, sea-like tinnitus sound. Pure silence is virtually absent from the performance. Moreover, my claim about the sea sound being an internal voice is partly based on the director's choice of a very artificial organ-like sea sound. It is a sound that indeed sounds 'so unlike the sound of the sea' (Beckett, 2006a: 197), as Henry explains. Also, my main point that the father and Henry are one single person, and that it is Henry who drowned with the father, is supported by the fact that the father has no separate voice in the play. Finally, the BBC production strengthens my underlying assertion about the play being specifically concerned with acoustic traumas. The repeated, extremely loud, unbearably loud '*wail[s]* ... *amplified to paroxysm*' (204) are so traumatising and uncomfortably loud that they may possibly even damage the listener's ear, thus continuing and contaminating the disturbing cycle of trauma.

In conclusion, although Henry is striving for a complete silencing of his traumatic memories, this is not a viable option. The distinction between sound and silence collapses through the body's insistence on being heard. It refuses to be silenced and it refuses to be laughed at. Moreover, the BBC production replaces all the pauses with the tinnitus sea sound – the object voice or *objet a* – thus making a powerful statement: a refusal to remain silent in the face of 'great trouble' (209) similar to Henry's refusal to laugh. The listener is implicated in this act of disobedience. By implicitly asking him or her to complete Henry's traumatic story, Beckett places responsibility on to him, especially since Henry – as a sound character – is completely isolated on the sound stage of this radio play. He is 'quite alone with [his] voice' (208), and it becomes clear that the listener is the only witness to the traumatic story, which Henry feels forced to tell and retell. Thus, for Henry, the traumatic past can arguably be represented and reworked through the affirmation of his tinnitus – by recognising it as a powerful bodily object voice and revealing its potential for resistance. However, it is also a disturbing head noise that reminds him of his mortality: a 'sound of dying, dying glow' (200) – the sound of embers.

References

Alpaugh, David J. (1973). '*Embers* and the Sea: Beckettian Intimations of Mortality', *Modern Drama* 16.3–4, 317–28.

Beckett, Samuel (2006a). *Samuel Beckett, Volume 3: Dramatic Works*. New York: Grove Press.

Beckett, Samuel (2006b). *Samuel Beckett: Works for Radio — The Original Broadcasts*. British Library Publishing Division, BBC [Audio CD].

Boulter, Jonathan (2004). 'Does Mourning Require a Subject? Samuel Beckett's *Texts for Nothing*', *Modern Fiction Studies* 50.2, 332–50.

Branigan, Kevin (2008). *Radio Beckett: Musicality in the Radio Plays of Samuel Beckett*. Bern: Peter Lang.

Caruth, Cathy (1996). *Unclaimed Experience: Trauma, Narrative, and History*. Baltimore, MD: Johns Hopkins University Press.

Cleveland, Louise O. (1968). 'Trials in the Soundscape: The Radio Plays of Samuel Beckett', *Modern Drama* 11.3, 267–82.

Dolar, Mladen (2006). *A Voice and Nothing More*. Cambridge, MA: MIT Press.

Hutchings, William (1986). 'Abated Drama: Samuel Beckett's Unbated *Breath*', *Ariel* 17.1, 85–94.

Kalb, Jonathan (1994). 'The Mediated Quixote: The Radio and Television Plays, and Film'. In John Pilling (ed.), *The Cambridge Companion to Beckett*. Cambridge: Cambridge University Press, pp. 124–44.

Kenner, Hugh (1962). *Samuel Beckett: A Critical Study*. London: Calder.

Lacan, Jacques (1977). *Seminar XI: The Four Fundamental Concepts of Psychoanalysis*. New York: W.W. Norton.

Latham, Alison (ed.) (2011). *The Oxford Companion to Music*. Oxford Music Online. www.oxfordmusiconline.com/public/book/omo_t114. Accessed 1 December 2015.

McMullan, Anna (2010). *Performing Embodiment in Samuel Beckett's Drama*. New York: Routledge.

McWhinnie, Donald (1959). *The Art of Radio*. London: Faber and Faber.

Salecl, Renata, and Slavoj Žižek (eds) (1996). *Gaze and Voice as Love Objects*. Durham, NC: Duke University Press.

Scott, Charles. E. (2009). 'Trauma's Presentation'. In Kristen Brown Golden and Bettina G. Bergo (eds), *The Trauma Controversy: Philosophical and Interdisciplinary Dialogues*. Albany, NY: State University of New York Press, pp. 115–24.

Smith, Russell (2007). '*Endgame*'s Remainders'. In Mark S. Byron (ed.), *Samuel Beckett's* Endgame. New York: Rodopi, pp. 99–121.

Worth, Katharine (1981). 'Beckett and the Radio Medium'. In John Drakakis (ed.), *British Radio Drama*. Cambridge: Cambridge University Press, pp. 191–217.

Zilliacus, Clas (1976). *Beckett and Broadcasting: A Study of the Works of Samuel Beckett for and in Radio and Television*. Åbo: Åbo Akademi.

Žižek, Slavoj (1989). *The Sublime Object of Ideology*. London: Verso.

Žižek, Slavoj (1991). *Looking Awry: An Introduction to Jacques Lacan through Popular Culture*. Cambridge, MA: MIT Press.

Part III

Historical and cultural contexts

6

Trauma and ordinary objects in Virginia Woolf and Samuel Beckett

Yoshiki Tajiri

Introduction: trauma and everyday life

While trauma studies and everyday life studies may be deemed two of the most salient trends in literary studies since the 2000s, they do not often seem to intersect with each other.[1] Current trauma studies began to flourish in the mid-1990s mainly through deconstructionists' attempts to re-engage with history, though the notion of trauma itself was elaborated in psychiatry and psychoanalysis from the late nineteenth century onwards, particularly in response to the shell-shocked soldiers produced by industrial warfare. On the other hand, everyday life studies, inaugurated by Henri Lefebvre and developed in post-war France, began to be repackaged and established as a distinct field in the English-speaking world in the 2000s, with some important books such as Ben Highmore's *Everyday Life and Cultural Theory* (2002). These two trends thus appear to have developed independently, which may be no surprise given the intrinsic incompatibility between the traumatic and the everyday.

There is no doubt, however, that they have common roots in the effects of the rapid urbanisation and modernisation in the late nineteenth and the early twentieth centuries. Fragmentation of life and the world was causing shock to the human mind and was in itself traumatic. Around the same time, as everyday life underwent drastic changes and the meaning of life and the world was more urgently questioned than before, Western culture was confronted with the question of being and the related problem of the existence of things themselves; phenomenology and existentialism emerged to explore these issues in the field of philosophy, and the art and literature of modernism, especially surrealism, began to discover the marvel of common everyday objects. With this broad outline in mind, it is worthwhile asking whether concerns with trauma and everyday life cannot be linked fruitfully in a discussion of literature and culture.

This essay is an attempt to explore one possible convergence between trauma studies and everyday life studies. It is often argued that a traumatised subject is compelled to return to the painful experience of the original traumatic event again and again in nightmares or daytime hallucinations. Yet even if that is the case, such a subject also needs to maintain its daily life, going through routines including eating and sleeping, even after a crucial event in which it could have died. While it lives in the special temporality of after-death as a sort of ghostly survivor, it is thrown out into daily life and ordinary objects. How do daily routines and ordinary objects appear to the traumatised subject? Focusing on this often overlooked dimension, I will discuss Virginia Woolf's *Mrs Dalloway* and Samuel Beckett's major plays, particularly *Happy Days*, as in my view they represent high and late modernists' attempts to come to terms with trauma in everyday life.

Virginia Woolf's *Mrs Dalloway*

Virginia Woolf is a privileged author in current studies of trauma and literature, mainly because her traumatic experience of childhood sexual abuse, the deaths of her family members while she was still young, and the two world wars so obviously underlie her texts (Henke and Eberly, 2007). Independently of this trend, much has been written on Woolf's concern with everyday life, particularly in relation to the rise of the distinct field of everyday life studies after the 2000s (Randall, 2007; Olson, 2009; Sim, 2010). As for her acute sense of ordinary objects as such, her 1920 short story 'Solid Objects', in which John sacrifices his career as a politician for his collection of valueless objects such as the fragments of glass he finds outdoors, has particularly attracted critics' attention. For Bill Brown, this story is a good reference point for a theoretical reappraisal of the value of things, as it represents the general tendency in the 1920s, 'the decade when things emerge as the object of profound theoretical engagement in the work of Georg Lukács, Heidegger, and Walter Benjamin, and which is the decade after objects and things are newly engaged by (or *as*) the work of art for Pound, Marcel Duchamp, Williams, Gertrude Stein' (Brown, 1999: 3, emphasis original). Lorraine Sim argues that in Woolf's story, John can look at things without preconceptions 'in the tradition of Merleau-Ponty's phenomenological reduction' (2010: 50).

Douglas Mao goes further and reads a Sartrean existential dimension in Woolf's attention to ordinary objects in this story and *Mrs Dalloway*. He says,

> [E]ven if *Nausea* and *Mrs. Dalloway* had nothing else in common, they would be linked by the sheer nakedness with which they raise the question of why anything, or everything, should exist; and indeed, with respect to the unembarrassed clarity with which they render this anxiety in their fictions, Woolf and Sartre are each other's only peers. (1998: 44)

For instance, Antoine Roquentin in *Nausea* and Septimus Warren Smith in *Mrs Dalloway* are both in a park, looking at a tree when they are confronted with the question of being. Mao claims that 'there is good reason to believe that Septimus is Roquentin's authentic park-bench precursor' (1998: 45), citing the revealing biographical fact that in a letter in 1931 Sartre mentioned Woolf (on whom he was actually lecturing) in relation to his own experience of realising the naked being of a tree which he later fictionalised as Roquentin's. This observation is invaluable in illuminating the overlooked Sartrean feature of Woolf's work. However, Mao's discussion of *Mrs Dalloway* moves away from Woolf's concern with ordinary objects to the epistemological question of how separate subjectivities are linked by their perception of the same objects in that novel. In the end he does not fully explore the specific nature of Clarissa Dalloway's attention to ordinary objects, which cannot be adequately explained by Sartrean existentialism alone because her concern is inseparable from the question of trauma.

In *Mrs Dalloway*, Septimus is an authentic specimen of a traumatised subject in that he is haunted by flashes of memories of
his war experiences. For him ordinary objects are too meaningful
and thus overwhelming: 'But real things – real things were too
exciting' (Woolf, 2000: 120). They might at any moment turn
into different things or send strange messages to puzzle him. For
a psychiatric patient like him, everyday life is simply horrifying
and painful due to his trauma. But we find the more intricate
way in which trauma and ordinary objects in everyday life are
intertwined if we turn to Clarissa Dalloway, who is afflicted with a
death anxiety related to trauma though she does not exactly suffer
from repetition compulsion like Septimus.

Clarissa is haunted by the keen sense of each moment passing
irrevocably. She obsessively concentrates on the particular
moment she is experiencing. What is interesting is that when
she does so, she also becomes sharply aware of the existence of
ordinary objects around her. Towards the beginning of the novel
when she is crossing Victoria Street, she thinks:

> In people's eyes, in the swing, tramp, and trudge; in the bellow and
> uproar; the carriages, motor cars, omnibuses, vans, sandwich men
> shuffling and swinging; brass bands; barrel organs; in the triumph
> and the jingle and the strange high singing of some aeroplane
> overhead was what she loved; life; London; this moment of June.
> (Woolf, 2000: 4)

In this manner, the ordinary objects of a June morning in a
London street which she accidentally perceives are connected to
her keen love of 'this moment'. A little later when she is walking
towards Bond Street, she similarly declares: '[W]hat she loved was
this, here, now, in front of her; the fat lady in the cab' (8). Again
'the fat lady in the cab' here is nothing more than a contingent
object of her vision. Some time later, in her own room while
making up, she feels as follows: '[A]s if to catch the falling drop,
Clarissa (crossing to the dressing-table) plunged into the very
heart of the moment, transfixed it, there – the moment of this
morning on which was the pressure of all the other mornings,
seeing the glass, the dressing-table, and all the bottles afresh [...]'
(31). Now ordinary objects like 'the glass, the dressing-table, and

all the bottles' in front of her appear afresh when she concentrates
on one particular moment.

The key to understanding Clarissa's unique psychological
mechanism can be found in her old friend Peter Walsh's recollec-
tion of their youth:

> But she said, sitting on the bus going up Shaftesbury Avenue, she
> felt herself everywhere; not 'here, here, here'; and she tapped the
> back of the seat; but everywhere. She waved her hand, going up
> Shaftesbury Avenue. She was all that. So that to know her, or any
> one, one must seek out the people who completed them; even the
> places. Odd affinities she had with people she had never spoken
> to, some woman in the street, some man behind a counter – even
> trees, or barns. It ended in a transcendental theory which, with
> her horror of death, allowed her to believe, or say that she believed
> (for all her scepticism), that since our apparitions, the part of us
> which appears, are so momentary compared with the other, the
> unseen part of us, which spreads wide, the unseen might survive,
> be recovered somehow attached to this person or that, or even
> haunting certain places, after death. Perhaps – perhaps. (129–30)

In this important passage, we can clearly see the link between
Clarissa's attention to ordinary objects around her (such as 'some
woman in the street, some man behind a counter – even trees,
or barns')[2] and her 'horror of death'. Because she is afraid of her
death, she is compelled to believe that the unseen part of her survives in other people or places after death; hence her 'affinities'
with the surrounding objects in the form of which she may survive
as a haunting ghost. She can feel that she has overcome her 'horror
of death' by dissolving into them, as it were. It is notable here that
this unseen part, which 'spreads wide' and becomes indistinguish-
able from its surroundings, does not work only after death. It is
always already living with her at present. That is why even before
death she has 'odd affinities' with 'some woman in the street, some
man behind a counter – even trees, or barns'. They are all herself
and therefore she is everywhere indeed. Here is a curious doubling
of the present and the future after death. This is because she wants
to anticipate the latter in the midst of the former in order to overcome her 'horror of death'. In other words, she is already living
like a ghost and this ghostly aspect manifests itself when her fear

of death compels her to pay attention to the surrounding objects.[3] It seems that, like a kind of vacuum, she needs to rely on them to maintain herself.[4] She darts and grabs at them to reassure herself that she exists now and even after death.

That Clarissa still keeps the theory of her youth becomes evident when we turn to the early scene where she is walking towards Bond Street. Immediately after declaring that 'what she loved was this, here, now, in front of her; the fat lady in the cab' as we saw earlier, she begins to think about survival after death:

> Did it matter then, she asked herself, walking towards Bond Street, did it matter that she must inevitably cease completely; all this must go on without her; did she resent it; or did it not become con-soling to believe that death ended absolutely? but that somehow in the streets of London, on the ebb and flow of things, here, there, she survived, Peter survived, lived in each other, she being part, she was positive, of the trees at home; of the house there, ugly, rambling all to its bits and pieces as it was; part of people she had never met; being laid out like a mist between the people she knew best, who lifted her on their branches as she had seen the trees lift the mist, but it spread ever so far, her life, herself. (8)

By picking up the accidental 'fat lady in the cab' in her love for the moment, Clarissa feels that she can overcome her fear of death.

This time, however, her fear of death is explicitly linked to the trauma of the First World War. Immediately afterwards she happens to read in a bookshop window the dirge in Shakespeare's *Cymbeline*, starting with 'Fear no more the heat o' the sun,/ Nor the furious winter's rages'; and then we read:

> This late age of world's experience had bred in them all, all men and women, a well of tears. Tears and sorrows; courage and endurance; a perfectly upright and stoical bearing. Think, for example, of the woman she admired most, Lady Bexborough, opening the bazaar [after her son was killed in the war]. (8)

The dirge in *Cymbeline* describes a peaceful state of the world after death. Its appearance here is logical given Clarissa's personal belief in survival after death. Even when she was young, she was seized with the 'horror of death', and thus traumatised, probably because, as Peter Walsh recollects, she had seen her own sister killed by a falling tree 'before her own eyes' (66). But now her fear of death has the added dimension of the trauma of the war that she shares with all people in her country. This theme is explored in relation to the shell-shocked Septimus, who comes to Clarissa's notice in the climactic scene towards the end of the novel.

In this scene, in the midst of her party, Clarissa meditates on Septimus's suicide, which she has just heard about. Septimus is a direct victim of the war and resorts to suicide because the doctors cannot treat his trauma adequately. First she is seized with her usual fear of death. She goes on to condemn herself, feeling it a disgrace that she 'had escaped' while 'that young man had killed himself' (157). But oddly she also feels happy in recollecting her past. She now tries to see the sky as she would often do in the past. And then, parting the curtains, she happens to see an old lady living opposite. This lady appeared earlier as an objective correlative of Clarissa's affirmation of life as it is. Opposed to the coercive force of love and religion, this lady represents the 'miracle' and 'mystery' of life or existence (107). As is now clear, however, she is fundamentally an extension of those accidental objects of perception such as 'the fat lady in the cab', to which Clarissa resorts in order to overcome the fear of death. The reappearance of this lady who curiously attracts Clarissa suggests that, as a ghost, she now 'spreads wide' and can identify with anyone or anything. It is then understandable that Clarissa feels 'somehow very like [Septimus]'. She also appropriately remembers the line 'Fear no more the heat o' the sun' which evokes the world after death. She can feel 'glad that he had done it; thrown it away while they went on living' (158), because as a ghostly being she has overcome her fear of death. But we should note that this overcoming is made possible by the mediation of the chance objects of perception such as the old lady in the room opposite.[5]

Clarissa is a traumatised survivor, both personally and socially. As such she is constantly seized with death anxiety.[6] When she thinks of Septimus's suicide, her fear of death is described in the following way:

> Then (she had felt it only this morning) there was terror; the over-whelming incapacity, one's parents giving it into one's hands, this

life, to be lived to the end, to be walked with serenely; there was
in the depths of her heart an awful fear. Even now, quite often
if Richard had not been there reading *The Times*, so that she
could crouch like a bird and gradually revive, send roaring up
that immeasurable delight, rubbing stick to stick, one thing with
another, she must have perished. (157)

Reading such a passage, typical of Clarissa in overcoming death
anxiety by relying on her daily life secured by her husband
Richard, we may be tempted to postulate a simple antithesis
between trauma (negative) and the ordinary (positive): the ordinary as a safe haven immune to trauma. Discussing the same
climactic scene, Liesl Olson argues in her *Modernism and the
Ordinary* that 'the narrative drive of *Mrs. Dalloway* – that is,
the way it ends – represents an affirmation of the ordinary, not
the traumatic' (2009: 75). She also claims that '[a]lthough *Mrs.
Dalloway* does not explicitly engage with ordinary experience as
a mode of opposing war and destruction, what it does advocate
is the ordinary as an individual choice against extreme forms
of violence' (76). As we have seen, however, Clarissa's peculiar
attention to ordinary objects is more deeply intertwined with her
traumatic fear of death than Olson's view suggests. While it is true
that Clarissa at times seems to feel secure amidst the ordinary,[7]
her preoccupation with each moment and ordinary objects – even
her love for them – is tinged with something compulsive suggesting that she is a traumatised subject beset with a 'horror of
death'. Daily life and ordinary objects become significant *because
of* trauma, not in opposition to it.

Samuel Beckett's *Happy Days*

'Fear no more the heat o' the sun': this line from the dirge in
Cymbeline functions as a reminder of the peaceful world after
death for Clarissa Dalloway. She feels that she can overcome the
fear of death when she quotes it. But when Winnie in Samuel
Beckett's *Happy Days*, who is another bourgeois woman of about
the same age, quotes this same line, it is simply in order to make
sure her husband Willie can hear her:

WINNIE: [*Same voice.*] Fear no more the heat o' the sun. [*Pause.*]
Did you hear that?
WILLIE: [*Irritated.*] Yes.
WINNIE: [*Same voice.*] What? [*Pause.*] What?
WILLIE: [*More irritated.*] Fear no more.
[*Pause.*]
WINNIE: [*Same voice.*] No more what? [*Pause.*] Fear no more
what?
WILLIE: [*Violently.*] Fear no more! (Beckett, 1986: 148)

Cut in half and abused in this manner, the phrase is disabled from meaning anything significant or profound as classics are supposed to do.[8] The same applies to many other phrases from classics that Winnie likes to quote. These fragments seem to imply that the whole of Western civilisation is ruined in the dreary landscape in which Winnie is situated, buried in the mound up to the waist in Act I and up to the neck in Act II. Oddly, however, she continues her daily routines such as brushing her teeth and making up in Act I, as if she were completely undisturbed by the oddity of her surroundings. The everyday objects she uses such as her bag, parasol, toothpaste, toothbrush and mirror make a sharp contrast with the 'blazing light' and 'the expanse of scorched grass' that suggest a hell. It is difficult not to see here a complete wreckage of human life, and behind that, the deep trauma of the catastrophe of the Second World War. 'What is the point of carrying on daily life after humanity has been totally ruined?', the play seems to be asking. Of course, Winnie herself is hardly conscious of any past disaster and therefore she cannot be called a traumatised subject like Clarissa Dalloway.[9] The presence of trauma is perceived through the entire situation of the play rather than Winnie's psychology. In other words, it is not Winnie as an individual but the subjectivity behind the play that is traumatised.

For Beckett, the primary trauma was simply his birth. It is important to pay attention to this personal trauma before returning to the historical trauma in his work. As is well known, Beckett was obsessed with the intrauterine state. When he was undergoing psychoanalysis with Wilfred Bion and reading various psycho-analytical works in the mid-1930s, he also studied, presumably with keen interest, Otto Rank's *The Trauma of Birth* (1924), the principal argument of which is that all human activities are an attempt to recover the ideal state before birth, thus overcoming the trauma of birth.[10] Due to his strong fixation on the womb, Beckett's work tends to be permeated with Schopenhauerian pessimism. Daily life is nothing but a superfluous residue that one is unduly obliged to face while one should never have been born. Birth is a traumatic event like death – 'Birth was the death of him', says a character in a late play *A Piece of Monologue* (Beckett, 1986: 425) – and life is already like a state after death where one floats like a ghost.[11]

Such an idea is already clear in his early works. In *Proust*, Beckett emphasises that Proust's creatures are 'victims and prisoners' of time: 'There is no escape from the hours and the days. Neither from to-morrow nor from yesterday' (1957b: 2). Habit makes life easier by effecting a compromise between the individual and his environment, but after all, it is merely 'the ballast that chains the dog to his vomit' (1957b: 8). The very first sentences of *Murphy* ironically express weariness with daily life consisting of eating, sleeping and so on: 'The sun shone, having no alternative, on the nothing new. Murphy sat out of it, as though he were free, in a mew in West Brompton. Here for what might have been six months he had eaten, drunk, slept, and put his clothes on and off [...]' (Beckett, 1957a: 1).

The idea of birth as trauma continues to underlie many of his later works and saturates them with the sense of tedium of daily life. The representation of two consecutive days with so many repetitions in *Waiting for Godot* strongly suggests the sheer meaninglessness of daily life itself. *Endgame* is more realistic in putting the characters in a shelter-like space with some ordinary objects, but it is also filled with the same kind of disgust at daily life, represented for instance by Nell's and Clov's remark, 'Why this farce, day after day?' (Beckett, 1986: 99, 107). *Happy Days* most sharply focuses on the absurdity of daily routines by putting Winnie in an extraordinary setting. Her very first words – 'Another heavenly day' (Beckett, 1986: 138) – are fiercely ironic in conveying to us the futility of starting another day, though she is not aware of it. But even she sometimes becomes conscious of the tedium: 'What *is* one to do? [...] All day long. [...] Day after day' (156). If the present everyday life does not seem so congenial to Beckett as it does to Joyce, Woolf or Stein, it may be because in his work everyday life is little more than a curse and there cannot be any positive engagement with it.

Now we can return to the historical trauma, which is in fact combined with the trauma of birth in these and other post-war works by Beckett, though they never directly deal with the Holocaust or the Second World War. As Alysia E. Garrison argues, 'Beckett's diminished and disembodied bodies are at once *the concept of being* subjected to trauma (what I call the condition of "ontological injury"), and also *particular beings' trauma* – the trauma of *social figures*, those sufferers and casualties of the violence of Nazi atrocity' (2009: 93, emphasis original).[12] Theodor W. Adorno was one of the first critics to point out the relevance of the Holocaust to Beckett's works. His following remarks on *Endgame*, which apply equally to other major post-war works by Beckett, clearly point to the burden of the trauma of the Holocaust:

> After the Second War, everything is destroyed, even resurrected culture, without knowing it; humanity vegetates along, crawling, after events which even the survivors cannot really survive, on a pile of ruins which even renders futile self-reflection of one's own battered state. (Adorno, 2000: 323)

> Beckett's figures behave primitively and behaviouristically, corresponding to conditions after the catastrophe, which has mutilated them to such an extent that they cannot react differently – flies that twitch after the swatter has half smashed them. (329)

Though Adorno does not use the term 'trauma', he suggests in effect that the characters in *Endgame* are living as (impossible) survivors with the profound trauma of the catastrophe of the Holocaust. In this context Adorno also notes the peculiar presence of 'pathetic details', which is important for our discussion:

> What becomes of the absurd, after the characters of the meaning of existence have been torn down, is no longer a universal – the absurd would then be yet again an idea – but only pathetic details which ridicule conceptuality, a stratum of utensils as in an emergency refuge: ice boxes, lameness, blindness, and unappetizing bodily functions. Everything awaits evacuation. This stratum is not

symbolic but rather the post-psychological state, as in old people and torture victims. (330)

The absurdity of living, or to be more precise, the absurdity of still living after the traumatic disaster, is conveyed more vividly by 'pathetic details' or 'a stratum of utensils' – to which ordinary objects surely belong – than by Sartre's philosophical 'idea'. In *Waiting for Godot*, as the characters are deprived of basic elements that constitute ordinary human life, common objects such as Estragon's shoes, Vladimir's trousers, and their turnips and carrots do look more conspicuous than in an ordinary context. Even Pozzo, who possesses many things, loses them one after another. In *Endgame*, Hamm and Clov are equipped with many more ordinary objects than the characters in *Godot*, as they have been sustaining themselves in a shelter-like space rather than on a bare roadside, but things are similarly disappearing one after another. In these two plays, ordinary objects are first and foremost personal possessions and they are presented in order to accentuate their loss and the characters' general state of deprivation.

In *Endgame*, the characters have developed a special attachment to certain objects (such as Hamm's toy dog). Russell Smith reads this play in terms of Freud's 'Mourning and Melancholia' and argues:

> But if the greater part of the play consists of parodies of mourning, particularly in the form of melancholy, in which lost objects are preserved through narcissistic attachments to their remainders, the *dénoument* consists of a sequence in which Hamm discards these remainders in a confrontation with the reality of loss, an ethical act of betrayal that constitutes the accomplishment of the tragic work of mourning. (2007: 115)

In the final scene Hamm discards Clov and 'a series of objects that function as melancholic metonyms of his losses' such as the gaff, the dog ('the melancholic fetish of the lost son') and the whistle. Hamm's acceptance of these losses means that he can now accomplish his mourning instead of lingering in melancholy after an unclear traumatic event. The objects that Hamm possesses could thus be interpreted as charged with psychoanalytic meanings.

The ordinary objects as 'pathetic details' in *Happy Days* seem to be rather different, though *Happy Days* does share with the previous two plays the general tendency to further deprivation. Winnie's possessions, which are contained in her bag or scattered around her on the mound, do not seem to suggest a narcissistic attachment that could generate a psychic drama of melancholy and mourning. They are more like the ordinary objects in one's daily life. This play coldly or even venomously objectifies Winnie's daily routines as if they were a specimen under a microscope.[13] Its focus on everyday life and ordinary objects is therefore much sharper than in the previous two plays.[14] And in my view, precisely for this reason, Adorno's idea that absurdity is better represented by 'pathetic details' and 'a stratum of utensils' is even more relevant to *Happy Days* than to *Endgame*. Let us turn to the opening scene to examine this feature.

When the play opens we see a big bag and a parasol around Winnie. She takes out from the bag a toothbrush and a tube of toothpaste and begins to brush her teeth. The stage direction here (as throughout the play) is extremely precise: '*She turns to bag, rummages in it without moving it from its place, brings out toothbrush, rummages again, brings out flat tube of toothpaste, turns back front, unscrews cap of tube, lays cap on ground, squeezes with difficulty small blob of paste on brush, holds tube in one hand and brushes teeth with other*' (Beckett, 1986: 138–9). Because tooth brushing is one of the most common activities of our daily life, and we do it almost automatically and unconsciously, its absurdity is all the more keenly felt against the dreary landscape in which Winnie is placed.[15] But here even the way she handles the cap of the toothpaste tube is specified. One may doubt that such a tiny detail of daily life has ever been focused on in the whole history of literature. Winnie begins to examine the handle of the toothbrush and read what is written on it with spectacles. She persists in examining it, even with a magnifying glass, until finally she discovers that the sentence is an empty commercial message: 'Fully guaranteed genuine pure hog's setae'. This is evidently an extremely minute detail that eludes our ordinary attention.[16] We come to realise that this play does not simply present Winnie's daily routines with detachment. There is a certain excess in the way it pays attention to ordinary objects.

At this point it is worthwhile to refer to past discussions of the ordinary in Beckett in order to explore the significance of ordinary objects in *Happy Days*. The American philosopher Stanley Cavell noted the ordinariness in Beckett's work in relation to his concern with Wittgenstein and ordinary language philosophy. He starts his essay on *Endgame* in *Must We Mean What We Say?* (1969) by asserting that the play is ordinary in both its human relationships (a family trouble, after all) and language (imitating ordinary conversation): 'To miss the ordinariness of the lives in *Endgame* is to avoid the extraordinariness (and ordinariness) of our own' (Cavell, 1969: 119). According to Simon Critchley, for Cavell, 'The ordinary is not a ground, but a goal. It is something we are in quest of, it is the object of an inquest, it is in question' (Critchley, 1997: 119). In other words, we are requested to discover or achieve the extraordinariness of the ordinary. Critchley says, 'On Cavell's reading, Beckett is not telling us that the universe *is* meaningless, rather meaninglessness is a task, an achievement, the achievement of the ordinary or the everyday' (179, emphasis original). He then argues that Beckett's work pares down or strips away illusory narratives of redemptive meaning that clutter the ordinary and conceal its extraordinariness. This is 'an approach to meaninglessness as an achievement of the ordinary without the rose-tinted glasses of redemption' (179). In opposition, David Rudrum contends, 'Beckett's characters are not so much in quest of the ordinary as imprisoned within it, and their impossible task is not so much achieving the ordinary but aspiring beyond or beneath it. That this is an unattainable quest, an impossible task, is, perhaps, the tragedy of the everyday' (2009: 546).

These philosophical discussions of the ordinary in Beckett, while valuable in themselves, do not at all pay attention to those ordinary *objects* in Beckett's work. They do not explain the bewilderingly poignant or 'pathetic' objects such as Winnie's toothbrush. But when we consider Winnie's weird attempts to examine the handle of her toothbrush, Rudrum's view that Beckett's characters are imprisoned within the ordinary is helpful. Indeed Winnie seems so firmly imprisoned in her daily life with its restricted routines that she is obliged to look into its minute details, such as the writing on the handle of her toothbrush. Everyday life reflects on itself pointlessly in confinement, as it were. It is to be noted that the apparent defamiliarisation of Winnie's toothbrush (which, in a sense, looks so strange as to tempt one to examine what is written on its handle) is certainly different from the surrealists' discovery of the wonder of ordinary objects that generated new artistic possibilities in the 1920s. Here it looks as though, confined in the mire – or chained to the 'vomit' if we remember *Proust* – of the everyday, Winnie is obliged to put her head deeper into it, to savour it. The defamiliarisation of ordinary objects here is forced by confinement and therefore devoid of liberating openness.[17] And the prison-like quality of daily routines is more keenly felt against the dreary background, which strongly suggests a traumatic disaster. As readers or spectators we understand that ontological and historical trauma accentuates the finitude of everyday life, although Winnie herself is hardly conscious of the trauma. We see the incredible fact that Winnie is still living with a limited number of 'pathetic' objects even after the catastrophe. The particular poignancy of Winnie's toothbrush and her bizarre attempts to examine its handle derive from trauma and the concomitant imprisonment in the everyday.

Conclusion

In the age of modernism, the 'thingness' of things emerged and became a serious concern in literature, art and philosophy, as everyday life was dramatically transformed by modernity and questions of being and existence came to the fore. In this general context, both Woolf and Beckett were exposed to the naked existence of ordinary objects. It is true that the destruction of human life is more fundamental and thoroughgoing in Beckett than in Woolf, as his generation saw more atrocities during the Second World War. In both cases, however, we observe the structure in which ordinary objects in daily life become significant against a backdrop of trauma. Trauma gives the singular acuteness to Clarissa Dalloway's 'some woman in the street, some man behind a counter – even trees, or barns' and Winnie's toothbrush. A traumatised subject or subjectivity survives after a deathly event, like a ghost or like 'flies that twitch after the swatter has half smashed them', to use Adorno's phrase, and its concern with death makes it highly conscious of the fact that it still needs to carry on its daily life of routines with ordinary objects. I would argue that in this structure lies a seminal field of study at the crossroads of trauma studies and everyday life studies. Trauma is, of course, far from an everyday phenomenon, but it can shed light on the nature of everyday life after the calamities of modernity, as we have seen in the cases of Woolf and Beckett. Conversely there may be ways of enriching trauma studies by incorporating reflections on everyday life. For instance, noting that the 'afterwardsness' that is deemed characteristic of trauma is in fact widely observed in our common experiences and not exclusive to trauma, Robert Eaglestone suggests that '[o]ne of the futures of trauma theory [...] is perhaps to look closely and more carefully not simply at the trauma, but at the structure of experience within which trauma is made manifest' (2013: 18). To consider trauma in relation to the way in which a traumatised subjectivity comes to terms with everyday life might be conducive to such a project to open up trauma studies, particularly when it is applied to literature.[18]

Notes

1 One exception is Bryony Randall's discussion of the relation between trauma and dailiness in H.D.'s texts based on her experiences of the First World War (2007: 124–54).

2 As this phrase implies, for Clarissa, there is ultimately no distinction between people and material objects such as trees or barns. She could be 'all that'. Therefore, I am going to use the term 'object' for her object of perception, even if it is a person.

3 This is suggested by the use of the word 'apparition' in the 'our apparitions, the part of us which appears' in the above quotation. Living in this world, she feels momentarily like an 'apparition', that is, like a ghost. The unseen part is permanent, but in 'haunting' places, it is also like a ghost after all.

4 The narrator of this novel works similarly as a ghostly being that needs to enter into characters' inner minds in order to maintain existence. See Miller, 1982: 180–1.

5 She feels that the sky holds 'something of her own in it' (Woolf, 2000:

157). It is thus implied that the sky is also one of the surrounding objects with which the 'unseen part' of Clarissa can identify.

6 Her husband Richard is far more naïve in appreciating the fact that he is still alive despite the war. At one point he thinks: 'Really it was a miracle thinking of the war, and thousands of poor chaps, with all their lives before them, shovelled together, already forgotten; it was a miracle. Here he was walking across London to say to Clarissa in so many words that he loved her' (Woolf, 2000: 98).

7 Earlier in the novel, when Clarissa comes back home and rediscovers the familiar conditions of her life ('The cook whistled in the kitchen. She heard the click of the typewriter. It was her life [...]'), she is explicitly grateful to Richard: '[A]ll the more [...] must one repay in daily life to servants, yes, to dogs and canaries, above all to Richard her husband, who was the foundation of it' (Woolf, 2000: 25). Later on, there is also a passage in which daily occurrences of events make Clarissa feel that death is 'unbelievable' (104).

8 It may be possible to argue that this phrase indirectly refers to the 'hellish light' under which Winnie is placed, but the way it is abused makes such an interpretation appear too deep.

9 However, Winnie is not completely devoid of apocalyptic imagination. 'Shower or Cooker' and his woman, the couple she imagines coming along, are called the 'last human kind' by her (Beckett, 1986: 157).

10 For Beckett and Rank, see Knowlson, 1996: 176–8; Baker, 1997: 64–72.

11 On the other hand, many Beckett characters are obsessed with the sense of being still in the womb. Their temporality is thus a paradoxical one of being at once after death and before birth; in the 'womb-tomb', to use a term from *Dream of Fair to middling Women*.

12 Using Dominick LaCapra's terms, Garrison also argues that Beckett's art 'witnesses the very oscillation between *constitutive absence* (the ontological, or trauma of being) and *historical loss* (historical trauma) that testifies to historically specific trauma while challenging the suppositions of humanism, ontology, and epistemology' (2009: 93, emphasis original).

13 This detached attitude to life will lead to the curiously scientific observation of human beings in *The Lost Ones*. We may also remember that Hamm in *Endgame* says, 'Imagine if a rational being came back to earth, wouldn't he be liable to get ideas into his head if he observed us long enough' (Beckett, 1986: 108).

14 This may be partly due to the fact that Winnie is a common bourgeois

woman. Beckett here follows the conventional association between women and immersion in daily life, exemplified also by Clarissa Dalloway.

15 In a different essay, which this present essay supplements, I discussed *Happy Days* as a post-Holocaust play in relation to Pinter, Levinas and Blanchot, arguing that Winnie's toothbrush is reminiscent of the piles of toothbrushes confiscated from the victims in the Nazi concentration camps. See Tajiri, 2012.

16 Winnie continues to use her ordinary objects such as spectacles, handkerchief, lipstick, mirror and so on. The only unusual object she has is a revolver. We feel that her revolver, which so directly symbolises the possibility of her suicide (that is, an escape from the imprisonment of her daily routines), is of a different order to the other objects. But in Act II, when she can no longer touch it, it is conspicuously laid beside her to suggest the impossibility of death.

17 Conor Carville discussed how Beckett inspired various post-war avant-garde artists in their attempts to open up the artwork to everyday life against Clement Greenberg's ideas of formalist autonomy and purity in modernism (Carville, 2011). For example, the video artist Bruce Nauman incorporated Watt's and Molloy's walking in his *Slow Angle Walk (Beckett Walk)*. In my view this was possible because Beckett had already foregrounded everyday acts such as walking as curious and uncanny. My suggestion in this present essay is that this aspect of Beckett's art, which puts him closer to Duchamp, Cage and other historical avant-gardists, could be linked to the question of ontological and historical trauma.

18 I am grateful to Dr David Tucker for commenting on an early draft of this chapter.

References

Adorno, Theodor W. (2000). 'Trying to Understand *Endgame*'. Trans. Michael J. Jones. In Brian O'Connor (ed.), *The Adorno Reader*. London: Blackwell, pp. 319–52.

Baker, Phil (1997). *Beckett and the Mythology of Psychoanalysis*. Basingstoke: Macmillan.

Beckett, Samuel (1957a). *Murphy*. New York: Grove Press.

Beckett, Samuel (1957b). *Proust*. New York: Grove Press.

Beckett, Samuel (1986). *Complete Dramatic Works*. London: Faber and Faber.

Brown, Bill (1999). 'The Secret Life of Things (Virginia Woolf and the Matter of Modernism)', *Modernism/Modernity* 6.2, 1–28.

Carville, Conor (2011). 'Autonomy and the Everyday: Beckett, Late Modernism and Post-War Visual Art', *Samuel Beckett Today/ Aujourd'hui* 23, 63–80.

Cavell, Stanley (1969). *Must We Mean What We Say?* New York: Cambridge University Press.

Critchley, Simon (1997). *Very Little… Almost Nothing: Death, Philosophy, Literature.* London: Routledge.

Eaglestone, Robert (2013). 'Knowledge, "Afterwardsness" and the Future of Trauma Theory'. In Gert Buelens, Sam Durrant and Robert Eaglestone (eds), *The Future of Trauma Theory: Contemporary Literary and Cultural Criticism.* London: Routledge, pp. 11–22.

Garrison, Alysia E. (2009). '"Faintly Struggling Things": Trauma, Testimony, and Inscrutable Life in Beckett's *The Unnamable*'. In Sean Kennedy and Katherine Weiss (eds), *Samuel Beckett: History, Memory, Archive.* New York: Palgrave Macmillan, pp. 89–109.

Henke, Suzette, and David Eberly (eds) (2007). *Virginia Woolf and Trauma: Embodied Texts.* New York: Pace University Press.

Highmore, Ben (2002). *Everyday Life and Cultural Theory: An Introduction.* London: Routledge.

Knowlson, James (1996). *Damned to Fame: The Life of Samuel Beckett.* London: Bloomsbury.

Mao, Douglas (1998). *Solid Objects: Modernism and the Test of Production.* Princeton, NJ: Princeton University Press.

Miller, J. Hillis (1982). *Fiction and Repetition: Seven English Novels.* Cambridge, MA: Harvard University Press.

Olson, Liesl (2009). *Modernism and the Ordinary.* Oxford: Oxford University Press.

Randall, Bryony (2007). *Modernism, Daily Time and Everyday Life.* Cambridge: Cambridge University Press.

Rudrum, David (2009). 'From the Sublime to the Ordinary: Stanley Cavell's Beckett', *Textual Practice* 23.4, 543–58.

Sim, Lorraine (2010). *Virginia Woolf: The Patterns of Ordinary Experience.* Farnham: Ashgate.

Smith, Russell (2007). '*Endgame*'s Remainders'. In Mark S. Byron (ed.), *Samuel Beckett's Endgame.* Amsterdam: Rodopi, pp. 99–120.

Tajiri, Yoshiki (2012). 'Everyday Life and the Pain of Existence in *Happy Days*'. In Mariko Hori Tanaka, Yoshiki Tajiri and Michiko Tsushima (eds), *Samuel Beckett and Pain.* Amsterdam: Rodopi, pp. 151–69.

Woolf, Virginia (2000). *Mrs Dalloway*. Ed. David Bradshaw. Oxford: Oxford University Press.

Woolf, Virginia (2001). 'Solid Objects'. In *The Mark on the Wall and Other Short Fiction*. Ed. David Bradshaw. Oxford: Oxford University Press, pp. 54–9.

7

Smiling tigers: trauma, sexuality and creaturely life in *Echo's Bones*

Conor Carville

This essay will draw on Eric L. Santner's work in order to read Beckett's early poetry, specifically the collection *Echo's Bones*, published in 1935. In Santner's thought the Freudian notion of trauma – or more accurately Lacan's interpretation of that notion – is allied with both Walter Benjamin's ideas of the creaturely, and Agamben's treatment of bare life and biopolitics (Santner, 2006).[1] This combination of ideas issues in an account of the relationship between the psychic and the social. To the extent that Santner draws on Freud to address issues of historical violence, his work bears some relation to the emergence of trauma studies in the 1990s, and to those critics and historians who have brought this body of theory to bear on the Holocaust. Yet Santner's recent books also depart from such antecedents, in that he is concerned, like Foucault, Lacan and Agamben in their different ways, to provide a general account of the formation of the subject in modernity. More specifically, and here the debt to Lacan is strongest, Santner sees trauma as constitutive of the subject, and not as an exceptional occurrence. Indeed it is the excitations of trauma – which Santner associates with Benjamin's idea of creaturely life – that provide the raw material, so to speak, on to which the biopolitical machinery of modern governmentality battens. Santner thus supplements both Agamben and Foucault by understanding the 'life' that is the focus of biopower as predominantly psychic life, desire and the symptoms through which the unconscious insists in everyday life. In this way he recognises the utility of trauma to power, and so avoids the tendency, which I have analysed elsewhere, for the discourses of trauma studies to repeat the assumptions of a more generalised trauma culture that is complicit with the ideological production of contemporary identities.[2]

Beckett's collection of thirteen poems, *Echo's Bones and Other Precipitates*, was published by George Reavey's Europa Press in December 1935. As Lawlor and Pilling point out, the book was 'written intermittently over about four years', and yet it has a strong sense of coherence. The poems, as the editors have it, 'fit well alongside one another' (Beckett, 2012: 259–60). This is indeed true: themes, motifs, images, settings and individual words return again and again in the collection. The poems also share some key concerns, and it is on these that I want to concentrate. Chief among them is the idea of life itself, conceived in terms of a propulsive, trans-individual, excessively animating force.

Take the first line of the very first poem, describing the vulture of its title 'dragging his hunger through the sky' (Beckett, 2012: 5). There is an echo here of the first line of a famous poem, Yeats's 'The Second Coming', and 'The Vulture' shares some of the former's concerns, while also departing from them. In 'The Second Coming' Yeats's hawk turns and turns in the circles of the gyres, and it is only later that the malign, anarchic 'desert birds' intervene. Beckett, however, begins with such a bird, the vulture, right away, and describes it 'stooping' or diving towards the 'prone' who lie below it. These same prone bodies must 'take up their life and walk' in order to escape. The reference here is to Matthew 9.5–6, where Christ commands the paralysed man to take his mat and walk. The allusion marks these prone bodies as human rather than animal, but more importantly it also distinguishes between them and the 'life' that they 'carry'. As with the vulture and its hunger, these figures drag their life with them: it is seen as a burden, an affliction. Such a reading is compounded by the next line's description of a 'tissue' or flesh that 'mocks' the self and, in another biblical reference, which 'may not serve'. 'The Vulture' thus breaks down boundaries between human and non-human forms of life, yet also insistently divides life from the self (or 'shell') that bears it. This notion of a life that is at once shared by all things, and yet retains an alien, extimate quality, is precisely what Santner refers to as the 'creaturely life' that is exposed to power at moments of trauma. If 'The Vulture' is a poem that seeks to shed this life, turning it into 'offal', it is because it is this creaturely life that makes the self vulnerable to the depredations of the biopolitical.

The period in which the poems contained in *Echo's Bones* were written saw Beckett move regularly between London, Paris and Dublin. As a result he was well placed to observe the ways in which the new biopolitical management of life was making itself felt across the continent. I have argued elsewhere that *Murphy* can be read as a response to the reorganisation of health, housing and working practices in 1930s London.[3] *Echo's Bones* brings in the two other cities where Beckett spent time, and which were also undergoing radical change. In Ireland the period between 1923 and 1935 saw the introduction of no less than eighteen separate pieces of legislation aimed at regulating sexuality, ranging from prostitution and indecent literature to illegitimacy and the age of consent.[4] In France and Belgium concerns about population decline led to laws being enacted against family planning, and widespread opposition to abortion and contraception.[5] 1930 also saw the publication of the papal encyclical *Casti Conubii*, highly influential in its condemnation of contraception and its insistence that sexual intercourse be linked with procreation.

The specific concerns to which the Irish legislation was designed to respond are well caught in J. P. F. Waters's 'Disease of the Social System', an essay that brings together health, economics and sexuality in a paradigmatically biopolitical form:

> If our social and economic disorder continues, it is obvious that the steady elimination of young people by emigration, the decline in the numbers born, the deterioration in the quality of children born due to the too late marriage age of mothers, and the decline in general health due to malnutrition can only lead to a complete sapping of the physical and mental vitality of the nation. (1938: 390)

It is clear from Beckett's writing of the 1930s that he had an acute sensitivity to the way that life, and the social reproduction of life in the name of the nation, was assuming a central position in governmental thought and practice not only in Ireland, but also in Britain and France.[6] More than this, however, in the mid-1930s he refracted these concerns through his own reading in psychology, and in particular his close attention to Otto Rank's book *The Trauma of Birth* (first published in German in 1924).[7] This book provides a link between 1930s concerns with sexuality and reproduction and trauma. In *On Creaturely Life*, Eric Santner extends Freud's notion of trauma to encompass the dialectic between parent and child in very early infancy. Rank's book does something oddly similar, conceiving of the universal experience of exiting the womb as an originary trauma that functions structurally in the constitution of subjectivity. Beckett's interest in Rank and trauma, together with his clear sensitivity to contemporary biopolitical discourses, thus brings him into proximity to Santner's ideas. And when we note the way that Rank, Beckett and Santner each see the question of animal life as also implicated in these concerns, the connections are strengthened still further.

Beckett himself remarked of his poem 'Sanies I' that it contained authentic reminiscences of the 'two primal traumata: birth and weaning' (2012: 275). This is a direct quotation from Rank, who writes of 'the painfully experienced primal traumata of birth and weaning', a phrase that Beckett carefully transcribes in his notes on the book. By calling these traumas primal, it should be noted, Beckett is explicitly commending Rank's heretical position, one that relegates the castration complex to third place in the production of later anxieties. For this, Rank was exiled from Freud's circle. *The Trauma of Birth* is thus a source for the poem, and for the book as a whole. The many images of animal life that we find in the poem and the collection generally are also present in Rank, who sees such images as central to the way birth trauma returns in later life. As he puts it 'the universal childish *fear of animals*' is a delayed consequence of the trauma of birth. He goes on to break down this fear into two types: fear of beasts of prey, and fear of small animals. In terms of the former Rank argues that 'the beasts of prey ... provide a rationalization ... of the wish – through the desire to be eaten – to get back again into the mother's animal womb' (Rank, 1993: 12). Similarly

> the feeling of weirdness or uncanniness in the presence of … small creeping animals, such as mice, snakes, frogs, beetles, etc., can be traced to their peculiar ability completely to disappear into small holes in the earth. They therefore exhibit the wish to return into the maternal hiding-place as completely accomplished. (Rank, 1993: 13)

The Trauma of Birth gives examples from actual case histories, as well as from myths and fairy tales, that serve to illustrate Rank's point. Several of these examples refer to spiders, toads and dogs. We will return to these and other images of creaturely life as they become relevant to our discussion of the poems.

Ostensibly the record of a bicycle ride around the suburbs of Dublin on Easter Saturday 1933, 'Sanies I' is more deeply concerned with the speaker's moment of birth, the absence of the father from this event, and the childhood experience of the proximity of the maternal body (Beckett, 2012: 12–13). As Beckett highlights in his letter to Thomas McGreevy, here birth is seen as a primal trauma. The poem also explores the subsequent assumption of object-relations and sexual identity. Yet the latter process is also undermined. Intimations of non-normative sexuation abound. Hence, for example, the first image of the speaker as he speeds home on his bicycle is a composite one:

> like a Ritter with a pommelled scrotum …
> Botticelli from the fork down (12)

The masculine, phallic image of the knight or 'Ritter' ends at his armoured codpiece, and from there (the fork of the legs) on downwards, it is (as Lawlor and Pilling surmise) Botticelli's *Venus* that is the model. The reference to the famous image of Venus, born fully grown from the sea, with the scallop shell on which she stands representing the vulva, is an indication that the largely upbeat description of the speaker's own birth, when it comes, might be taken as similarly idealised. Indeed the line following the allusion to Botticelli, although it ostensibly describes the speed of the bicycle, is more likely, with its references to 'bleeding' and 'voiding', an early trace of the painful physical business of giving birth. This movement between the real and the idealised continues throughout the poem. For example, one corridor of images depicts a kind of suburban idyll of swans and weekend promenaders, through which the young cyclist zooms, eyeing up 'the billows of the nubile', but 'bound for home like a good boy'. Yet this image of the well-adjusted, healthy and normatively masculine young man is undercut, not only by the indeterminacy of the Ritter/Venus, but by deliberately abject sexual identifications:

> clipped like a pederast as to one trouser-end
> sucking in my bloated lantern behind a Wild Woodbine
> cinched to death in a filthy slicker. (13)

Perhaps as a result of this failure to adopt a normative sexual identity, the speaker's ultimate desire is, as Beckett puts it, to 'be back in the caul', i.e. to leap back over the terror of birth and childhood, and to refuse even to attempt to take up the kind of position in the symbolic order that the primal trauma sponsors. In this amniotic utopia there will be, as Beckett puts it, 'no trusts, no fingers, no spoilt love'. It is worth tarrying with this trilogy of terms for a moment. The middle phrase presumably refers to the lack of differentiation in the embryo's body (though fingers are in fact developed relatively early). The mention of trusts is a thornier issue. Beckett's use of the plural suggests that the reference is to the legal instrument whereby property is held by one person, in order to use it for the benefit of another. Such arrangements are often familial, a parent managing an estate for the benefit of a child, or vice versa. Then there is also the more general sense of confidence, belief, reliability: the reliance of the child on the parent's judgement and assistance. If one was going to evoke the notion of the law in both its ethical and more broadly commercial meanings one could do a lot worse than trusts. We could paraphrase the first two words in the line as 'no law, no body', then.

Which brings us finally to the 'spoilt love'. A quote that Santner adduces from Laplanche is useful here. According to the former, unconscious formations arise from:

> an encounter between an individual whose psycho-somatic structures are situated predominantly at the level of need, and signifiers emanating from an adult. These signifiers pertain to the

satisfaction of a child's needs, but they also convey the purely inter-
rogative potential of other messages – and those other messages are
sexual. These enigmatic messages set the child the difficult, or even
impossible, task of mastery and symbolization and the attempt to
perform it inevitably leaves behind unconscious residues. (Santner,
2006: 33)

One can read spoilt love as a reference to the encounter with the
'dauntless nautch-girl' of the final lines of the poem.[8] However, a
broader reading is also available, which sees the phrase as referring to the speaker's experience of a traumatic, enigmatic kernel
at the heart of the mother's loving gaze, the question that the child
attempts to answer by him or herself asking 'Che Vuoi?' What do
you want of me? What is that you want me to become in order to
satisfy you?[9] The love of the parent is spoilt because it carries the
traumatic stain of the real.

It is the presence of such a stain on the gaze of the other that
structures the account of birth and weaning that the speaker gives
us in 'Sanies I'. 'I was born with a pop with the green of the
larches' says the speaker, and then a few lines later:

Oh the larches the pain drawn like a cork
the glans he took the day off up hill and down dale
with a ponderous fawn from the Liverpool London and Globe
back the shadows lengthen the sycamores are sobbing
to roly-poly oh to me a spanking boy
buckets of fizz childbed is thirsty work
for the midwife he is gory
for the proud parent he washes down a gob of gladness
for footsore Achates also he pants his pleasure
sparkling beestings for me. (Beckett, 2012: 12)

There are several things to say about this. Although the tone is
remarkably jaunty for the most part, with the theme of celebration uppermost – born with a pop, drawn like a cork, buckets
of fizz – these are for the most part clichés, and other, darker
elements roil beneath. Standard images of sexuation are proposed
only to be ironised elsewhere in the poem. The passage includes
two such normative images: first there is the basic marker of 'the
glans', the first glimpse of which confirms the biological sex of the
child. This is then succeeded by the more confident, symbolically

coded identification of a 'roly-poly … spanking boy'. But note the effects of Beckett's use of syntax and lack of punctuation here. The speaker's self-identification as a boy coincides with the father's return: the father comes 'back … to … oh to me', so that the assumption of a defined position in the symbolic order is triggered by the father's naming of the gender of his child. And yet this is also shadowed by the enigmatic image where, in an alternative reading to the one where it is the father who is return-ing *to* the child, the sycamores are 'sobbing/ *to*' him. The implicit violence of 'spanking' intensifies the unease here.

Most importantly, however, the section ends with a further small drama of interpellation, where the child seeks to play the role that he thinks he should adopt for each of the adults present. The pronoun changes from first to third, so that 'he' is covered in blood for the midwife and gulping with pleasure for his father. The presence of footsore Achates, the man from the Liverpool London and Globe, an enormous insurance company, ensures that the symbolic network into which the child is being inculcated is not limited to the family unity but encompasses the social, and ultimately the globe. For Achates too the child anxiously performs the role that he assumes he is expected to.

In return the infant receives the reward of his mother's milk. This brings together two important motifs: the breast and the animal. It is 'sparkling beestings' that the child receives from the mother, beestings being the colostrum of a cow. Jean Laplanche sees such a moment as a paradigmatic example of the traumatic enigma of parental–child relations:

> Can analytic theory afford to go on ignoring the extent to which women unconsciously and sexually cathect the breast, which appears to be a natural organ for lactation? It is inconceivable that the infant does not notice this sexual cathexis … it is impossible to notice that the infant does not suspect that this sexual cathexis is the source of nagging question: what does the breast want from me, apart from wanting to suckle me and, come to that, why does it want to suckle me? (quoted in Santner 2001: 34)

As Santner comments: 'What Laplanche is describing here is nothing short of the birth of the drama of legitimation as con-

stitutive of human subjectivity' (2001: 34). Beckett's introduction of this drama of the breast in his account of the trauma
of birth provides a bridge to the poem's final section. Here the
speaker returns to the present, and a chance encounter with his
beloved, 'gliding towards me dauntless nautch girl on the face
of the waters/ dauntless daughter of desires in the old black and
flamingo' (Beckett, 2012: 13). As Lawlor and Pilling inform us, a
nautch girl is an Indian professional dancing girl, and the phrase
also occurs in *Dream of Fair to middling Women* as 'the hard
breastless Greek slave or huntress the hard nautch girl'.[10] The
nautch girl is thus an androgynous figure that links back to the
ambiguous sexuation of the Ritter/Venus image of the poem's
beginning. The suggestion that the woman is 'gliding' on 'the face
of the waters' strengthens the connection with Botticelli's *Venus*,
and this association with birth is clinched by the fact that she
lives in Dublin's Holles Street, home of the National Maternity
Hospital. If the poem's final encounter is with a 'dauntless daughter of desires' then, it is also one with the disturbingly powerful
desire of an enigmatic figure that recalls earlier moments in a
highly unstable, undetermined way. The chance meeting with the
nautch-girl is a shocking, traumatic one that reworks in a more
unnerving form the primal scene of birth and sexuation. It is this
that accounts for the speaker's urgent, excessive, seemingly panic-
stricken reaction to her.

This final encounter also brings the poem's pervasive animal
images to a head, through the flamingo-coloured clothes the woman
wears, and the more sinister description of her house as a web at the
centre of which she sits. In *The Trauma of Birth* Rank argues that
'the spider is a clear symbol of the dreaded mother in whose net one
is caught'. He then quotes from one of Ferenczi's patients:

Hypochondria surrounds my soul like a fine mist, or rather like a
cobweb ... as though I had to stretch out my head so as to be able
to breathe. I want to tear the cobweb, to tear it. But no, I can't do
it! The web is fastened somewhere – the props would have to be
pulled out on which it hangs. If that can't be done, one would have
slowly to work one's way through the net in order to get air. Man
surely is not here to be veiled in such a cobweb, suffocated, and
robbed of the light of the sun. (Rank, 1993: 15)

The manner in which the speaker commands the nautch-girl back to 'the cob of your web in Holles Street' confirms the encounter with her as a traumatic one. Her presence troubles the success of the original traumatic separation in the way that, as Rank suggests, all small creeping animals do, representing a complete assimilation to the maternal body. In this respect it is significant that another animal is subsequently added to the menagerie, when the speaker evokes a tiger 'that funds ways home' instead. Here we have an example of Rank's alternative strand of animal imagery, the beast of prey that supposedly stages the desire to be eaten and so return to the womb. For the speaker of 'Sanies I' it seems that the lesser of two evils is the return to the smiling tiger of the mother, from whom he has successfully separated once, rather than the web of the estranged lover, whose androgyny reminds him once again of the turmoil of his sexual identifications.

There are many other creatures mentioned or implied in the poem: Achates (Ulysses' dog), some sneering fauns, chickens, pigs, a knight's trusty steed and the swans of the opening lines. In this 'Sanies I' is typical of the collection as a whole: animals stalk through its pages and in some cases displace the human characters almost completely. In several poems they are described in the anthropomorphic terms that Santner calls creaturely. Following Benjamin, but again reading him through Lacan, Santner understands this term to indicate something different from a sheerly animal or instinctual existence. To speak of the creaturely is not to attempt to isolate the purely biological functioning of the human animal. It is not, in other words, to distinguish between *zoe* and *bios* in Agamben's Aristotelian terms. Rather the creature marks the point where 'life' intersects with the law, with the symbolic, the social and the political. The template for this intersection is the primal traumatic encounter with the parents' desire. But Santner argues that this moment is constantly negotiated later in life in much wider contexts, and it is at these moments that what he terms the creaturely makes its presence felt:

> creaturely life – the peculiar proximity of the human to the animal
> at the very point of their radical difference – is a product ... of

[man's] exposure to a traumatic dimension of political power and social bonds whose structures have undergone radical transformation in modernity. The 'essential disruption' that renders man 'creaturely' … has, that is, a distinctly political – or better, biopolitical – aspect; it names the threshold where life becomes a matter of politics and politics comes to inform the very matter and materiality of life. (Santner, 2006: 12)

This quotation and my short summary preceding it are problematic in that they condense an argument that unfolds across the length of Santner's book, and draws, apart from Freud, on Rilke, Heidegger, Benjamin, Agamben, Kafka, Rosenzweig, Lacan, Žižek and others. I hope that an analysis of a second poem from *Echo's Bones*, one that explicitly engages with the animal, might help to fill in some more detail, however.

In 'Serena II' the speaker's dreaming dog dreams of giving birth. An earlier draft of the poem, sent to McGreevy in 1932, complicates the scenario described, but links it more surely to 'Sanies I' and to Rank's *The Trauma of Birth*:

> In her dreams she leaps again
> way back in the good old dark old days
> in the womb of her dam panting
> in the claws of the Pins in the stress of her hour
> the womb writhes bagful of ferrets
> first come first served no queuing in the womb. (Beckett, 2012:
>   246)

In this version it is the dog's own birth that is the focus, and the struggle to be born is emphasised. In this, the following quotation from Rank seems pivotal: 'the dreams of animals which pass through a foetal development may be assumed to reproduce the situation in the womb, only they lack the means for linguistic expression so characteristic of human beings' (1993: 101). The speaker proceeds to describe the dog's dream, but in doing so the subject changes from the act of being born to the act of giving birth, a shift from progeny to mother. In the earlier variant of the poem there is more stress on the debilitating effects of multiple births than in the published version: 'in a hag she drops her young/ the asphodels come running the flags after/ cloppety-clop all night she drops them/ ... she wakes whining' (Beckett, 2012: 247).

In terms of Santner's creaturely life, what is significant here is the way Beckett dramatises the dream by introducing emotional, social and symbolic inflections. The poem is not an attempt to somehow occupy an animal's bodily experience. Rather, the description of the dream is an amalgam of the materiality of sexual reproduction with cultural and political codings. Some of these codings are very much of the historical moment in which Beckett is writing. The early draft of the poem contains a reference to Pavlov 'toiling on second gear through the Celtic mizzle' (247), for example. As Lawlor and Pilling argue, this suggests that the 'damfool twilight' of the first verse is a reference to the cultural nationalism that Beckett often dismissed. There are many other such references. The setting of the first half of the poem in Connemara, for example, as clearly suggested by the references to the Twelve Pins mountain range, and to Clew and Blacksod bays, locates the poem close to the geographical heart of Irish nationalist discourse of the early twentieth century. All of these are significant sites in the folklore and mythology of the Irish Revival. Blacksod Bay is divided from Clew Bay by Achill Island, and there are hundreds of other small islands and islets in these waters. One of these is Inishglora, which is the source of the phrase 'islands of glory' in the poem.

Inishglora was one of the places where, in medieval Irish myth, the Children of Lir settled, after having been turned into swans by their jealous stepmother Aoife. Lady Gregory has a version of the story in *Gods and Fighting Men* (1905: 140–58). The human-to-beast transformation of the myth accords with the poem's own strategies, and the lines 'with a yo-heave-ho of able-bodied swans/ out from the doomed land their reefs of tresses' surrealistically entwines the dog's throes with the Celtic myth. More importantly, these references momentarily – and bathetically – place the dog's travails in a recognisable ideological context, that of the heroic nationalism of 1930s Ireland. The poem, in other words, operates at the precise point where the material, physiological processes of social reproduction are traversed by the mythic and the symbolic

– the threshold where, as Santner describes it, 'life becomes a matter of politics and politics comes to inform the very matter and materiality of life' (2006: 21). In response to the spectacle of the whining, trembling body of the dog as it sleeps, the speaker's own creaturely life is called forth, excited, and his fantasy of the dog's dream ensures. Crucially, however, this fantasy is not simply a personal one, but partakes of a more general structuring of creaturely life in which the material, intimate, felt processes of the body *in extremis* are caught up and traversed by the law of the social and the symbolic.

Lawlor and Pilling suggest that the second section of the poem, set in the Wicklow mountains, sees the dog of the first part replaced by the speaker's mother. There is no direct evidence of this, but certainly a concentrated network of images emerges which suggests a close relationship with the maternal figures of 'Sanies I'. The following lines are particularly notable in this respect:

> with whatever trust of panic we went out
> with so much shall we return
> there shall be no loss of panic between a man and his dog
> bitch though he be (Beckett, 2012: 19)

The 'trust' here picks up on the 'trusts' of the previous poem, which we associated with both parental support and legal instruments. The idea of a 'trust of panic' (panic, from Pan), however, brings the term into line with the creaturely connections that are the subject of 'Serena I'. The 'trust' of panic that man and dog share can be read again in legal terms as something held for us in reserve, a creaturely life that is always there for us, if not directly accessible. At the same time, if we take panic in the more familiar sense of distress or affliction, a 'trust of panic' is an exact description of the kind of primal trauma of birth and identification with paternal authority with which 'Sanies I' is concerned. Certainly the going out and the returning spoken of in these lines are the events of birth and death, as much as they are the everyday acts of taking a pet out for a walk. The multiply perplexing last line, meanwhile, repeats the questions of disidentification that play out also in 'Sanies I'.

In the closing stages of the poem Rank again makes his presence felt, by way of an otherwise bizarre reference to 'toads' and 'their snares' (19). For Rank, the toad is another creature, like the spider, that stands for an undifferentiated union with the maternal. Hence *The Trauma of Birth* refers to 'the very ancient popular practice of picturing the womb as an animal' and then, in a footnote, suggests that 'this animal is most frequently a toad, which creeps into dark and inaccessible holes' (1993: 16). Rank goes on to provide a series of scholarly authorities for this claim, taken from the comparative study of myth, including Karl Speiss's analysis of the 'uterus-toad', and Jacoby and Spiegelberg's essay on the 'frog-headed' Egyptian goddess of birth. Once again we get the movement from birth trauma, to creaturely life, to the symbolic realm of myth, ideology and law. Beckett again relates birth, the animal and nationalist myth by also evoking 'the fairy-tales of Meath' here. The speaker's rejection of the snares of the toads repeats the rejection of the womb-like web of the nautch-girl at the close of 'Sanies I'. Indeed, the end of 'Serena II' rehearses a very similar situation to the one found at the end of the previous poem. There, as I argued earlier, the nautch-girl's implied androgyny troubles the speaker, a reminder of a failure to conform to conventional sexual difference earlier in the poem. Here too, at the end of 'Serena II', normative gender-imagery is evoked only to be compromised, resulting in a traumatic torrent of images that suggests a massively disturbed, stricken relation to the assumption of an approved sexual identity:

> sodden packet of Churchman
> muzzling the cairn
> it is worse than dream
> the light randy slut can't be easy
> this clonic earth
> all these phantoms shuddering out of focus...
> all the chords of the earth broken like a woman pianist's (Beckett,
>   2012: 19)

Note the focus on gender roles and imagery here. The first line refers to the conventionally masculine signifier of the cigarette, but specifically to the brand name or logo on the packet.

This 'Churchman' is thus the Name-of-the-Father or paternal metaphor, the symbolic term by which the body of the mother is replaced in any successful accession to the realm of language and law. Here, however, the term is abjected as 'sodden', flaccid, impotent. The second line similarly 'muzzles' or neuters the phallic cairn or standing stone. 'Muzzled' leads back to the crea-turely life of the female dog, however, and seems also to anticipate the 'slut' of a later line. The implication of the attempted muzzling is that the cairn is an all-devouring mouth, an implacable hunger. (In *Seminar IV*, at the end of chapter entitled 'The Phallus and the Insatiable Mother', Lacan refers to the mother's mouth in the same terms – 'comme un guele ouverte'.) Significantly, the muzzling fails, the rage of sex and life cannot be 'easy', indeed it affects the very light, which is mobile, 'randy', while the earth itself is 'clonic', subject to spasms of desire. All of which leads to the subject's affliction with uncontrollable phantoms, and the sense of an insurgent, exorbitant, all-pervading life that renders a stable subjectivity impossible. Finally, 'all the chords of the earth [are] broken like a woman pianist's' again introduces a reference to gender, but more importantly smuggles in the homophonic 'woman's penis'. This points to the way that the end of the poem sees the failed paternal authority of the Churchman replaced by an imaginary maternal phallus. That is to say, the knees of stone, at which the now infantilised speaker prays and goes to sleep in the closing lines, is another reiteration of the stone cairn, now properly petrified and erect. This reading is reinforced by Lawlor and Pilling's contention that the final image is based on a well-known photograph of the young Beckett praying at his mother's knee (Beckett, 2012: 290).

At the end of *The Trial*, Santner reminds us, Josef K. exclaims 'like a dog', and immediately after, in the last line of the novel, we read 'it was as if the shame would outlive him'. The last line of the dog's dream in 'Serena II' reads 'she thinks she is dying she is ashamed' (18). Santner quotes Agamben:

> To be ashamed means to be consigned to something that cannot be assumed. But what cannot be assumed is not something external.

Rather it originates in its own intimacy; it is what is most intimate in us (for example our own physiological life). Here the 'I' is thus overcome by its own passivity, its ownmost sensibility; yet this expropriation and desubjectivication is also an extreme and irreducible presence of the 'I' to itself. It is as if our consciousness collapsed and, seeking to flee in all directions, were simultaneously summoned by an irrefutable order to be present at its own defacement. This double movement, which is both subjectification and desubjectification, is shame. (2006: 23–4)

For Santner, this shame when the sheerly physiological emerges publicly is a trace of the traumatic moment when the subject is formed and sexual identity is assumed. The shame in 'Serena II' can be termed creaturely, in Santner's terms, in that the intimate, physiological activity of giving birth is presented by Beckett in the context of a broader politico-mythic-symbolic network, present in the poem through the setting in the west of Ireland and the allusions to the Children of Lir. For Santner, the operations of biopower are reliant on and revealed by such traumatic moments of exposure. In this way the creaturely body in its vulnerability and pain is analogous to the 'bare life' that Agamben sees typified by the figure of *Homo Sacer*. Beckett's reading of Otto Rank furnished him with a notion of the 'primal traumata' that brought *Echo's Bones'* explorations of sexuation and identification into close proximity with contemporary biopolitical concerns with birth, reproduction and population. It is this parallel between the public and the personal that links 'Sanies I' to 'Serena II'.

Beckett also refers to shame in 'Serena III': 'or on Butt Bridge blush for shame/ the mixed declension of those mammae/ cock up thy moon, thine and thine only' (2012: 20). A variant has the following:

> on Butt bridge take thought for yer buzzum
> the mixed declension of those mammae
> cock up thine arse there is no other word for it. (2012: 291)

And so we have here a final traumatic encounter to add to the series. As in each of the other poems, this encounter seems to trigger a traumatic return of repressed memories of separation from the mother as well as intimations of the speaker's non-normative sexual identifications. It is for the latter reason that in both 'Sanies I' and 'Serena II' the poem ends through the termination of trauma by a return to the real mother, as bones of stone or smiling tiger, the latter intriguingly reminiscent of Lacan's description of the traumatic, devouring mother in *Ecrits*: 'intentional aggressiveness gnaws away, undermines, and disintegrates; it castrates; it leads to death: "And I thought you were impotent!" growled a mother, with a tiger's cry, to her son, who, with not without great difficulty, had confessed to her his homosexual tendencies' (2006: 104).

Notes

1 Santner continues this project in *The Royal Remains: The People's Two Bodies and the Endgames of Sovereignty* (2011), which concludes with a short account of Beckett, and most recently *The Weight of All Flesh: On the Subject Matter of Political Economy* (2015).
2 See Carville, 2012: 67–89.
3 See Carville, 2016: 74–88.
4 See Crowley and Kitchin, 2008: 355–72; McAvoy, 1999: 253–66; and Smith, 2004: 208–33.
5 See Schneider, 1990.
6 Social reproduction refers to the crucial, unpaid work – childbirth and childcare – that women carry out to supply capital with labour power. An important strand of feminist theory explores this crucial gendering of the biopolitical. See, for example, Federici, 2012.
7 Rank's book was a source of fascination for the avant-garde of the 1930s.
8 See Beckett, 2012: 279.
9 See Žižek, 2008: 95–145.
10 See Beckett, 2012: 279.

References

Beckett, Samuel (2012). *The Collected Poems of Samuel Beckett*. Ed. Seán Lawlor and John Pilling. London: Faber and Faber.
Carville, Conor (2012). *Ends of Ireland: Criticism, History, Subjectivity*. Manchester: Manchester University Press.
Carville, Conor (2016). 'Murphy's Thanatopolitics', *The Irish Review* 53.1, 74–88.

Crowley, Una, and Rob Kitchin (2008). 'Producing "Decent Girls": Governmentality and the Moral Geographies of Sexual Conduct in Ireland (1922–1937)', *Gender, Place & Culture* 15.4, 355–72.

Federici, Silvia (2012). *Revolution at Point Zero: Housework, Reproduction and Feminist Struggle*. Oakland, CA: PM Press.

Gregory, Lady Augusta (1905). *Gods and Fighting Men: The Story of the Tuatha de Danaan and the Fianna of Ireland, Arranged and Put into English by Lady Gregory. With a Preface by W.B. Yeats*. London: John Murray.

Lacan, Jacques (2006). *Écrits*. Trans. Bruce Fink. New York: Norton.

McAvoy, Sandra (1999). 'The Regulation of Sexuality in the Irish Free State, 1929–35'. In Greta Jones and Elizabeth Malcolm (eds), *Medicine, Disease and the State in Ireland, 1650–1940*. Cork: Cork University Press, pp. 253–66.

Rank, Otto (1993 [1924]). *The Trauma of Birth*. New York: Dover Publications.

Santner, Eric L. (2001). *On the Psychotheology of Everyday Life: Reflections on Freud and Rozenzweig*. Chicago: University of Chicago Press.

Santner, Eric L. (2006). *On Creaturely Life: Rilke, Benjamin, Sebald*. Chicago: University of Chicago Press.

Santner, Eric L. (2011). *The Royal Remains: The People's Two Bodies and the Endgames of Sovereignty*. Chicago: University of Chicago Press.

Santner, Eric L. (2015). *The Weight of All Flesh: On the Subject Matter of Political Economy*. Oxford: Oxford University Press.

Schneider, William H. (1990). *Quality and Quantity: The Quest for Biological Regeneration in Twentieth Century France*. Cambridge: Cambridge University Press.

Smith, James M. (2004). 'The Politics of Sexual Knowledge: The Origins of Ireland's Containment Culture and the Carrigan Report (1931)', *Journal of the History of Sexuality* 13.2, 208–33.

Waters, J. P. F. (1938). 'Disease of the Social System', *Irish Ecclesiastical Record* 52, 390.

Žižek, Slavoj (2008). *The Sublime Object of Ideology*. London: Verso.

8

The global trauma of the nuclear age in Beckett's post-war plays

Mariko Hori Tanaka

The Holocaust and the development of nuclear weapons changed the world at the end of the Second World War. These two horrific events still weigh heavily on our lives. As Theodor Adorno warned, 'Today something worse than death is to be feared' (2001: 106). Both events proved that human beings can be infinitely savage and that we can potentially even destroy our species. Referring to his own famous words, 'After Auschwitz one could no longer write poetry' (2001: 110), Adorno explains that the statement does not deny art but '[i]t is the question whether one can *live* after Auschwitz' (110). In a culture where an individual identified as a burden on society might be victimised at any time, how can one escape the world of torture and 'live', sustaining human dignity? Nowadays, this question has no limits. Today, it is no longer the issue of victims and those who narrowly escaped Auschwitz or other forms of genocide, but a global issue faced by every one of us.

Inhuman violence and the global crisis have been recognised since the news of the Holocaust and of Hiroshima and Nagasaki were disclosed after the war. The exposure of such ferocity severely shocked people. Lack of knowledge about the events simultaneously led to panic. The horror was heightened after the war when powerful nations began competing to manufacture weapons of mass murder and destruction, particularly atomic and hydrogen bombs. Far from reflecting on history and creating international harmony, the leaders of the superpowers built up their defences, creating ideological enemies. Ordinary people's fear and anxiety about nuclear wars became nightmarish.

In the tension between politically divided worlds that was termed the Cold War, people were affected by the conditions and even traumatically afflicted. The notion of human annihilation and the end of the world took on an air of feasibility in the 1950s, when Beckett, with the success of *Waiting for Godot*, began to write frenziedly. It is unthinkable that so sensitive a writer as Beckett would not feel the influence of such a collective cultural nightmare. He could not have been indifferent to the widespread imaginative fear and anxiety. As Andrew Gibson rightly says, 'From the mid-1950s onwards, there is a strain in Beckett's art which seems less abstract than global … [His works] clearly respond to a historical condition, that of the Cold War' (2010: 133).

Herbert Blau, recalling the Cold War era, also confesses:

> What seemed to me evident then was that, at the psychic level at least, the nerve ends of perception itself, it was the Balance of Terror that Beckett was writing about … along with the Energy Crisis, paralysis, *debility*, the exhaustion of Western culture, before the idea of an energy crisis was materialized as economic fact in the geopolitics of a postindustrial world, with what seemed inevitable in *due* time, the debility of a debit, in the distressing modulations of the microphysics of power and the ominous emergence of OPEC. (1991: 2)

As if responding to Blau's insightful thinking on Beckett, Peter Boxall discusses Beckett's perception through the lenses of globalisation:

> [W]hile Beckett's representation of the global is in part an imagination of the frozen limits of perception – a presentiment of a global death that is carried in the image of stone spreading across the earth, evoking another ice age or a genetic global ecological disaster – it is also, and at every point, a performance of a surplus, or a supplement, a continued trembling movement that arises from the erosion of the partition – that same erosion that opens on to the rigidity of stone. […] The mechanics which lead to the global in later Beckett – the variously political and aesthetic forces which erode the boundaries between zones and between nation states

– produce at once a stony rigidity and trembling movement, a vibrating movement between elements which maintain their difference, even within the identity produced by Beckett's globalization. (2009: 164)

Although Boxall, referring to Francis Fukuyama's *The End of History and the Last Man*, defines 'globalisation' in a positive sense, it connotes domination by a superpower and the possibility of military supremacy over the deprived. Beckett, who always sided with the underprivileged, calling them 'margin people like me' (Beckett, 2011: 65), must have watched the world in sadness and despair. He was certainly one of 'the artistic and literary elites' and 'many sophisticated thinkers' who responded early to the bleak post-war mood, speaking of 'an anguished hollowness' and making connections with 'the problem most particularly with nuclear bombs' (Weart, 2012: 287). 'With the news from Hiroshima', states Weart, 'sensitive thinkers quickly realized that doomsday was no longer just a religious or science-fiction myth, but as real a part of the possible future as tomorrow's breakfast. Worse, the future might lead into blank nothingness' (287). Beckett, in what Blau calls 'a verbal hallucination, a mutilated sentence' (1991: 6), portrayed the terrified world that can be described as 'hollowness' and 'blank nothingness'.

H. Porter Abbott is right when he says, 'Already, in *Godot*, the emptied, unfruitful, and barely populated landscape suggests a world left over after global calamity' (1996: 133–4). Abbot categorises Beckett's works after *Endgame* as 'utopian fictions', dealing with 'the far distant future of *The Time Machine*' (133). Veronica Hollinger also finds in *Endgame* 'a typical SF [science fiction] scenario' (1992: 189), but separates it from conventional types of SF, calling the play 'specular SF', because it 'functions as a kind of allegory which appropriates the icons and images of SF as a way of commenting not on time future but on time present' (1992: 187); this means 'it is the *present* that is read through the *future*' (187).

In *The Sense of an Ending*, Frank Kermode remarks that in Beckett's writing, any order is 'no longer usable except as an irony' (2000: 116), and Hollinger regards *Endgame* as a dramatisation of 'the apocalypse with irony' (1992: 188). Beckett, deeply touched by the nuclear age and its perception of future global crisis, is aware that irony best expresses 'the sense of an ending' in this culturally traumatic age that he shares with his contemporaries. He suggests global trauma in his calculated, allegorical choice of words and images that convey deep ironies. This chapter aims to analyse and discuss how Beckett uses words and images to reveal collective apocalyptic trauma and ironise it in his plays.

Symbols and metaphors of the nuclear age

After the Second World War, 'the bombs – or nuclear energy in general – served as a condensed symbol for the worst of modernity' (Weart, 2012: 287). Beckett does not refer to bombs, but they appear suggestively as mysterious symbols, which often perplex us. From them stem ominous feelings about living with an energy that could annihilate human beings. In *Happy Days*, Winnie's parasol explodes like a bomb. The parasol itself provides an image of an atomic bomb's mushroom cloud.[1] In *Krapp's Last Tape*, Krapp's recorded voice reminisces about a time when a younger Krapp threw a black ball to a white dog (Beckett, 1990: 220). The black ball arouses an ominous feeling, especially in an age of nuclear anxiety, if we think of the sphere-shaped blackness of the bomb. In *All That Fall*, the boy Jerry brings something he picked up to Mr Rooney, saying, 'You dropped something, sir' (Beckett, 1990: 198). Mrs Rooney, examining it, asks him, 'What is this thing, Dan? … It looks like a kind of ball. And yet it is not a ball' (198). At first, Mr Rooney denies that the ball belongs to him, but then admits, 'It is a thing I carry about with me' (198). We never know what that ball is or whether Mr Rooney actually carries it about. Just as the radio play ends mysteriously, hinting that Mr Rooney might have pushed a little child from the train, killing him, the ball puzzles the drama's listeners. Furthermore, the ball even evokes fear, more so than Krapp's black ball, because it is not improbable that Mr Rooney might be plotting to pay back or kill the children who bother him. He asks his wife when they are jeered at by 'the Lynch twins', rascals in their neighbourhood, 'Did you ever wish to kill a child? [*Pause.*]

Nip some young doom in the bud' (191). It might be surmised that the ball is a weapon.[2]

If a parasol or mysterious balls are emblematic in Beckett's work, dust is another symbol of nuclear disaster that is often mentioned. Dust – the fallout after the explosion of a nuclear bomb – placed a great issue before the world:

> By the end of the 1950s anxiety over fallout had become a powerful force around the world, with the full support of many governments. [...] Never before in history had there been such worldwide concern about a scientific issue. [...] A risk is especially likely to be feared if it is largely unknown – not only invisible but something new, outside normal experience, mysterious. (Weart, 2012: 114)

Radioactive fallout exists in the air, but to human eyes it is imperceptible. It certainly harms us, but we have no way of avoiding it. It is 'invisible' and 'mysterious'. Beckett, who was interested in existential questions of self and others, life and death, and body and mind, responded to the anxiety and terror his contemporaries felt towards the unknown, the invisible and the uncertain by philosophising imperceptibility and impenetrableness. Beckett's characters attempt to look at tiny things or to look at something as if to pierce it.

From biblical times, dust has symbolically expressed the mortal human body or death. However, Beckett's audiences and readers cannot help perceiving references to dust from the perspective of their time. At the end of *That Time*, a recorded voice narrates that the aged protagonist, wandering in the library, sees only dust around him, but this disembodied voice also suggests an uncanny atmosphere – the earth uninhabited. The end of the world with no one left alive is imagined as a post-nuclear hazard.

The earth uninhabited is often mentioned in Beckett's plays. In *Krapp's Last Tape*, this idea is repeated three times when the voice of young Krapp on the tape recorder refers to the silence around him: 'The earth might be uninhabited' (Beckett, 1990: 221, 223). Although there is no mention of 'dust' in the text, Krapp dusts the tin boxes when he takes out the tapes. Indeed, he is almost turning to dust himself, as are Beckett's later ghost protagonists. Anthony Kubiak observes that 'Krapp's final stage, then, is the site of history's ruin, and the site of the ruin is a staged event' (1991: 119). If Krapp is the site of ruin, almost all post-war Beckett characters are also sites of ruin, where dust covers not only them but also the things around them. Beckett's references to ashes, embers and fire also evoke apocalyptic images. *Endgame* is more obviously set in the post-apocalyptic world where all human beings except the four characters in the play are dead. So is *Happy Days* set in an outdoor desert, where the only human survivors are a middle-aged couple. Even Mrs Rooney in *All That Fall* imagines the post-apocalyptic landscape:

> All is still. No living soul in sight. There is no one to ask. The world is feeding. The wind – [*Brief wind.*] – scarcely stirs the leaves and the birds – [*Brief chirp.*] – are tired singing. The cows – [*Brief moo.*] – and sheep – [*Brief baa.*] – ruminate in silence. The dogs –[*Brief bark.*] – are hushed and the hens – [*Brief cackle.*] – sprawl torpid in the <u>dust</u>. We are alone. There is no one to ask. (Beckett, 1990: 192, emphasis mine)

What is 'the dust' in which 'the hens sprawl torpid'? Fallout, perhaps?

Dust is usually unseen and microcosmic, neglected at the site of ruin. Ironically, dust is not much acknowledged in ordinary life. Through his plays, Beckett helps us notice things normally unnoticed in our daily lives, whether they are human or not. For instance, in *Happy Days*, Winnie shows her excitement at finding 'a live emmet' (Beckett, 1990: 149).[3] She experiences happiness at finding something alive on that post-nuclear, desolate earth where 'nothing grows' (152). Beckett has a strong attachment to particular words, but in his choices lie his irony. Here *emmet* is archaic, not generally used, but it is suggestive because it means not only 'an ant' but also 'an unwelcome visitor/traveller', with which the author must have identified his position in France, or perhaps even in his home country. Adorno finds in such a character, who exhibits sympathy even to such an unwelcome pest, Beckett's deep understanding of the downtrodden under the Third Reich, which buried Jewish people, homosexuals, political prisoners, gypsies and so on as society's 'pests':

> [T]he dramas of Beckett … seem to me to be the only truly relevant metaphysical productions since the war […] Beckett can never get away from urns, refuse bins and sand-heaps in which people vegetate between life and death – as they actually vegetated in the concentration camps – this jibe seems to me just a desperate attempt to fend off the knowledge that these are exactly the things which matter. (Adorno, 2001: 117–18)

The people who live in 'refuse bins' and 'sand-heaps', mentioned above, are Nagg and Nell in *Endgame*. They symbolise those confined to concentration camps or prisons, but they are also in the universal condition of aged people who, unable to move, wait for death – wait to return to dust. These people's lives disappear like ashes, another of Beckett's favourite words, or what Derrida terms 'the cinders'. However, they were 'there' (Derrida, 1991: 33) and perhaps still hover around us as dust or ghosts.

Endgame contains another reference to a thing as tiny as dust or ash, that is, 'grain'. Grain appears in Clov's opening lines: 'Finished, it's finished, nearly finished, it must be nearly finished. [*Pause.*] Grain upon grain, one by one, and one day, suddenly, there's a heap, a little heap, the impossible heap' (Beckett, 1990: 93). This metaphor of the heap of grain

> invoke[s] the paradox of the grains posed by Eubulides of Miletus, a contemporary of Aristotle. The paradox is usually stated in its positive or additive version: Which grain by being added makes the heap? […] [T]he paradox was also well known in a negative or subtractive version: Which grain by being removed unmakes the heap? (Halpern, 2014: 746)

Clov, sensing no possibility of changing his situation, metaphorically expresses that there is no more grain, 'the last straw' (Beckett's phrase, quoted in Gontarski and Ackerley, 2006: 175, 661), necessary to make or unmake the heap. Of course, lack of grain suggests that the day of starvation is nearing. Behind Clov's metaphysical thought lurks the horror of death – the death of the human species.

The world of Beckett's post-war works is thus filled with references suggesting that our world, which we believe will continue forever, might end any day. Let us explore one more example of a tiny thing evoking nuclear fear in Beckett's works. In *All That Fall*, Mrs Rooney, deploring her difficulty in moving, screams, 'Oh to be in atoms, in atoms! ATOMS!' (Beckett, 1990: 177). The presence of atoms, like the paradox of the grains, is rooted in ancient Greek philosophy; for example, Democritus advocates that all things in nature form, change and die, with numberless atoms repeatedly uniting and disuniting. Therefore, Mrs Rooney's scream manifests Beckett's favourite wish, to absent himself from the painful world like an atom that transforms and dies. However, this radio play was written in 1956 and broadcast in 1957, when the word 'atom', thanks to global campaigns, was popularly received as something good, to sweep away people's fear.[4] Many radio listeners to *All That Fall* must have laughed at Mrs Rooney's scream, and some of them must have perceived the author's irony towards the light-hearted campaign and boom of 'Atom'. Like Mr Rooney's enigmatic ball, the sound of Mrs Rooney's 'ATOMS!' might have acted on listeners to arouse obscure anxiety in the depths of their minds.

The sense of the endless endtimes

As discussed so far, in many of his plays Beckett imagined, through allusions and symbols, the earth uninhabited and a landscape of ruins, with the last human beings barely alive. Fear about the earth's crisis intensified as the millennium neared. In the 1980s, Beckett, always sensitive, became even more strongly conscious than in the previous two decades of a deserted world with no one alive: the dying protagonist of *A Piece of Monologue*, for example, could be the last inhabitant on earth, while ghostly figures disappear one by one in *What Where*. Indeed, in the 1980s the nuclear imagination was rekindled. After the Cuban missile crisis was over, anxiety and fear about nuclear power subsided for a while because of the détente that encouraged many people to '[cling] to a culture of stability' and '[rely] on the nuclear predominance of the U.S. to keep the world safe' (Weart, 2012: 145). Andrew Gibson, considering the flare-up of a crisis regarding human annihilation, points out especially that Beckett dealt with 'the Cold War scenario' (2010: 137) in the mid-1950s, and his 'responses to the era of the New Cold War' (142) in the 1980s.[5]

It is ironic that Beckett died in 1989, just after the Berlin Wall collapsed and the Cold War ended. In the last few years of his life, his short plays gave the impression that he was reflecting on situations during the Cold War. *A Piece of Monologue* ends with short phrases: 'The globe alone. Alone gone' (Beckett, 1990: 429). These phrases suggest that only the 'globe' is left after the last human being, the narrative's protagonist, dies. Beckett brilliantly plays with the well-known Shakespearean metaphor of the stage as a globe, and with modern apocalypse. *Catastrophe*, performed at the Avignon Festival in 1982, was written for Václav Havel, ex-president of Czechoslovakia (1989–92) and the Czech Republic (1993–2003), who was a political prisoner when the play was written. From this timing, it is clear that Beckett was critical of totalitarian governments during the Cold War era. The torturous situation illustrated in *Catastrophe* is again depicted in *What Where*, Beckett's last play, which foregrounds the ominous circle of torturers and the tortured, both ignorant of why the torture goes on. The play ends with no one on stage; only Voice reverberates, saying 'I am alone. In the present as were I still. It is winter. Without journey. Time passes. That is all. Make sense who may. I switch off' (Beckett, 1990: 476). Four protagonists disappear one by one in each of the four seasons, and the play ends with the coming of 'winter', which might connote 'nuclear winter'. Again, *What Where* ends with the desolate end-world of the human species, not just with reference to the Beckettian cycle of human life. The play's horror also lies in the cycle of a torturer becoming a victim tortured, like a child's make-believe game. From it emerges a horrified world where distinguishing between perpetrators and victims is difficult and where men are buffeted without knowing why.

This is actually the traumatic condition we now face daily. As Slavoj Žižek explains, with the support of Catherine Malabou's psychoanalytical study, trauma has become a daily condition in the post-Holocaust era. It is thus impossible to use Freudian explanations for our contemporary trauma:

> [F]or Freud (and Lacan), every external trauma is 'sublated,' internalized, owing its impact to the way a pre-existing Real of 'psychic reality' is aroused through it. [...] Today, however, our socio-political reality itself imposes multiple versions of external

intrusions, traumas, which are just that, brutal but meaningless interruptions that destroy the symbolic texture of the subject's identity. (Žižek, 2011: 292)

Such traumatic conditions have been yearly augmented, and 'the single most crucial factor spurring this acceleration was the creation of nuclear weaponry' (Quinby, 2014: 27), which caused panic among people in the early 1950s, when the European continent was divided in two and nuclear war was not inconceivable. Then, 'the basic message was "Keep Calm!"' (Weart, 2012: 71). In *Waiting for Godot*, in reaction to Vladimir's admonition, Estragon, in panic, retaliates, 'Calm ... calm ... The English say cawm. [*Pause.*] You know the story of the Englishman in the brothel?' (Beckett, 1990: 17). The repetition of 'calm', with its cynical tone towards the genteel, must have sounded witty to the audience who saw the play's premiere.

In such a panicky period, building nuclear shelters was seriously considered, and creating SF fantasies of survivors in a nuclear shelter was in vogue. 'Home shelters fitted nicely with the image of a new frontiersman who "could venture forth" after the bombs, as *Time* said, "to start ensuring his today and building for his tomorrow"' (Weart, 2012: 149). Charles Carpenter discusses *Endgame* as a play that generates 'a perceptible metaphor of a family shelter after a nuclear holocaust, and an unobtrusive but distinct analogy to the dilemma that might have faced the person in charge' (1999: 137). In his essay, Carpenter quotes various allusions to shelter in *Endgame*, though he emphasises that Beckett never refers to it as a 'nuclear' shelter. In fact, Beckett objected to the American Repertory Theater's production of *Endgame*, with the set changed to the New York subway damaged by a nuclear bomb. However, it is still possible to read *Endgame* as a work 'directly promoted by the existence of first the atomic and then the hydrogen bomb' (Mercier, 1977: 174), and such a reading 'has since become a commonplace in both critical and directorial contexts' (Halpern, 2014: 749 n. 4).

Beckett must have been particularly intrigued by a shelter fitting his view of a man born from a womb and waiting for his return to it. This view is rooted in Otto Rank's *The Trauma of*

Birth, which Beckett read. Rank explains, 'the thought of death is connected from the beginning with a strong unconscious sense of pleasure associated with the return to the mother's womb' (2010: 24), because the womb, like a shelter, 'protect[s]' from any outside catastrophe.[6] Beckett's elderly dying protagonists confine themselves in a shelter that resembles a womb. *Krapp's Last Tape* is set in a windowless room – an isolated shelter – while *Rockaby* ends with the protagonist shutting herself in a dark, windowless space. Speaker in *A Piece of Monologue* stands on a set with no window or entrance.

Beckett thus continued to reflect upon human existence as being locked in a shelter, an image shared by his contemporaries. At the same time, he must have felt deeply the irony of another image of the time – nuclear energy as a substitute for Eden: 'The campaign [led by Eisenhower's "Atom for Peace"] taught people everywhere to believe what until then had seemed convincing only to a few elites: an atomic Eden could be reached within their lifetimes' (Weart, 2012: 83). Beckett subverts this image of Eden; every character he creates is Adam/Eve, the prototype of human beings, but Beckett shows his prototypes living on this planet in today's critical condition. In the first act of *Happy Days*, for example, Winnie is buried to her waist in a mound of earth, looking almost as if she reigns over the earth itself. This image resembles that of Leviathan in the frontispiece of Thomas Hobbes's eponymous book. In Hobbes's scheme, Leviathan, the giant man with a crown, a sword and a sceptre, is emblematic of the nation-state ruled by an (often despotic) sovereign. Hobbes strives to balance the private sovereignty of the individual against the sovereign authority of the state in the interests of civil harmony. In Beckett's play, however, Winnie represents a vulnerable human being with no sovereignty, in the stateless circumstances at the end of the world.

Beckett seems to wonder how, in such circumstances, human beings can go on living after experiencing a terrible disaster. However, he never mentions what the disaster was, or where or when it occurred. We never know if it was a nuclear disaster, a deluge or some other catastrophe. 'I was never there', says Hamm in *Endgame*. 'Absent, always. It all happened without me. I don't know what's happened. [*Pause.*] Do you know what's happened? [*Pause*] Clov?' (Beckett, 1990: 128). Hamm repeats the question, to which Clov answers, 'When? Where? … What for Christ's sake does it matter?' (128). Hamm, a miraculous survivor of some calamity, cannot grasp the event, just as in many cases a traumatised victim does not comprehend the origin of his or her trauma.[7] Clov, who was little when the calamity occurred, does not even remember it. The survivors' memory is blank. However, Hamm tells a story of 'a madman who thought the end of the world had come', having reported to Hamm that 'All he had seen was ashes' (113). It was the same sight that Hamm makes Clov see outside their 'old refuge' (126) – 'Zero' and 'Grey' (107). But certainly, 'outside of here [their refuge] is death' (126), and 'the earth is extinguished' (132). At the play's end, Clov, hoping that 'it'll never end, I'll never go', admits that '[t]hen, one day, suddenly, it ends, it changes, I don't understand, it dies, or it's me, I don't understand that either' (132). Although we never know what happened in the world outside Hamm and Clov's shelter, there is a feeling that they found themselves vulnerable due to some sudden, uncontrollable, sociopolitical catastrophe.

A similar comment is made by Pozzo in the second act of *Waiting for Godot*, when Vladimir asks when Lucky had become dumb:

> When! When! One day, is that not enough for you, one day like any other day, one day he went dumb, one day I went blind, one day we'll go deaf, one day we were born, one day we shall die, the same day, the same second, is that not enough for you? (Beckett, 1990: 83)

This exclamatory question indicates that numerous things happen to us regardless of our will and desire. In addition, the number of things we cannot control has been increasing at an accelerated pace since the second half of the twentieth century. Thus, we feel that some devastating catastrophe is approaching.

Beckett never exposes the disaster's causes, but behind his writings are anger and fear, targeting unseen Kafkaesque dictators who might have caused such disasters. Andrew Kincaid, discovering the coincidence of the naming of 'Endgame' in the political document published by US Homeland Security in the wake of 9/11, summarises Beckett's intention as follows:

> Beckett speaks to the fear of contemporary lives, from alienation to intimate acts of violence to nuclear war. But while identifying and stirring up anxiety, he never plans its palliative. Anxiety conjures up the desire to name its roots and trace its causes but the very fact that the definition remains outside of Beckett's orbit leaves its remedy a fantasy. (2013: 177)

If we consider our fear that the war with terror will not end simply through controlling terrorists by means of violence, the 'Endgame' sounds hollow. 'Endgame' connotes the sense of forever unending, as Beckett's original *Endgame* seems to continue even after the play's end, so that the title suggests the author's irony. Hollinger, claiming that the play is '*the* emblematic re-presentation on the stage of our postmodern "sense of an ending"', explains that '[w]ithin the brief theatrical event that is *Endgame*, we seem to encounter the end of the world, but also an end endlessly deferred, as well as the suggestion that the end has always already occurred' (1992: 187). That is why 'Hamm fears to leave the last flea alive' (188). In her discussion of the post-9/11 novel by William Gibson, *Pattern Recognition*, Hollinger suggests that it is 'an SF novel set in the endless endtimes of the future-present' (2006: 452). But *Endgame* already possesses such a lack of closure: 'The calculated, apocalyptic ending of *Endgame* remains deferred and the origins of life in the shelter lost to memory. Hamm struggles to hold together life in the shelter with a series of narratives – fragmented, incomplete, yet unending' (Gontarski, 2009: 141).

Similarly, in *Happy Days*, even though Winnie will die if her whole body is buried, ironically she still lives on not only at the play's end but also at the very end of the world. At the play's beginning, she prays 'World without end Amen' (Beckett, 1990: 138). This might be interpreted as the world being endless both in time and in space – ironic in the context of forever 'endless endtimes'.

This sense of the 'endless endtimes' permeates what Hollinger calls 'postmodern' (1992: 182) scenes, in other words, the post-Holocaust world.[8] It is the apocalypse scenario of our age: fear of the global crisis never ends. Apocalypse and trauma are thus inseparable in our age. In what Hollinger calls 'specular SF', future cannot be separated from present, or fantasy from reality.

Conclusion: resisting oblivion

It is true that fear and anxiety about the end of the world have become traumatic. Even so, people, especially those who did not go through hell, readily forget such atrocities as the Second World War and the Holocaust, so that they have turned into a kind of fantasy, having lost their reality as time passes. Forgetfulness and oblivion are rampant among many who live next to disaster today, although somewhere in their minds they know that such a state cannot be right. Adorno explains this as the mechanism of 'feeling of guilt':

> One is pushed, as it were, into forgetfulness, which is already a form of guilt. By failing to be aware at every moment of what threatens and what has happened, one also contributes to it; one resists it too little; and it can be repeated and reinstated at any moment. (2001: 113)

He warns against this tendency as characterising traumatised victims, but the situation can be applied to every one of us who is facing the danger of becoming a traumatised victim at any time. It is important, Adorno emphasises, for us to be conscious of 'each moment of identification with the victims, and of alert awareness and remembrance' (113).

Oblivion is a disease in our time. The horror of nuclear energy grows greater and greater. We know this from repeated accidents at nuclear power plants, such as Three Mile Island, Chernobyl and most recently Fukushima, but the efforts to eliminate nuclear plants from our new Cold War world remain insufficient. Many nations seem to ignore the fact that they are endangered. Weart recalls that after Chernobyl, 'they [the Ukrainians] did not call themselves by the positive term "survivors." They identified themselves, and were officially identified, as "victims"' (2012: 248). Behind the psychology of referring to victims as 'survivors' might lie the desire to ignore those one considers unpleasant and obstructive by making them honourable. By calling them 'survivors' and welcoming them almost as heroes, one can behave as if nothing serious has happened. This is the mechanism of moving victims from outside society to inside, an assimilation mechanism of a globalised world that does not tolerate difference. Such mechanisms operate through a dangerous logic of justification, as Naoko Miyaji critically asserts:

> Men can resort to violence and easily become perpetrators by the logic of justification, that is, by holding what they believe to be the correct judgment. [...] Men accept or support violence when they are convinced they are on the side of the victims and forget that they actually stand on the side of the assailants. (2013: 192, my translation)

One can easily become an aggressor, so that the vicious cycle of perpetrators and victims can never be eliminated from our society.

When Beckett portrays such vicious cycles in works such as *How It Is* and *What Where*, he characterises those who are truly traumatised as they repeatedly narrate their painful past experience, never able to forget. They repeatedly remember their traumatic past. 'Remembering', says Elizabeth Barry, 'the repetition of inevitably painful experience for Beckett's narrators, is always felt as a form of torture, albeit an inescapable one' (2006: 70). No matter how torturous remembering is, it is not easy for Beckett's narrators to forget their memories. They pick up unheard voices of victims undergoing some kind of torture, even when they are hidden in their silence. Barry praises the protagonist of *Catastrophe* as 'the culmination of all of the images in Beckett's work of humankind being moulded like clay, or made out of dust and ashes' (205). The protagonist, however, has not lost his human dignity, even in that image of death. The silent Protagonist/prisoner, reminding us of Václav Havel, to whom Beckett dedicated the play, stands at a podium at the mercy of Assistant/aide who obeys the orders of the Director/dictator. However, at the play's end, he raises his head and casts a sharp glance, showing his fortitude and dignity as a human being.[9]

In *Writing of the Disaster*, Maurice Blanchot attempts to pick up the unheard voices of those who died (and may die) in disasters such as wars, concentration camps, etc. For Blanchot, an act of writing is 'to speak of passivity' (1986: 15), in which

> silence is perhaps a word, a paradoxical word, the silence of the word *silence*, yet surely we feel that it is linked to the cry, the voiceless cry, which breaks with all utterances, which is addressed to no one and which no one receives, the cry that lapses and decries. (51)

One who is silent might look passive and listless, but he or she might be aggressively saying a great deal or even crying inside his or her mind. The protagonist of *Catastrophe* is such a man; he does not speak a word, but his muteness tells us plenty of things. He shows his human dignity. If one has dignity, one can express it without words even when treated as dust, ash or trash. One can manifest one's inner thoughts with facial expressions or demeanour, not with words. Rather paradoxically, Beckett is a writer who experimented with saying more with fewer words.

The importance of narration, or what Blanchot calls 'writing', is conveyed through much of Beckett's oeuvre, wherein numerous narrators appear even when communication is impossible. These narrators cannot obliterate the internal narratives that emerge from their minds, and this can even become the motive for continuing to live. Žižek, focusing on narrative as a process of hatching new thoughts after some traumatic event, says that 'the truly New emerges through narrative, the apparently purely reproductive retelling of what happened – it is this retelling that opens up the space (the possibility) of acting in a new way' (2014: 133). Beckett, rather than optimistically philosophising the need for narrative, as Žižek does, portrays narrative as the compulsion of a traumatised person. Even if the thought-narrative were incongruous, it would be the only way its author could face his or her trauma. With unheard voices, Beckett's characters – those suffering from trauma – address the society that drives them into the isolated and forgotten place. To borrow an expression from Blanchot, in that way those silenced people maintain 'the silent murmuring' (1986: 43). In Beckett's words, they 'go on' with their lives in the state of 'stirring still'.

Weart warns that such oblivion has turned into repression

and denial in recent years because 'the imagery [of nuclear war] was mixed up with fantasies involving primitive fears and desires that many people hid even from themselves' (2012: 155), and that denial 'almost to the extreme of blindness' spread on a mass scale: 'The refusal to face up to dreadful reality was infectious, [psychologist Robert Jay] Lifton argued, a numbness that spread into entire regions of public thinking, from international politics to thoughts of death itself' (288–9). Adorno also condemns such defence mechanisms, which are widespread in today's globalised society, calling it the 'principle of inertia' or 'new protectedness' (2001: 115).

In such circumstances, people have lost interest in expressing their opinions openly, so that they can easily be controlled by a nation-state if it attempts to ignore democracy and oppress its people. A totalitarian nation such as the Third Reich might appear and the madness might recur, as depicted in recent British 'political' plays by Beckett's successors such as Harold Pinter, Sarah Kane and Caryl Churchill. These playwrights admonish us regarding the danger of repeating the evils of history, but 'without actually showing them [torture or other forms of political oppression]' (Scolnicov, 2014: 47) and 'without overtly relating the action of their plays to contemporary political events' (Taylor-Batty, 2014: 74). Beckett provided a new way of expressing such terror – the play form without any actual political particularity. His illustration of vulnerable people, the cynicism in his portrayals of the last human beings and of the vicious cycle of torturers and tortured, and symbolic allusions to the nuclear age all make us aware of global danger in the post-Holocaust, nuclear era. With deep irony in his unique fantasies, Beckett seriously questions the blindness of human beings living on this planet in the age of nuclear fear.

Notes

1 Weart notes the terms that observers of the first Trinity test used for the shape of the A-bomb cloud, now commonly called a mushroom cloud: 'the *parasol*', a 'great funnel', a 'geyser', a 'convoluting brain' and even a 'raspberry'. 'One Japanese witness of the Hiroshima

explosion thought it looked like a "jellyfish"; a Bikini test in 1946 was accurately described as a "cauliflower cloud"' (2012: 283, emphasis mine).

2 The confrontation between the old people and the children in *All That Fall* is unpleasant, for both of them are socially disadvantaged. Mr Rooney's reprisal might be read as a representation of the unbalanced power relationship, in which perpetrators and victims can be interchangeable any time. Such menacing situations between perpetrators and victims are often seen in Beckett, leading to the reversal of the power relation, as in the relationship between Pozzo and Lucky in *Waiting for Godot*: blinded Pozzo in the second act cannot help depending on Lucky, who is enslaved by Pozzo in the first act.

3 Winnie, then, seizes magnifying glass and inspects the emmet, saying that it '[h]as like a little white ball in its arms' (Beckett, 1990: 149). We hear the word 'ball' again – this time a 'white' ball that contrasts with a 'black' ant. If the ball is a burden to the emmet, it may connote the situation in which the bomb is a burden to us human beings.

4 In the United States, for example, 'the comic book *Inside the Atom* … the 1952 animated color film *A Is for Atom* … Walt Disney's *Our Friend the Atom*, shown on television and in schools beginning in 1957' (Weart, 2012: 87) were distributed effectively, while in Japan, Osamu Tezuka's comic book and television animation *Astro Boy [Tetsuwan Atom]* really caught on with children.

5 The new Cold War phenomenon was triggered in the 1980s by Ronald Reagan's 'proposals to push the nuclear arms race into space' (Boyer, 1994: 360) and 'this Reagan-induced wave of nuclear awareness found dramatic expression not only in the political arena but also in the mass media and the cultural realm' (361).

6 Weart writes, 'A few critics noted sardonically that a shelter somewhat resembled a womb' (2012: 149).

7 The basic definition of trauma is that traumatised victims develop symptoms much later than the time at which they experienced the traumatic incident, a mechanism that Freud termed 'belatedness'. Cathy Caruth examines Freud's theory of trauma, which characterises its 'belatedness and incomprehensibility' (1996: 92).

8 Russell Smith analyses the postmodern 'sense of an ending unending' (2004: 411) in Beckett, comparing it with temporality as theorised by Fredric Jameson, Frank Kermode and Jean-François Lyotard.

9 Referring to a source for the raised head of the protagonist in *Catastrophe*, James Knowlson mentions 'the baited bear' in Hugh

Walpole's novel *Judith Paris*, which Beckett had read, in which the bear 'raises his head to stare at the onlookers, distancing himself from them, and becoming a symbol of dignity in suffering' (1996: 327). Beckett, like Walpole, considers both human beings and animals – living creatures – as equally dignified, and therefore neither should be debased. It could be said that the end of the play exemplifies not just 'human' dignity but a dignity of being and of living.

References

Abbott, H. Porter (1996). *Beckett Writing Beckett: The Author in the Autograph*. Ithaca, NY: Cornell University Press.

Adorno, Theodor W. (2001). *Metaphysics: Concept and Problems*. Ed. Rolf Tiedemann. Trans. Edmund Jephcott. Stanford, CA: Stanford University Press.

Barry, Elizabeth (2006). *Beckett and Authority: The Uses of Cliché*. Basingstoke: Palgrave Macmillan.

Beckett, Samuel (1990). *The Complete Dramatic Works*. London: Faber and Faber.

Beckett, Samuel (2011). *The Letters of Samuel Beckett 1941–1956*. Ed. George Craig, Martha Dow Fehsenfeld, Dan Gunn and Lois More Overbeck. Cambridge: Cambridge University Press.

Blanchot, Maurice (1986). *The Writing of the Disaster [L'Ecriture du désastre]*. Trans. Ann Smock. Lincoln, NE: University of Nebraska Press.

Blau, Herbert (1991). 'Quaquaquaqua: The Babel of Beckett'. In Joseph H. Smith (ed.), *The World of Samuel Beckett*. Baltimore, MD: Johns Hopkins University Press, pp. 1–14.

Boxall, Peter (2009). *Since Beckett: Contemporary Writing in the Wake of Modernism*. London: Continuum.

Boyer, Paul (1994). *By the Bomb's Early Light: American Thought and Culture at the Dawn of the Atomic Age*. Chapel Hill, NC: University of North Carolina Press.

Carpenter, Charles A. (1999). *Dramatists and the Bomb: American and British Playwrights Confront the Nuclear Age, 1945–1964*. Westport, CT: Greenwood Press.

Caruth, Cathy (1996). *Unclaimed Experience: Trauma, Narrative, and History*. Baltimore, MD: Johns Hopkins University Press.

Derrida, Jacques (1991). *Cinders*. Trans. and ed. Ned Lukacher. Lincoln, NE: University of Nebraska Press.

Gibson, Andrew (2010). *Samuel Beckett*. London: Reaktion Books.

Gontarski, Stan E. (2009). 'A Sense of Unending: Samuel Beckett's Eschatological Turn', *Samuel Beckett: Today/Aujourd'hui* 21, 135–49.

Gontarski, Stan E., and Chris J. Ackerley (eds) (2006). *The Faber Companion to Samuel Beckett*. London: Faber and Faber.

Halpern, Richard (2014). 'Beckett's Tragic Pantry: *Endgame* and the Deflation of the Act', *PMLA* 129.4, 742–50.

Hobbes, Thomas (2009 [1651]). *Leviathan*. Oxford: Oxford University Press.

Hollinger, Veronica (1992). 'Playing at the End of the World: Postmodern Theater'. In Patrick D. Murphy (ed.), *Staging the Impossible: The Fantastic Mode in Modern Drama*. Westport, CT: Praeger, pp. 182–96.

Hollinger, Veronica (2006). 'Stories about the Future: From Patterns of Expectation to Pattern Recognition', *Science Fiction Studies* 33.3, 452–72.

Kermode, Frank (2000). *The Sense of an Ending: Studies in the Theory of Fiction with a New Epilogue*. Oxford: Oxford University Press.

Kincaid, Andrew (2013). 'Mapping the Future: *Endgame*, Premediation, and the War on Terror', *Samuel Beckett Today/Aujourd'hui* 25, 169–82.

Knowlson, James (1996). *Damned to Fame: The Life of Samuel Beckett*. London: Bloomsbury.

Kubiak, Anthony (1991). 'Post Apocalypse with Out Figures: The Trauma of Theater in Samuel Beckett'. In Joseph H. Smith (ed.), *The World of Samuel Beckett*. Baltimore, MD: Johns Hopkins University Press, pp. 107–24

Mercier, Vivian (1977). *Beckett/Beckett: The Classic Study of a Modern Genius*. Oxford: Oxford University Press.

Miyaji, Naoko (2013). *Torauma [Trauma]*. Tokyo: Iwanami-shoten.

Quinby, Lee (2014). 'Apocalyptic Security: Biopower and the Changing Skin of Historic Germination'. In Monica Germanà and Aris Mousoutzanis (eds), *Apocalyptic Discourse in Contemporary Culture: Post-Millennial Perspectives on the End of the World*. London: Routledge, pp. 17–30.

Rank, Otto (2010 [1924]). *The Trauma of Birth*. Mansfield Centre, CT: Martino Publishing.

Scolnicov, Hanna (2014). 'Bearing Witness and Ethical Responsibility in Harold Pinter's *Ashes to Ashes*'. In Mireia Aragay and Enrich Monforte (eds), *Ethical Speculations in Contemporary British Theatre*. Basingstoke: Palgrave Macmillan, pp. 42–58.

Smith, Russell (2004). 'Beckett's Endlessness: Rewriting Modernity and the Postmodern Sublime', *Samuel Beckett Today/Aujourd'hui* 14, 405–20.

Taylor-Batty, Mark (2014). 'How to Mourn: Kane, Pinter and Theatre as Monument to Loss in the 1990s'. In Mireia Aragay and Enrich Monforte (eds), *Ethical Speculations in Contemporary British Theatre*. Basingstoke: Palgrave Macmillan, pp. 59–75.

Weart, Spencer R. (2012). *The Rise of Nuclear Fear*. Cambridge, MA: Harvard University Press.

Žižek, Slavoj (2011). *Living in the End Times*. London: Verso.

Žižek, Slavoj (2014). *Event: A Philosophical Journey through a Concept*. London: Melville House.

Index

Lightning Source UK Ltd.
Milton Keynes UK
UKHW022250180620
365223UK00010B/658